The Story of Drama

RELATED TITLES FROM BLOOMSBURY PUBLISHING

Contemporary Adaptations of Greek Tragedy
Edited by George Rodosthenous
IBSN 978-1-4725-9152-4

English Renaissance Tragedy
by Peter Holbrook
ISBN 978-1-4725-7280-6

Reader in Comedy
ISBN 978-1-4742-4788-7
Edited by Alan Ackerman and Magda Romanska

Reader in Tragedy (forthcoming)
Edited by Marcus Nevitt and Tanya Pollard
ISBN 978-1-4742-7042-7

Rethinking the Theatre of the Absurd
Edited by Carl Lavery and Claire Finburgh
ISBN 978-1-4725-0667-2

Visions of Tragedy in Modern American Drama (forthcoming)
Edited by David Palmer
ISBN 978-1-4742-7693-1

The Story of Drama

Tragedy, Comedy and Sacrifice from the Greeks to the Present

Gary Day

Bloomsbury Methuen Drama
An imprint of Bloomsbury Publishing Plc

B L O O M S B U R Y
LONDON · OXFORD · NEW YORK · NEW DELHI · SYDNEY

Bloomsbury Methuen Drama
An imprint of Bloomsbury Publishing Plc

Imprint previously known as Methuen Drama

50 Bedford Square	1385 Broadway
London	New York
WC1B 3DP	NY 10018
UK	USA

www.bloomsbury.com

**BLOOMSBURY, METHUEN DRAMA and the Diana logo are trademarks of
Bloomsbury Publishing Plc**

First published 2016

© Gary Day, 2016

British Library Cataloguing-in-Publication Data
A catalogue record for this book is available from the British Library.

ISBN: HB: 978-1-4081-8415-8
PB: 978-1-4081-8312-0
ePDF: 978-1-4081-8488-2
ePub: 978-1-4081-8353-3

Library of Congress Cataloging-in-Publication Data
A catalog record for this book is available from the Library of Congress.

Cover design: Louise Dugdale
Cover image: Gaston Batistini

Typeset by Integra Software Services Pvt. Ltd.
Printed and bound in India

To Kate, for being there.

Man was made for Joy and Woe
And when this we rightly Know
Through the World we safely go.
WILLIAM BLAKE, AUGURIES OF INNOCENCE

'*I stopped believing in God [but] I still needed ritual.*'
MARTIN SHERMAN, ROSE

CONTENTS

ACKNOWLEDGEMENTS

I would like to thank my editor, Mark Dudgeon, for his patience, encouragement, thoughtfulness and insights; Elizabeth Goodridge for friendly criticism of the first two chapters; and all the students who contributed to my drama course at De Montfort. Any errors or omissions are my own.

1

Sacrifice

The aim of this book is to sketch a history of tragedy and comedy in the West through a discussion of individual plays. Each chapter will begin with a brief sketch of the status of tragedy and comedy in that particular period, touching on such matters as their role in society and how they relate to other forms of entertainment. A key part of the book will be to show that sacrifice is an important element of both genres. This is not a new idea. It was Aristotle who first declared that tragedy developed from hymns to Dionysus and comedy from phallic songs, but he was also the first to dissociate them from their atavistic beginnings. His treatise on comedy has never been found but his theory of tragedy, expounded in the *Poetics* (350 BCE), has resonated down the centuries. Aristotle stated that tragedy is the imitation of a single action that occurs in one time in one place. These are the famous unities. Tragedy aroused pity and terror in the audience but it also served to purge them of these emotions, a process Aristotle called catharsis. Its success depended on the precise organization of what he identified as the six characteristics of tragedy: plot, character, theme, diction, spectacle and song. The order in which Aristotle lists them is significant. Rationality, ethics and decorum are prized over vulgar display and showmanship. The former belong to civilization, the latter smack of barbarism.

In general, theorists of tragedy have followed Aristotle in taking an intellectual approach to the genre. One of the most important was the German philosopher Georg Friedrich Wilhelm Hegel (1770–1831). He claimed that tragedy lay in the hero or heroine being compelled to choose between two right courses of action, both leading to destruction. In Sophocles' *Antigone* (441 BCE), for instance, the eponymous heroine has to opt either to obey the gods and bury her brother, the traitor Polynices, or to obey the law and leave his body to rot. She chooses to bury him and is sentenced to death but she would have suffered the same fate, in a different manner, if she had not. The difference between classical tragedy and 'modern' tragedy, Hegel adds, is that in Aeschylus, Sophocles and Euripides the protagonist is faced with incompatible external demands whereas in Shakespeare he or she is riven by internal conflict. There is no catharsis in Hegel's account of tragedy; instead there is a sense that all opposition is an illusion and that beyond pity and fear we glimpse an 'eternal justice'[1] where all differences are reconciled.

Since it requires a leap of faith to believe in the existence of an 'eternal justice', this is not a particularly convincing argument, but it does demonstrate how thinkers on tragedy tend to stress its spiritual or philosophical aspect at the expense of its relation to ritual. This trend has caused them to overlook parallels between Aristotle's theory of tragedy and the operation of sacrifice. In both cases an arrangement of formal elements leads to an act of cleansing. Sacrifice purges society, tragedy the individual. What's more this very basic model seems to be deeply embedded in Western culture. It appears, in modified form, in both Catholic confession and Freudian psychoanalysis. The one is designed to free the penitent of sin, the other the patient of their neurosis. To the extent that catharsis is their aim, both confession and psychoanalysis function like tragedy. Of course there are huge differences, historical, cultural, generic and institutional between all three; but that just makes their fundamental similarity all the more striking.

The diversity and longevity of sacrifice is largely the subject of the following chapters. The purpose of this one is to provide a brief introduction to the term itself.[2] Sacrifice is derived from the Latin *sacrificium*, made up from the Latin *sacer*, holy, and *facere*, to make. It therefore means to 'make holy'. What sacrifice makes holy in particular is the sacrificial victim. Whether animal or human it is first separated from the community, purified, revered and then slain on the altar. It is the immolation of the victim which finally makes it holy. Sacrifice has many functions: to commune with the gods; to ask for blessing; to ensure a good harvest; to prevent disaster; to make reparation for wrongs and so on. It also changes over time from simple meal to elaborate ceremony and, in the process, the notion of god becomes increasingly abstract, moving from totemic figure to spirit in the sky to intellectual construct. How exactly sacrifice develops is a matter of some dispute, as is its relation to ritual and myth. To cover all the different aspects of these issues would take us too far out of our way and so we will touch on them only as and when necessary.[3]

The study of sacrifice really begins in anthropology. One of the first to analyse its workings was Edward Burnett Tylor (1832–1917). At first sacrifice was simply a present of food or valuables to gods who were thought of more as social superiors than divine beings. These offerings sometimes had the additional purposes of appeasing or enlisting their help. Tylor called this the 'gift-theory'[4] of sacrifice. It involved little or no ceremony and there is 'as yet no definite thought how the receiver can take and use it'.[5] The second type of sacrifice, 'the homage theory' is characterized by devotion and/or 'expiation of sin'.[6] It was a response to a new view of the gods as beings who cared for humans and who sought their praise. In addition they would act on their behalf in exchange for offerings of food and drink. This made the sacrificial meal the most important part of this ceremony. Tylor called the third and final kind of sacrifice 'the abnegation theory'.[7] Here the person performing the sacrifice does so mainly for his or her own benefit rather than for that of the deity, for example choosing to forego pleasure in this life in order to enjoy bliss in the second, though the deity is presumably pleased to welcome another soul into paradise.

The relevance of Tylor for our purposes is that he serves to introduce some aspects of sacrifice – exchange, feast and expiation – which will crop up in the discussion of individual texts. Moreover, in showing that it evolves, he gives some support to the main proposition of this book: that sacrifice, in one form or another, has been a feature of drama from Athens to Broadway. William Robertson Smith, a Scottish scholar of Biblical literature (1846–1894) also believed that sacrifice changes over time, but he disagreed with Tylor that it originated in the 'gift theory', a notion he summarily dismissed. First, it rested on the absurd assumption that the gods were dependent on man for their nourishment and, second, since it frequently failed either to win the deity's favour or avert its wrath no one seriously believed in it.

Robertson Smith's thesis was that sacrifice sprang from a belief in the oneness of existence. In his words 'all sacred relations and all moral obligations depend on the physical unity of life, and that physical unity of life can be created or reinforced by common participation in living flesh and blood'.[8] The act of eating the flesh of the sacrificial victim and drinking its blood was a means of communing with the gods, nature and one's fellow human being. Any later meanings of sacrifice, such as the need for atonement, are simply variations of the original need 'to maintain the bond of holiness that kept the religious community together'.[9]

Robertson Smith makes a strong link between sacrifice and the social structure. He argues that sacrifice and society appear together and that its rituals change as society changes. The classicist Walter Burkert (1931–2015) takes this one step further claiming that sacrifice is the very foundation of society: 'all orders and forms of authority in human society are founded on institutionalised violence'.[10] For Burkert, the origin of society lies in the hunt, which he regards as the precursor of sacrifice: both rely on ritual, both involve the killing of an animal and both end in a shared meal. Robertson Smith's ideas about the interrelations between sacrifice and the social are echoed in the works of sociologists Henri Hubert (1872–1927), Marcel Mauss (1872–1950) and Émile Durkheim (1858–1917). Hubert and Mauss observe that sacrifice is both a social and economic phenomenon. It puts social relations on display – royalty, priests, worshippers and so forth – and it is also a type of exchange between humans and the divine. The gods, moreover, symbolize the ideals of society. In honouring them, sacrifice endorses the hierarchies, institutions and values of the social order. Durkheim shared this view and added that sacrifice was necessary to sustain belief in the gods, for if we cease to believe in them, we cease to believe in society. 'The sacred principle' of sacrifice, he writes, 'is nothing but society hypostasised'.[11]

Sacrificial ritual enacts the norms, beliefs and ideas that bind society together. It promotes social feelings which counter 'the antagonistic tendencies which the demands of the daily struggle awaken and sustain'.[12] The idea that sacrifice prevents the outbreak of conflict is found in a different form in the work of the historian, critic and social philosopher René Girard (b. 1923). Ritual killing, he argues, 'serves to protect the community from its own violence'.[13] The bloodshed of sacrifice is a safeguard against aggressive impulses that might otherwise destroy society. It is a bulwark against anarchy, a boundary line between civilization and savagery. But, Georges Bataille (1897–1962), author of the notorious *Story of the Eye* (1928),[14] has a different conception of sacrifice. He regards the excessive violence of some rites not as a way of protecting society but of protesting against what he saw as its miserly, utilitarian nature. The spectacular nature of sacrifice, the squandering of life, is a demonstration of plenty. It is stating, so to speak, that 'we have life to waste'. 'Death', declares Bataille, 'reveals life in its plenitude'.[15] The celebrations of sacrifice are also a way of immersing ourselves in the oneness of existence. Robertson Smith made a similar point but for him this did not entail revelling in bloodshed.

Although his work has been attacked in the past, no discussion of sacrifice can ignore James George Frazer (1824–1941). Indeed, there are signs that his reputation is undergoing something of a revision.[16] His monumental study, *The Golden Bough* (1890–1915), is one of the urtexts of modernism. Its account of the origins and meaning of myth offered the sort of spiritual anchorage that Christianity, weakened by textual scholarship and the theory of evolution, no longer could. But, at the same time, it redeemed the essential elements of the faith – death and resurrection – by showing that they were permanent features of myth the world over. Myth also appealed to the modernist imagination because it appeared to sanction the instinctive life whose repression, according to Sigmund Freud (1856–1939), was the cause of so much misery.[17] Another attraction of myth was that it was the product of relatively small communities whose supposed integration and coherence stood in enviable contrast to the fractured nature of contemporary existence.

Finally, the seeming continuity of myth hinted at a way of reconnecting with the past. Advances in science, technological innovation, the growth of mass society and the carnage of the First World War (1914–1918) severed the link with previously sustaining institutions, traditions, habits and beliefs. Probably the closest historical parallel would be the Reformation (in England 1529–1537). Then, too, a series of traumatic events transformed the social order. But the break with Rome did not spell the death of Christianity merely, in spite of all the turmoil, another stage in its development.

The situation at the beginning of the twentieth century was quite different. Even the Victorian age, whose artists and thinkers had struggled with many of the problems that future generations would, seemed like a foreign country.[18] The result was drift and dislocation. What could be done? Myth was not the answer but its universal themes of creation and death suggested that it could transcend time and therefore be a means of engaging with past ages as if they were present. More than that, as the work of W. B. Yeats (1865–1939), James Joyce (1882–1941) and T. S. Eliot (1888–1965) shows, myth had the power to draw the fragments of modern life together, alchemizing base existence into significant being.[19]

For these reasons, Frazer's work was a source of fascination for some modernists, especially Eliot.[20] In many ways Frazer is an enlightenment figure, believing in the progress of human reason. He demonstrates to his satisfaction, if not that of his critics, that humans move steadily from magic to religion to science. Frazer starts with a question. Why did the candidate for the ancient priesthood at Nemi have to kill the incumbent to succeed him? His answer, after much research, is that the priest, also known as the King of the Wood[21], was a spirit of fertility and that he, along with his feminine consort, was responsible for the fecundity of the land. When he got sick, the land got sick; when he got old, the land got old. To ensure that nature did not suffer in this way, the king was killed by which means his spirit was transferred to the new, younger king.

Frazer claimed this process of death and resurrection is present in myth and folklore. Dionysus, for example, is torn to pieces but then reborn and the same pattern is found in the tale of *Gawain and the Green Knight*. Gawain beheads the Knight, who symbolizes spring, but he rises up unhurt. It was not only humans who were thought to embody the spirit of fertility. It could also inhabit trees and corn. Effigies of both could be destroyed in the belief that this was the way to ensure their continued growth.

Frazer claims that sacrificial ritual is the womb of organized religion. He shows, in some detail, that Christ's arrest, imprisonment, torture and crucifixion have close connections with the Roman Saturnalia but more especially with the Feast of Purim which celebrates the Jews' deliverance from Haman. The story is told in the Old Testament book of Esther. Not content with these links Frazer also traces Christ's fate to the fertility myths of Ishtar and Marduk. The success of Christianity, he concludes, was due to its consonance with these much older stories of 'the mournful death and happy resurrection of a divine being celebrated annually with alternate rites of bitter lamentation and exultant joy'.[22]

If one purpose of sacrifice is to guarantee fertility, another is to get rid of the 'accumulated misfortunes and sins' of the whole community.[23] These can be heaped upon a thing, an animal, a man or even a God. On the Jewish Day of Atonement, for example, the high priest would lay his hands on the head of a live goat and confess over it all the iniquities of the Children of Israel 'and, having thereby transferred the sins of the people to the beast,

sent it away into the wilderness'.[24] And, of course, Christians believe that
Christ died on the cross for the sins of all mankind. To believe in him is to
be cleansed of all crimes and misdemeanours. The term 'scapegoat' is used
to describe the animal or human who is made to bear the faults of everyone.
After the scapegoat has been dispatched, there are festivities marked by
feasting, sexual promiscuity and the mocking of authority.

Where does Frazer fit with the other writers on sacrifice that we have
mentioned? Unlike Tylor he does not take a markedly evolutionary
approach to sacrifice. For him, its meaning remains fairly constant whether
it is primitive ritual or high mass. Nor does he stress its social aspect in
the way that Robertson Smith and others do. But what Frazer does show
is that sacrifice is a highly elaborate attempt to cope with the mystery,
awfulness and inevitability of death. It is a ceremony designed to take
control of it and give it a meaning by, in effect, making death the condition
of new life. Moreover, Frazer's account of the scapegoat offers an insight
into the nature of the mind; it implies that we have difficulty in accepting
responsibility and that our default setting, when faced with difficulty, is to
blame someone or something else. Eliot famously said that 'humankind/
Cannot bear very much reality'[25] and the examples Frazer offers of groups
offloading their guilt and wrongdoing onto a solitary figure would suggest
that he was right.

Frazer was not the only person to touch on the psychological aspect of
sacrifice. So too did Robertson Smith. His stress on sacrifice as a means
of promoting a feeling of oneness with the divine is nothing other, Freud
argues, than the desire to recreate the feeling of contentment that the infant
enjoys at the breast.[26] Robertson Smith also notes 'the close psychological
connection between sensuality and cruelty'.[27] Freud explains this connection
in terms of the development of the sexual instinct. It goes through the several
stages during early childhood but can become 'fixated' on any one of them if
there is exposure to a traumatic sexual experience, for example abuse. Freud
identified the anal stage, the period during which a child gains pleasure from
control of its bowels, as the source of the connection between sensuality
and cruelty.[28] He returns to a version of this relationship in his theory of the
pleasure principle which, among other things, considers how the instinct for
life and the instinct for death battle each other in the human mind.[29]

Robertson Smith was no psychoanalyst, but like Frazer, he touched
on the darkness of the mind and Freud was influenced by both men. He
was particularly interested in totemism. The term comes from the Ojibwa
language of the Algonquin people of Canada and can be translated as 'he is
a relative of mine'. Totemism is one of the early forms of religion and is
characterized by the worship of an animal. There are various views as to the
meaning of totemism. Robertson Smith claims the totem contains the spirit
of the god and Frazer claims that it is the receptacle of a man's life while for
Durkheim it is simply the clan itself. But for Freud, the totem was the father.
His theory, partly influenced by Darwin, goes like this.[30]

The earliest humans lived in small communities with one male, the father, having sole access to the females. When his sons came of age he drove them out, but they returned and killed him. Appalled at what they had done they introduced the totem as reparation for their crime. The totem was the source of two taboos: not to kill the totemic animal and not to have sexual relations with anyone from the same tribe. Freud argues that these taboos correspond to the prohibitions laid on the little boy in the Oedipus complex: he must not have sex with his mother or kill his father. Despite the taboo against killing the totem animal, there are times when it is sacrificed. Robertson Smith says that this is to renew communion with the god, and Frazer says that it ensures the survival of the species. But for Freud the killing of the totem simultaneously re-enacts the primal murder of the father and makes restitution for the deed – the victim being an offering to the slain parent.

The ceremonial slaying of the animal is accompanied by a sense of both guilt and liberation. Robertson Smith claims that guilt is the product of later religious ideas about remorse and the need for atonement as in the story of the Fall. Frazer claims that guilt arises from the belief that all living creatures had a soul and that to kill one, even for food, was to anger its spirit and rouse its desire for vengeance. Freud says that the guilt stems from the ancient memory of murdering the father. Frazer interprets the sexual licence following sacrifice as a way of encouraging nature's fertility. Freud, on the other hand, sees it as the expression of incestuous desire, for this is the one occasion when members of the same tribe are permitted to indulge in sexual relations with one another.

Freud also claims that the feelings of enmity and bitterness towards the father eventually gave way to a longing for him and 'it became possible for an ideal to emerge which embodied the unlimited power of the primal father'.[31] This psychological development marked the transition from totemism to organized religion but the sense of guilt remains. Freud even suggests that Christianity recapitulates the original murder because the worship of Jesus rather than God means 'a son-religion displaced the father-relation'.[32]

There is, of course, no empirical evidence whatsoever for Freud's interpretation of sacrifice as the repetition of and reparation for the murder of the primal father. But if it serves no other purpose than to draw attention to the almost universal theme of rebellion against authority as a problem that needs explaining, then it has done its work. In one sense the answer is easy. Wherever there is oppression, there will be opposition. Historians have shown the reasons why, in different times and different places, the powerless have risen up against the powerful. It is more difficult, however, to understand why the unequal distribution of power should be a constant in human society. It therefore seems sensible to consider psychological as well as social explanations for this phenomenon. Freud may not have the answer, but he can help us to think differently about the question.

Sacrifice, psychoanalysis and anthropology all come together in the West's most famous tragedy, Sophocles' *Oedipus Rex* (429 BCE). Freud always claimed that the poets got there before him and the play stages the central drama of psychoanalysis: the little boy's struggle to overcome his desire for his mother and his hostility to his father. Oedipus learns that he will murder his father and sleep with his mother. He tries to escape his destiny by running away from his parents. But, unbeknown to him, they are not his real parents and, in fleeing from them, he encounters his true ones with the result that the prophecy is fulfilled. Hence, for Freud, the play demonstrates that our conscious intentions are deeply at odds with our unconscious desires. And, moreover, Oedipus becomes the prototype of the patient – someone who, like the tragic protagonist, must undergo a journey that ends in self-knowledge.

Oedipus Rex also has a very clear sacrificial structure. Thebes is cursed. The crops won't grow, animals are dying and women can't give birth. What can have caused this terrible blight? The Delphic oracle has the answer. The murderer of Laius, the previous king of Thebes, is living unpunished in the city. If fertility is to be restored to the land, he must be expelled. During the course of the play, Oedipus will discover that he is that murderer and that Laius was his father. When he learns the terrible truth not just about Laius but about how his wife, Jocasta, is also his mother, Oedipus blinds himself and goes into exile with his two daughters, Antigone and Ismene. The basic elements of sacrifice are very clear here. An evil has stopped nature in her cycle. She can only start to turn again when that evil has been removed.

The centrality of Sophocles' play to psychoanalysis prompts the question of whether or not Freud's invention itself has a sacrificial form. Burkert certainly seems to think so. Sacrifice begins with the experience of evil, then a religious person interprets why the evil has arisen and finally he or she recommends appropriate acts of atonement. Similarly psychoanalysis begins with the symptom, then the analyst interprets the symptom using his or her specialized techniques and finally he or she is able to effect a cure.[33] As we said at the beginning, the operations of sacrifice and psychoanalysis are consonant with Aristotle's theory of tragedy, in particular the notion of catharsis. But, as Freud noted in a late essay, 'Analysis Terminable and Interminable',[34] psychoanalysis cannot guarantee to cure all patients of their illness. Hence some must learn to live with it. Tragedy, at least in the field of psychoanalysis, does not always end in purgation but with a recognition that, since some things cannot be changed, they must be borne. But Freud also observes that there are other patients who choose not to be cured because their illness in some way defines them. They look to the analyst for recognition of their condition which they can endlessly elaborate. On this reckoning, tragedy is what we secretly desire.

There is a great deal more to sacrifice than I have been able to indicate here. Hopefully, enough has been said to indicate something of its complexity. Sacrifice, for our purposes, is best considered as a narrative, that is, something which gives shape and meaning to existence. It creates a connection between life and death and establishes a relation between humans and the wider cosmos. One of the reasons why there has been a revival of interest in sacrifice has to do with our attitude to death.[35] For centuries religion eased our encounter with mortality. It spoke of how we were to live, how we were to die and what lay beyond the grave. The decline of organized religion has left us with the problem of how we are to understand death.

George Steiner (b. 1929) wrote that 'What is central to a true culture is a certain view of the relations between time and individual death.'[36] The appeal of sacrifice is that it holds out the possibility of giving meaning to death in a culture which would rather not talk about it except as something that, with the help of science, can be put off – perhaps indefinitely. There is no equivalent in contemporary culture to the Medieval *memento mori*. I am not, of course, advocating the reintroduction of ritual slaughter to remedy this situation; what I am suggesting is that we can use sacrifice as a tool for thinking about the relation between life and death and our place in the greater scheme of things not, it should be emphasized, in a religious way, simply in a holistic one. The example of sacrifice shows that we can give a meaning to death that has a life-enhancing effect.

The following chapters develop some of the ideas discussed here. The next one gives a brief account of the relationship between tragedy and comedy and how they are connected to ritual.

2

Tragedy, Comedy and Ritual

Although tragedy and comedy are closely entwined, it is the former which has fascinated critics the more, largely because of the problem of suffering. Why does it happen, what does it mean and what can be done about it? We might even say that tragedy is a response to the problem of evil. Why does a supposedly loving God create a world where privation, misery and wretchedness seem to be the common lot of all creation? Such serious questions seem to preclude comedy and yet it too is concerned with the fall of man, not because he ate an apple, but because he slipped on a banana skin.

This chapter will look at the differences between tragedy and comedy before arguing that they have a common origin in sacrificial ritual. It will show that the kinship between tragedy and comedy is evident, to a certain extent, in their etymology and in the myth of Dionysus, the god of theatre. It will then look at Nietzsche's theory of tragedy, which puts Dionysus at its heart, before moving on to consider the Cambridge Ritualists and some of their critics. Finally it will clarify the relationship between drama and ritual and say why it is important to appreciate the spectral presence of ritual in tragedy and comedy as they develop over time.

Tragedy and comedy: The same or different?

The differences between tragedy and comedy are easy to spot. Tragedy ends in death, and comedy in marriage; tragedy focuses on the high-born, and comedy on the low-born; tragedy focuses on an individual, and comedy on the community; tragedy celebrates resignation, and comedy celebrates improvisation; tragedy is of the mind, and comedy is of the body; tragedy is the acquisition of self-knowledge and comedy thrives on self-ignorance; and so on. No doubt the reader can add to this list. But while these distinctions have a certain validity, they are by no means absolute. Tragedy, for example, does not always end in death as the example of *Cresphontes* (425 BCE)[1] shows, nor does comedy always end in marriage, as is apparent in Shakespeare's *Love's Labour's Lost* (1598).

Nor does the distinction between high- and low-born characters stand up to scrutiny. Willy Loman in Arthur Miller's *Death of a Salesman* (1949), as his name suggests, is not a high-born figure but he is often regarded as a tragic one, while Alceste in Moliere's *The Misanthrope* (1666) is both comic and high-born. And while there are certainly tragic heroes like Oedipus and Lear who suffer into truth there are others, such as Sophocles' Antigone and Shakespeare's Coriolanus, who make little progress in understanding themselves. They are much poorer in self-knowledge than some comic characters. By the close of Shakespeare's *Much Ado About Nothing* (1598/1599), Benedick and Beatrice realize that they really love each other, while Glyn in Alan Ayckbourn's *Time of My Life* (1993) has to face the consequences of his affair and learn the true meaning of happiness.

This is not to say that there are no differences between tragedy and comedy, only that they are ones of emphasis rather than substance. Tragedy and comedy are closely related because they both grew out of sacrificial ritual which connects death with the celebration of new life. As such, sacrificial ritual may itself be an expression of what Freud considers to be the two main instincts of human beings, Eros and Thanatos: the one strives for ever more complex forms of life, and the other for its dissolution, for a return to an inorganic state. These instincts are separate but they are also 'fused, blended and alloyed with one another'.[2] Of course we cannot prove this, and Freud's theory of the instincts may well have been supplanted by the science of genetics, but it remains an intriguing proposition.

The story of tragedy and comedy is one of divergence as they develop from their common origin. Not only do they appear different from one another but, over the centuries, each genre begins to internally diversify so that tragedies from one period barely resemble those from another and the same applies to comedies. These changes are largely to do with the conventions of tragedy and comedy; their nature, possibly rooted in the structure of the human psyche, remains largely the same. But, as the genre of tragedy in particular begins to decline due to urbanization, the rise of science and the development of democracy, this nature seeks new forms of expression. We will come to those in their proper place.

Etymology

Tragedy and comedy are usually considered separately. Yet they are linked not just by sacrifice but also, though more tenuously, by terminology. The Greek *tragōidia*, from which we get our term 'tragedy', meant both serious and *sportive* tragedy.[3] *Tragōidia* is formed from *tragos* meaning 'goat' and *ōidē* meaning 'song'. The term could also refer to the prize of a goat for the best actor or tragic chorus. *Tragos* has one further meaning, 'spelt', a form of Athenian grain used in brewing beer which connects the term with Dionysus, the god of theatre who was the god of beer before he was the god of wine. The word 'comedy' has several derivations. At one time it was believed to be a combination of *kōma* sleep and *ōidē*. In sleep we dream, and dreams, so Freud tells us, are the expression of forbidden desires which are analogous to the scatological humour, slapstick violence and anarchic sexuality of comedy. Another possible derivation of the word 'comedy' is the word *kōmē*, which means 'country village'. *Kōmē* is related to comedy because behaviour that was prohibited in the city was permitted in the country. Erich Segal says that the 'orgiastic indulgence'[4] of country festivities were socially sanctioned activities providing outlets for excess energies that might otherwise disrupt the smooth working of society. But the most likely source for our word 'comedy' is *komoidia*, the song of the *kōmos*, a procession characterized by singing, dancing and drinking. Those taking part wore masks and costumes and shouted abuse at individuals along the way. They also carried with them a huge phallus to promote fertility.

Although tragedy and comedy are different words they are both forms of song and they have similar connotations. Each is associated with intoxication – tragedy because of its etymological links with beer, and comedy because drink was an integral part of the *kōmos*. Both tragedy and comedy are also associated with the instinctual life – tragedy because it is derived from the ancient Greek for goat, a creature which symbolizes animal passions, and comedy because it arose from the celebrations which gave free rein to such passions. In short, tragedy and comedy overlap to the extent that they were originally types of song both of which were associated, in their different ways, with the pleasures of sensuous existence. But etymology alone will not disclose their various meanings. Segal, indeed, wonders whether we can ever exhaust the explanations for comedy. In his delightfully witty phrase, it is 'a revel without a cause'.[5]

Dionysus

Aristotle (384–322 BCE) said that tragedy and comedy had their roots in religious ritual. Tragedy arose from the dithyramb which was a hymn in honour of Dionysus, while comedy arose from phallic songs which were also associated with his worship. Given that Dionysus seems to be the source of both tragedy and comedy, it is not surprising to learn that he was the god of theatre. The story of Dionysus is similar to that of other deities described by Frazer in *The Golden Bough*. That is to say, he is killed and brought back to life.

The basic elements of the myth are constant but the details vary. Zeus, the king of the Olympians, is Dionysus' father and his mother, in most accounts, is Semele, a mortal woman. Hera, Zeus' wife, is jealous, and wants to kill Dionysus. In one version of the myth she tries to do this by tricking Zeus into incinerating the pregnant Semele; in another she asks the Titans, a race of giants, to kill the infant Dionysus which they do by cutting him into little pieces, a ritualistic act known as *sparagmos*. In the first version of the myth Zeus rescues Dionysus from the flames and sews him into his thigh; in the second, the Titans eat every part of him except his heart which is rescued and used to bring him back to life.

Zeus then has Dionysus transformed into a kid or ram and sends him to be educated by nymphs on Mount Nysa where he invents wine. The constant presence of females makes Dionysus often appear womanly in appearance and behaviour. Hera recognizes him when he eventually leaves Mount Nysa and drives him mad. He wanders all over the world introducing the cult of the vine[6] and demanding recognition for his divinity. After various adventures, including battling the Amazons, a tribe of warlike women, and escaping from pirates, he enters Greece. Having established his worship throughout the world he ascends to heaven and sits on the right hand of Zeus.

The killing of Dionysus supplies tragedy with its theme of death while his rebirth supplies comedy with its theme of life. This reflects the two parts of the ancient ritual, the sacrifice and the celebrations of new life that followed. The sacrifice evolves into the death of the high-born hero in tragedy and the celebration of new life evolves into the marriage with which comedies conventionally end, at least until the eighteenth century. There are other aspects of the Dionysian myth that underpin tragedy and comedy. He is, for instance, a supreme actor, being able to transform himself at various times into a bull or a goat. He is also a rather androgynous figure, mainly due to his upbringing by nymphs, an experience that proves useful when he pretends to be female. This aspect of his identity feeds into the play with gender found in particularly Shakespearean comedy, where a part like Viola in *Twelfth Night* (1601–1602) calls for a boy actor to dress as a girl to dress as a boy.

Disguise is a prominent feature of comedy, a lot of its humour arises from cases of mistaken identity. But it is also featured in tragedy. Hamlet, for example, pretends to be mad while Edgar, in *King Lear* (c. 1603/1606), disguises himself as a beggar. In tragedy disguise is related to questions about the nature of man. Is he no more than the part he plays? But it is also an attempt to escape the confines of the self, a desire that has its roots in Dionysian ecstasy. The wine and the collective worship did not, though, just offer the chance of liberation; they were also a way of getting in touch with fundamental life forces, of being in contact with cosmos and feeling the unity of creation.

On a more mundane level Dionysus is also the prototype for hubris because, by mounting his father's throne and 'mimicking the great god by brandishing the lightning in his tiny hand',[7] he exhibits the pride that causes the tragic hero's downfall. He may also be seen as an early draft for the tragic villain since he commits a number of brutal murders in order to gain recognition of his divinity.[8] This ruthlessness is certainly in evidence in Euripides' *The Bacchae* (405 BCE). King Pentheus bans the women of Thebes from worshipping Dionysus. The god therefore causes them to escape to the Mount Cithaeron, led by Pentheus' mother Agave. He also tricks Pentheus into spying on the women's activities but, in their frenzy, they mistake him for a wild animal and tear him apart, as Dionysus was once torn apart by the Titans.

Dionysus' final contribution to drama was the satyr play which was performed after the trilogy of tragedies at the festival of the City Dionysia in Athens. The satyrs themselves were a combination of human and animal characteristics. They accompanied Dionysus on his travels along with the Maenads, his female followers. Satyr plays were an ancient form of tragicomedy based on the stories of Greek mythology but the form in which they were sung, the dithyramb, was exclusive to the god. From the little evidence we have, the satyr plays appear to have been a mixture of drunkenness, brazen sexuality and general merriment.

Nietzsche (1844–1900), *The Birth of Tragedy* (1872)

Nietzsche's *The Birth of Tragedy* revives the importance of Dionysus for the modern world. He contrasts him with Apollo claiming that the former stands for the world of reality and the latter for the world of appearance. From this basic distinction flow several others which, in many ways, parallel Freud's characterization of the conscious and the unconscious. Apollo, for example, is intellect while Dionysus is instinct. In Nietzsche's view, the tragic hero represents Apollo and the satyric chorus represents Dionysus. Each symbolizes a different state of being. The hero stands for the individual while the chorus stands for the unity of all things. We experience the first through speech and the second through music. Music gives us direct access to this unity; speech gives us the idea of it. The satyric chorus plunges us into the very heart of it, and the tragic hero presents it for our contemplation. By doing so he or she protects us from too great an exposure to the ecstasy that is the essence of the 'primal Oneness'.[9] But the tragic hero doesn't just mediate between us and the 'primal Oneness'; he or she also stands for the value of the individual. The individual is the ground of a number of values including beauty, moderation and self-knowledge.

Nevertheless, the greatest desire of the tragic protagonist is 'to achieve universality ... to escape the spell of individuation'.[10] He or she does this by destroying the moral and social order. Consequently all distinctions, such as those between good and evil, are dissolved, and all sense of separation between self and other, self and world, are abolished. For Nietzsche, the supreme act of destruction is incest. That is why he hails Oedipus as the greatest hero of tragedy. His actions break the taboo on which society is founded in order to experience the deep truth about the nature of existence, namely that everything is one. It has to be said that this interpretation is hard to sustain for the simple reason that Oedipus, far from wanting to commit incest, actually tries to avoid doing so. All the same Nietzsche's point about the desire to merge with the life force cannot be completely dismissed because it harks back to tragedy's origins in ritual where one aspect of the celebrations was indeed a desire to transcend the self by becoming one with divinity and the vital forces of nature.

The echo of ritual is also apparent in Nietzsche's claim that the tragic hero is a sacrificial figure because he or she endures life's violent beauties and fierce energies on our behalf. He or she takes 'the entire Dionysiac world on his back and relieves us of its burden'.[11] He or she is destroyed by the Dionysiac force in order that we might live. And yet the death of the tragic hero is not a real death at all; it is a return to 'the Primal Mother, eternally creative, eternally impelling into life, eternally drawing satisfaction from the ceaseless flux of phenomena'.[12]

This, indeed, is the basic doctrine of tragedy. The satyr chorus consoles us with the thought that whatever superficial changes may occur, no matter how heart-rending they may be, 'life is, at bottom, indestructibly powerful and joyful'.[13] Tragedy initiates us into an 'understanding of the unity of all things'; it teaches us that individuation is 'the prime source of evil' and that art breaks 'the spell of individuation'[14] and hopefully restores us to a state of oneness with nature. Nietzsche tries to make us experience this by writing in a heightened, dramatic, intoxicated style – a style, in short, that is Dionysiac.

Nietzsche's ideas may tell us less about Greek tragedy than they do about the time in which he was living. *The Birth of Tragedy* was first published in 1872 at the dawn of the modern age – a time characterized by growing mechanization, the spread of urban living, the rise of mass culture, growing secularization and the spread of democracy. One consequence of these changes was that many felt cut off from traditions and ways of life that had previously sustained them. Nietzsche talks about this in *The Birth of Tragedy* when he writes that 'modern man has begun to sense the limitations of the Socratic delight in knowledge, and yearns for a shore from the wide and barren sea of knowledge'.[15] His characterization of Greek tragedy is therefore intimately related to his sense of the spiritual impoverishment of late nineteenth-century Europe. In a world drained of meaning and significance, argued Nietzsche, we look to art to save us 'to heal the wound of existence' by turning it into an 'aesthetic phenomenon'.[16]

The Cambridge Ritualists and Tragedy

A more detailed consideration of the part Dionysus plays in the genesis of tragedy and comedy can be found in the work of the Cambridge Ritualists. They were influenced by Frazer's *The Golden Bough* and also, like Nietzsche, by the upheavals of modernity. In particular they sought in myth a connection to the past, the old ones having been broken by the industrial revolution, the growth of mass society and 'the death of god'. The group's main members were the poet Francis Macdonald Cornford (1874–1943), the linguist and feminist Jane Harrison (1850–1928) and the public intellectual Gilbert Murray (1866–1957).[17] They were all also classical scholars who attempted to explain myth and early forms of drama in terms of ritual, chiefly those dealing with the death and resurrection of the 'Year Spirit', that is gods like Baal, Adonis and, of course, Dionysus.

Harrison's epic work *Themis: A Study of the Social Origins of Greek Religion* (1912) provided the intellectual underpinnings of the group. She argued that religion began as the sacrifice of a 'year-god', or *eniautos daimon*, whose death and resurrection was a ritual re-enactment of the life cycle of the crops, but which then developed into the god's promise of immortality to all men in the form of the great mystery religions of Dionysus and Orpheus. Murray applied some of these ideas to the study of Greek tragedy. It originated, he argued, in a ritual dance in honour of Dionysus, but it was also shaped 'by the epic, by hero cults and by various ceremonies not connected with Dionysus'.[18] Nevertheless, Murray continues, while the content of tragedy may have strayed from the story of Dionysus, 'the forms of tragedy retain clear traces of the original drama of the Death and Rebirth of the Year Spirit'.[19]

He identifies six elements which can be found in the myth of Dionysus and other gods. First there is an *agon* or contest; secondly there is the *pathos*, the ritual slaying of the god; third a messenger announces the death of the god; fourth there is a *threnos* or lamentation; fifth there is *anagnorisis*, a recognition of the mutilated god; and sixth there is *theophany*, the resurrection of the god and a change from sorrow to joy. Murray detects this basic pattern in the tragedies performed at the City Dionysia, a festival held in honour of the god. Each playwright presented three tragedies, followed by a satyr play. Collectively, they were known as a tetralogy.

A number of these elements can be found in *The Bacchae*. The *agon*, whose source is the conflict between winter and spring, lies in the confrontation between Dionysus and Pentheus over the worship of the god; the ritual slaying of the god is evident in the Bacchae tearing Pentheus to pieces, and the messenger announcing the death of the god is evident when a messenger in the play recounts that horror. Murray says that the other two elements would have appeared in the satyr play which 'represented the joyous arrival of the Reliving Dionysus and his route of attendant *daimones*'.[20]

The fact that Murray locates the fifth and sixth elements in the satyr play is a reminder that, in general, the elements he describes are distributed over the tetralogy as a whole. Most Greek tragedies have survived as single plays. The exception is Aeschylus' *Oresteia* (458 BCE). This highlights a big difference between our experience of tragedy and that of the ancient Greeks. We see tragedies as individual works; the ancient Greeks saw them as a trilogy ending with a satyr play. So while we may think of tragedy in terms of loss, the Greeks were more likely to view it in terms of loss and restoration, hence Aristotle's remark that the best tragedies end happily.[21]

The Cambridge Ritualists and Comedy

But what of comedy? Can we find elements of ritual in comedy as well as in tragedy? Cornford's answer is a resounding 'yes'. Looking particularly at Aristophanes, he examines the phallic songs from which Aristotle said that comedy sprang. While no one can be sure of the exact forms of the songs, they were certainly a feature of the worship of Dionysus. From the available sources it seems that phallic songs were divided into two parts. The first was an invocation to Phales, a satyr and companion to Dionysus, and the second consisted of abuse and invective. The first part was intended to promote fertility and the second was meant to expel any evil influences. The songs, which were divided between a leader and a chorus, were part of a drunken procession called a *kōmos*, which moved to the place of sacrifice and then onto another place where, most likely, there would be more singing, dancing and drinking.

Cornford's analysis of phallic songs and their relation to comedy is more subtle than I can indicate here. He shows that the phallic songs began to evolve into folk drama when people started to impersonate Phales or the spirits which had to be expelled if the harvest was to be successful. Driving out those spirits gradually evolves into a conflict between good and evil that is personified by two antagonists, which represents another stage in the development of drama. The battle between good and evil corresponds to 'the succession of the seasons, each in his turn has his separate reign, the period during which he triumphs over his rival'.[22] Many folk dramas feature a battle between a young and old king which, Cornford argues, is really a battle between summer and winter. The claim is familiar from Frazer. The old king is a force of evil and obstruction because he has grown senile and yielded to the decay of winter. The young king is a force for good. Standing for the vigour of youth, he facilitates sexual union and fertility. His association with marriage has its roots in the *kōmos* which was also a wedding procession. In some versions of the conflict, it is the young king who is killed but then, like Dionysus, he is later restored to life.

How, then, does all this relate to the comedies of Aristophanes (c. 445 BCE–c. 383 BCE)? Cornford begins his study by noting that the plays usually conclude with the chorus leading the hero out of the orchestra in triumph.[23] He was also accompanied by a female character who appears only at this point in the play. She is not related to what has gone before nor has anyone mentioned her existence. Her sudden entrance is a mystery. Who is she? Why is she partnering the hero? Cornford suggests that we look for the explanation in ritual. The singing and dancing of the chorus, the *kōmos*,

the uniting of male and female together with the honours with which the
hero was in some plays bestowed, are all reminiscent of the sacred marriage
where the bride and bridegroom represent spirits of fertility. Furthermore,
Cornford continues, the celebrations surrounding the hero have their roots
in those ceremonies designed to greet the new king after he has successfully
banished the old one.

Not content with general parallels, Cornford argues that the basic
structure of Aristophanes' plays has the formal character we associate
with religious ritual. First there is the *prologue* which establishes the scene,
introduces the characters and signposts the main themes; second there is the
parodos, or entry of the chorus; third there is the *agon*, or contest; fourth
there is the *parabasis* or address by the chorus to the audience; fifth there are
several miscellaneous scenes, usually of a farcical nature; and sixth there is
the *exodus* or final scene which usually involves festivities of some kind. The
most important element in this list is the *agon* for this is the central feature
not only of Aristophanes' comedies, but also of rituals and folk drama.
One example is the contest in *The Frogs* (405 BCE) over who is the best
dramatist to inspire Athens to beat back the Spartans gathering at her walls,
Euripides or Aeschylus. Such arguments, claims Cornford, can be traced
back to the conflict in folk drama between summer and winter, which itself
reaches back to the ritual of sacrifice to ensure a successful harvest.

The *parabasis*, which has seven parts,[24] comes after the *agon*. Cornford
argues that the *parabasis* 'closely resembles the Phallic Songs'[25] in that,
like them, it contains invocation and invective, the calling up of the god,
and the satire used to scatter evil spirits. Moreover, the very form of the
parabasis mirrors how the phallic songs were performed, that is by a leader
and a chorus. But despite the obvious parallels between the *parabasis* and
the phallic songs the two are not the same. The biggest difference is that
invocation and invective are not directed at gods or spirits but at social
problems. The *parabasis* in *The Wasps* declares that the poet's aim is to drive
off 'all those plagues, fears and nightmare shapes/That came and hovered by
your beds at night,/Smothering fathers, choking grandfathers,/And pinning
lawsuits, summonses, and writs,/On harmless, peaceful folk'.[26] This is the
secular version of the expulsion of evil spirits. The poet, too, is the human
version of the god, taking on monsters, 'to purge the land of grievous ills'
and 'sow a crop of new ideas'.[27]

The miscellaneous scenes and the *exodos* evoke, either separately or
together, the sacrificial feast that follows the sacrifice. After the killing of
the god, usually in the form of an animal, the meat was shared between
the worshippers, an act that expressed both oneness with the deity and
communal solidarity. Cornford detects references to the sacrificial feast in
Aristophanes. In *The Wasps* (422 BCE), for instance, the debate between
Procleon and his son Anticleon[28] about the worth of the jury system
concludes with preparations for a ceremony followed by the drinking of
soup. Incidentally, this conflict between father and son is an echo of that

between the old and the young king. Freud will eventually rewrite this struggle in terms of the Oedipus complex, with the small boy wishing to eliminate his father.

Coming after the *agon*, the feast is a victory celebration. It has echoes of the festivities surrounding the death of the god. His various body parts were either devoured by his worshippers or scattered across the fields to help fertilize the crops. In either case, it was believed he would be resurrected. Cornford's claim is that the *agon* recalls the original sacrifice because it is ultimately about death and new life. The eating and drinking which follow the *agon* resemble the consumption of the god, while the practice of throwing little barley cakes in the form of phalli to the audience is strongly reminiscent of strewing the god's parts across the land. In both cases the intention is to spread 'the beneficent influence of the fertility rite throughout the community'.[29] It should be added, however, that Aristophanes disapproved of this custom. In *The Wasps*, Xanthias, a slave, tells the spectators that no one is going to come on with a basket and distribute food to them. *The Wasps* is the sort of play that is 'a bit more intelligent than the usual knockabout stuff'.[30]

Ritual and Drama

Not everyone agrees that the origins of Greek tragedy and comedy, let alone the later manifestations of both genres, lie in sacrificial ritual. A. W. Pickard-Cambridge (1873–1952) famously stated that tragedy and ritual were quite different because in one the central character does not return to life and in the other he does.[31] But this assumes that the Cambridge Ritualists were arguing for exact parallels between ritual and tragedy which they were not. They were simply pointing out those features of tragedy which suggested it had developed from ritual, something which Pickard-Cambridge himself accepted since he wrote that the dithyramb was 'primarily Dionysiac [in] character', that tragedy was 'originally Dionysiac' and that both tragedy and comedy are closely associated with 'intoxication'.[32] In fact Pickard-Cambridge's real quarrel with the Cambridge Ritualists is aesthetic. He simply cannot countenance the idea that 'the noble seriousness of tragedy can have grown...out of the ribald satyric drama'.[33]

Bertolt Brecht (1898–1956) does not share Pickard-Cambridge's views on the nobility of tragedy but he too downplays the role of ritual in theatre. 'Theatre may be said to be derived from ritual', he says, 'but this is only to say that it becomes theatre once the two have separated'.[34] Brecht's criticism of ritual was part of his desire to create a new type of theatre, one which encouraged the audience to take a more critical approach to the events portrayed on stage – to think how they came about, how characters respond to them and how the social order can always be changed. Ritual had no place in this project because it reinforced the religious message that suffering was inevitable and that, if people wanted to please God, they should accept their lot in life. What's more Brecht had seen the danger of putting ritual at the heart of society. The Nazis with their parades, torchlight rallies and ideology of the Volk had brought disgrace and ruin to Germany and devastation to Europe.

Others, though, had a more positive view of ritual. Colonialism had made European populations more aware of different cultures. A number of modernist artists such as Paul Gaugin (1848–1903) in painting, D. H. Lawrence (1885–1930) and T. S. Eliot (1888–1965) in literature and Igor Stravinsky (1882–1971) in music saw the world of myth and ritual as offering a more authentic, spiritual and fulfilling way of life than could be found in their own supposedly more advanced societies.[35] Drama also saw a turn to ritual which resulted in a greater emphasis on dance, music and gesture than on the interactions of character. The stage designer Gordon Craig (1872–1966) advocated getting rid of 'the play' to concentrate on the true art of theatre: action, words, line, colour and rhythm. The French director and drama theorist Antonin Artaud (1896–1948) also wanted to dispense with the script and return to a theatre of masks, costume and stylized actions. Both men were convinced that by reviving the ritualistic element of theatre they would put the audience in touch with vital forces, pure emotion and profound truths about humanity and its relation to the cosmos.

Conclusion

The debate about ritual and drama often seems to be asking us to choose one or the other, but it is sometimes hard to tell them apart. For example, the claim that ritual is religious and drama is secular collapses as soon as we think of Medieval morality plays. Another frequently cited difference is that ritual is efficacious and that is it is intended to bring about a desired result, while drama is entertainment. But this ignores how, from the time of the ancient Greeks right up to at least the nineteenth century, it was believed that plays should promote good behaviour by rewarding virtue and punishing vice. It has also been argued that drama is an expression of a freer and more egalitarian society, while ritual suggests hierarchy and compunction. Can Shakespeare's England be described as free and egalitarian? Yet again the boundary between ritual and drama begins to blur.[36] The argument is not that there are no differences between the two, only that they are much more closely related than we sometimes think. It is time we gave ritual the recognition it deserves.

We can start by acknowledging that there is a kinship between sacrificial ritual and tragedy and comedy. And, despite the development of drama over the centuries and the decline of tragedy this kinship is still evident. Which prompts the question of what ritual brings to drama. This is very difficult to answer without reference to specific plays which we will do in the following chapters. However we can say that ritual gives shape to drama. It provides it with a template, the death of a god, and the celebrations which follow. Both are a means of understanding such things as the origin of society, the meaning of community, the nature of divinity and the relationship between life and death. In short, ritual provides drama with a framework that allows us to comprehend the world and our place in it.

It is important to be clear on this point. Sacrificial ritual does not supply drama with a set of beliefs about these matters; rather it is a mode of perceiving them. In that respect it seems to tell us something about human psychology, namely that our minds are predisposed to look at the world from a particular point of view; for example, it seems we must always deal with problems by finding a scapegoat for them. Thus one reason for the survival of sacrificial ritual in drama is that it reflects our mental make-up, the particular way that our brain makes us apprehend the world and organize all its various phenomena. Again it is important to be clear. The claim is not that sacrificial ritual is the key to how our minds perceive things, only that it appears to be a factor in how we see and conceive them. There are many other factors that shape our vision and understanding but what is remarkable about sacrificial ritual is that, despite the rise and fall of different belief systems, all of which drama registers, it remains a fairly constant presence. The following chapters will attempt to flesh out this claim.

3

Greek Drama

Greek tragedy was a product of fifth-century Athens though it did spread to other Greek cities, like Thebes and Corinth, during the fourth century. Comedy had more diverse beginnings. Sixth-century vases from different parts of Greece show costumed choruses that anticipate those found in Athenian Old Comedy. Aristotle was hampered in his search for the source of comedy because, he said, it was not taken seriously and therefore there were no records of its development. In addition, he added, 'the form was already partly fixed before the first recorded comic poets and so we do not know who introduced masks, prologues, numerous actors and so on'.[1] Aristotle does, however, suggest that comic plots came from Sicily. He did write more on comedy but the work, which was to have formed the second half of *Poetics*, has been lost.

The First actor and reactions to Tragedy

The first actor was a man called Thespis who lived in the sixth century. The introduction of the actor was a crucial step in the change from ritual to drama. The actor represented a person separate from the chorus and he spoke with a single voice to their collective one. The dialogue between self and society had begun. It was reputed that Thespis disguised his face either with white lead or a white mask. Thespis is also credited with taking his 'plays' round the local villages and performing them on wagons. Ritual remained a key ingredient of these performances, partly because they centred round the death and resurrection of the god and partly because they were shown at local Dionysiac festivals.

Solon (c. 638 BCE–c. 558 BCE) was a statesman and lawmaker who had laid the foundations for democracy by, among other things, establishing an assembly where male citizens would meet to discuss and vote on decrees that affected every aspect of Athenian life.[2] The Greek historian and biographer Plutarch (c. 46–127 CE) tells the story of his perhaps apocryphal encounter with Thespis. Because he himself was a poet and because he was, as Plutarch tells us, naturally fond of learning anything new, he was keen to find about this latest thing called tragedy. Plutarch does not tell us what Solon saw but he does tell us about Solon's reaction. The old man accosted Thespis and asked him if he were not ashamed to tell such lies in the presence of so many people. Thespis replied that there was no harm in saying such things in a play to which Solon responded by 'striking the ground sharply with his staff declaring: "Soon, however, if we give plays of this sort much praise and honour, we shall find them in our solemn contracts."'[3] Solon, in short, thought that tragedy glorified lying and that, as a result, falsehood would permeate the polity.

The Athenian tyrant Peisistratus (c. 668 BCE–c. 527 BCE) was unencumbered by such worries. He brought rural festivals honouring Dionysus into the city. He was also responsible for introducing tragedy into the Panatheniac Festival for which Thespis won the first ever prize. The Festival, which consisted of religious ceremonies, athletic competitions and cultural events such as the reciting of Homer, was created by Peisistratus to consolidate his power and promote pride in Athens. After him came Cleisthenes (570 BCE–508 BCE) whose reforms earned him the nickname 'the father of Athenian democracy'. One of the most important was the replacement of a political system based on a small number of aristocratic families with one based on areas of residence known as *demes*. This also involved increasing the number of tribes from four to ten, each being named after one of the legendary heroes of Athens. The effect of these changes was to make the various institutions of the city, such as the *Boule* or council, which governed Athens on a day-to-day basis, more representative and to make the inhabitants loyal to the city rather than to their village or small town. The emergence of the actor, the inclusion of tragedy in the Panatheniac Festival and the first tentative steps towards democracy form the backdrop to the Great Dionysia which was established in about 500 BCE.

The Great Dionysia

The Great or City Dionysia was established in about 500 BCE and took place annually at the end of March or the beginning of April. A competition for the best tragedy and satyr play, it was both an act of worship and a display of civic identity. As a big, international event it was different from the other two drama festivals held in honour of Dionysus. The first, the Lenaea, was also held in Athens, or just on the outskirts, and took place in January while the second, the Rural Dionysia, was celebrated in December. Each festival had a slightly different conception of Dionysus. In one he was the liberator, in the other he was the god of wine and, in the third, he was Dionysus of the field. A reminder, perhaps, that Dionysus had a number of identities, which made him an ideal deity for the theatre.

There were several events in the days leading up to the Great Dionysia which lasted four days. The first was the procession of the statue of Dionysus to a temple in Eleutherae, a village near Athens. The statue was then returned to the theatre in Athens where sacrifices and hymns were performed. The presentation of playwrights and performers, known as the *proagōn*, was the second event leading up to the Great Dionysia itself and this was followed by a grand ceremonial procession called a *pōmpe*, in which the participants carried a variety of sacred objects as well as the phalluses associated with the worship of Dionysus. The procession concluded with the sacrifice of bulls in the sanctuary of the god. Finally, there was the *kōmos* the celebratory revel which was discussed in the previous chapter.

All citizens, that is adult males with the right to vote, were required to attend the Great Dionysia. Those who could not afford the entry fee were subsidized from the city's Thoric or Festival Fund. There is some controversy over whether foreigners, resident aliens and women could attend the theatre but there is partial evidence that they did.[4] The seating arrangements reflected the different sections of society. One block, for example, was reserved for the council or government of Athens, another for visiting ambassadors, priests and other dignitaries, while still another was for *ephebes*, young men whose fathers had been killed in combat and who now were about to join the armed forces. The survival of lead tokens, used as tickets, bore the names of different tribes, suggesting that seating was also organized on tribal lines.

Before the plays began, there were four rituals. The first, performed by a priest, was a sacrifice of piglets whose blood was scattered round the playing area. This was followed by a libation poured out by ten leading political and military figures. The second ritual consisted of a herald reading out the names of citizens who had made a contribution to the state and received, in return, a crown. The third was a show of tributes paid to Athens by her allies. Servants carried in bars of silver bullion and paraded them round the theatre. Finally, the *ephebes* were exhibited to the audience. The state had paid for their upbringing and education and now, appearing in their military uniform, before approximately 18,000 people, they swore by the gods to fight and die for Athens as their fathers had done. They then took their seats in their designated spot and the performances began.

It is clear that these rituals were designed to glorify Athens and to uphold a model of democratic citizenship. How then, asks the classics scholar Simon Goldhill, are we to make sense of tragedy since it 'show[s] a world ripped apart, civic foundations shattered and the noble values of citizenship turned against themselves in violence, confusion and horror'.[5] In part, the answer lies in the fact that most Greek tragedies were set in the distant past and in places other than Athens. Audiences were therefore asked to contrast their well-ordered city with the chaos that had reigned in ancient Thebes or Corinth. Athens represented advancement, progress, and civilization. But the warnings were clear. Tragedy showed what can happen when things go wrong. Those who did not honour the gods, those who went against the order of nature, those who put their own interest above those of the *polis*, or city, brought anarchy and destruction in their wake.

Tragedy, then, reinforced the social order but, as Edith Hall argues, it also subverted it by giving voice to those like women, foreigners and slaves who were 'silenced in the public discourse of the city'.[6] More generally, tragedy taught the audience the art of debate. Many citizens had received little formal schooling and what they learnt from the exchanges between the protagonist and the chorus was how to discuss an issue and to be aware that it could be viewed in different ways, an important skill if Athenian democracy was to work. They also had to learn to distinguish between substance and style in discussion, a key theme in Euripides' plays. Tragedy, in short, did not simply reflect moral and political ideas; it also explored and questioned them and, in the process, helped to create an informed, self-aware body of citizens. It valued hierarchy but it also uprooted it; it promoted conformity but it was also a form of critique.

Aeschylus (525–456 BCE), *The Oresteia* (458 BCE)

Aeschylus is regarded as the father of Greek drama because he introduced a second actor into his plays. Prior to that time there was only a single actor and a chorus. Aeschylus is reputed to have worked in a vineyard until Dionysus appeared in a dream and told him to write tragedies. His encounter with Dionysus is a reminder of the relation between drama and ritual. Sacrifice involves violence. So too does revenge. The relationship between the violence of sacrifice and the violence of revenge is one of the most complex in the history of tragedy. Both are forms of exchange. The priest sacrifices to the gods in the hope of something in return while those seeking vengeance are intent on repaying an injury done to them. In the first case the violence is public and socially cohesive; in the second it is private and socially divisive.

Both types of violence are evident in Aeschylus' trilogy, *The Oresteia*. Indeed, they are closely linked to one another for it is Agamemnon's sacrifice of his and Clytemnestra's daughter, Iphigenia,[7] that initiates the cycle of revenge in the play. Clytemnestra murders Agamemnon who is then murdered by their son, Orestes, who, in turn, is pursued by the Furies[8] only escaping their vengeance by the intervention of Athena who establishes the law and replaces revenge with justice: 'the time of brute force is past./ The day of reasoned persuasion,/With its long vision,/With its mercy, its forgiveness,/Has arrived'.[9]

As these words show, *The Oresteia* deals with the passage from savagery, defined as revenge, to civilization, defined as law, a process that culminates in the Furies renouncing their primal urge to destroy those who murder members of their own family in return for a position of honour and respect in Athens. In addition, they will receive tributes 'at marriage and childbirth/Where strangers are united in love/And a new being is brought out of chaos'.[10] These tributes are a reminder of the uses of sacrifice, how it strengthens communal ties and promotes fertility. The Furies' renunciation of their powers will result in healthy animals and large harvests. 'We can', they say, even 'persuade great Pan/To bring twin lambs/From every ewe.'[11]

The meaning is clear: civilization is built on sacrifice, especially that of giving up the right of revenge. This accords with those theories which state that sacrifice marks the boundary between the domestic and the wild, between nature and culture.[12] But the position is a little more complicated than that, if only because the act of revenge already implies some form of social organization. That apart, the true sacrifice in *The Oresteia* is not the self-sacrifice of the Furies but the killing of Clytemnestra. At first glance her death does not look like a sacrifice but like revenge. Orestes stabs his mother – itself a sexually symbolic act – because she killed his father. However, from another angle, Clytemnestra's death takes on the appearance of a sacrifice. Why? Because it was demanded by Apollo. He it was who 'appointed the stroke of the sword-blade/That dispatched [Orestes] mother'.[13]

But the fact that Apollo required Clytemnestra's death is not, of itself, sufficient to turn it into a sacrifice. For it to acquire that status it also needs to have a beneficial effect. And what the slaying of Clytemnestra achieves is nothing less than the establishment of a new pantheon of gods and the founding of the new Athens. Athene and Apollo represent the new gods and the Furies the old ones, the latter recognizing that their laws are now 'obsolete'[14] and so they accept the invitation to be part of the new order. Athene establishes a new Athens by creating a permanent court and instituting trial by jury, two things that will make the city's name 'resound throughout the nations'.[15]

Clytemnestra's death, in short, makes Athenian civilization possible. Or to put this in a more extreme manner, without her death, there would be no poetry, philosophy or democracy. The whole edifice of Western civilization rests on her butchered body. It is the dramatic equivalent of the ancient Greek custom of sacrificing an animal or, in some cases, a human, whose remains were buried under the foundation of a new building in order to give it 'strength and stability' and 'to guard it against the intrusion of enemies'.[16] This civilization has a distinctly masculine character. Athene may be a female goddess but she represents law, restraint and rationality, traditional 'male qualities' that she uses to douse the fiery instincts of the female Furies. Clytemnestra is like the Furies to the extent that she is female and because she acts from vengeance. The difference is that she is killed and the Furies are incorporated into the new society.

Why is this? One reason is that Clytemnestra exhibits both male and female qualities. She has 'a man's dreadful will in the scabbard of her body'.[17] Such gender confusions could not be tolerated as they may lead to the dangerous blurring of social boundaries. If women came out of the home, what was to stop slaves from rebelling? There was also a fear that women's desires could disrupt the ordered world of men.[18] Clytemnestra's taking a lover, Aegisthus, is one example of how female sexuality could undermine the institutions of society. This sexuality was most evident in fertility goddesses such as Gaia and Demeter. Cybele, known as the 'great mother', was another important goddess and her rites, celebrated in spring, were accompanied by drinking, wild music and abandoned dancing.[19]

Such behaviour was a threat to the social order and the killing of Clytemnestra can be seen, in part, as the repression of the anarchic female goddess and her powers of generation. If civilization was to flourish, the feminine had to be repressed. This is apparent in the difference between the rites associated with Cybele and those invoked by Athene at the end of *The Oresteia*. The former belong to the tradition of the *kōmos*, the drunken wedding procession, but the latter is an altogether more stately and dignified affair. 'Pour out the wine./Let the pine bough crack and blaze .../ So God and Fate, in a divine marriage,/Are made one in the flesh/Of all our people–/ And the voice of their shout is single and holy.'[20] This is a cleaned-up *kōmos*, one that aims at political unity rather than sexual release.

The killing of Clytemnestra represents the removal of the excess associated with the feminine. It therefore fulfils one of the functions of sacrifice, the expulsion of 'evil' by projecting it onto another who is either ceremonially slain or cast out from the community. Nancy Jay's theory of sacrifice may also be relevant here.[21] She argues that sacrifice is a response to the fear of female sexuality which, because it cannot be contained, creates doubts about paternity. Sacrifice addresses this anxiety by creating an artificial form of patrilineal descent. Only males are allowed to perform sacrifice, and they pass on its various offices to their descendants.

William Beers (b. 1948) argues that sacrifice is the result of men's 'narcissistic anxiety'.[22] The male infant cannot identify with the all-powerful mother and resents his dependence on her. In sacrifice this anger – even rage – is directed at the scapegoat, but it can also erupt against women as the source of the problem. Orestes' murder of his mother may have a deeper source than her killing of Agamemnon. But while Clytemnestra's death has some of the features of sacrifice, it lacks others. She is not, for example, made holy or consecrated, which, as we saw in the first chapter, is a vital part of the sacrificial process. Nor is she killed in a ritualistic manner and the motive for her murder remains revenge. So is her death a murder or a sacrifice? It appears to be both.

A similar ambiguity attends the death of Agamemnon. On the one hand it is a murder; on the other it has the appearance of a sacrifice. The chorus refer to it as a 'murder' and an 'unfathomable evil',[23] a view echoed by Orestes who damns his mother as a 'killer'.[24] Yet the description of Agamemnon's killing recalls the ritualistic slaying of sacrifice. He arrives in a chariot, is hailed by the chorus and has a purple cloth spread at his feet before being ritually cleansed. Clytemnestra even refers to him as 'a sacrificial victim...ready at the altar'.[25] She makes a display of his remains in a manner reminiscent of the ritualistic display of the slain god and when she describes his death she tells the chorus that his blood showered her 'like a warm spring rain/That makes the new-sown corn swell with joy/And the buds split into blossom',[26] words that suggest that Agamemnon's death, like that of the sacrificial animal, brings about fertility.

The ambiguous nature of killing in The Oresteia suggests that the violence of revenge and the violence of sacrifice are not as distinct as we earlier claimed. Each has elements of the other, but both are spectacular forms of violence. Burkert believes that this shared dramatic quality was derived from the hunt and developed in sacrifice. The hunters' dance, enacting the killing of the prey, laid the foundation for the elaborate rites leading up to the ritual slaughter of the animal on the altar.[27] The key motive for the killings in The Oresteia is revenge which Burkert again relates back to hunting and sacrifice. He claims that the hunter had to make reparation to the animal for killing it; otherwise its spirit would seek retribution. Sacrifice generated a similar anxiety, with some participants objecting to the whole blood-soaked affair.[28]

These anxieties were to some extent allayed by making the creature live again. Hunters did it by adopting a reverential attitude to its bones or by using its skin for warmth and its teeth for decoration. In sacrifice, too, the animal could be resurrected. After the ox was killed in the ancient Athenian sacrifice known as the Bouphonia or 'murder of the ox',[29] its skin was filled with straw, sewn up and the stuffed animal was then harnessed to a plough. More generally, sacrifice justified ritual slaying on the grounds that the god whom the creature represented had to die in order to be reborn. The main point, however, is that these various elements of hunting and sacrifice – spectacle, revenge and the fear that the dead will return – may account for why murder, sacrifice and revenge are all mixed up together in The Oresteia.

The way the past moulds the present helps us to understand another aspect of The Oresteia, the tension between fate and free will which, incidentally, is one of the recurrent themes of tragedy. Clytemnestra, who appears to be both free and not free, embodies this tension. On the one hand she accepts full responsibility for killing Agamemnon. 'See my work perfected,' she says when she displays his body. 'I don't disown it.'[30] But, on the other, she says to Orestes, 'Do not blame me I was in the hands of Fate.'[31] How can we account for this apparent contradiction? The simple answer is that Clytemnestra makes these conflicting remarks in different circumstances. She utters the first as a queen and the second as a mother pleading for her life at the hands of Orestes, and her words reflect her state of mind at those times. But while this may explain Clytemnestra's behaviour within the terms of the play, it does not help us understand the more general condition, that of destiny versus self-determination, which afflicts so many tragic protagonists, of whom Clytemnestra is only one example.

Perhaps some light may be thrown on this wider problem if we look at the strange behaviour of the participants in the Bouphonia. The sacrifice is unusual in that it had the character of a serious crime.[32] No one wanted to take responsibility for the killing of the creature, not even the priest who struck the fatal blow. Instead, everyone blamed everyone else for the ox's death until, in the end, the knife used to kill it was held to be responsible and cast into the sea.[33] The fact that the participants point the finger at each other implies that the ox was killed as a matter of choice. But the ceremonial nature of the slaying implies the opposite – that the ox's death was the result of a divine demand, an obligation laid upon the community to perform the sacrifice or else suffer the consequences. In short, what we find in the *Bouphonia* is the same impasse between human autonomy and divine diktat that we find in tragedy.

This is not to say that the *Bouphonia* alone is the source of that clash between fate and free will which is part of the dynamic of tragedy but if we accept that drama grew out of ritual, then it is reasonable to assume that it was, to some extent, shaped by it. Certainly we find a fatalistic strain in the act of sacrifice. In one Babylonian ceremony the priest would address the bull he had just killed with these words: 'This deed was done by all the gods, I did not do it,'[34] words which closely echo Clytemnestra's defence of her actions quoted above and also those of Orestes who, like his mother, first of all declares that he is a free agent, 'we must find the means in ourselves',[35] but later states that 'the great god commanded me [to kill my mother]'.[36]

It should be clear from the above that past and present are mixed together. Despite Athene's fine words at the end of *The Oresteia*, there is no complete transition from 'savagery' to 'civilization'. Athens can always regress to an earlier stage of development, as an individual can regress to an earlier stage of his or her instinctual development. Indeed, *The Oresteia* can be loosely interpreted in terms of the Oedipus complex. First the underlying cause of the drama is a variation of the Oedipus story, as the young Paris steals the wife of King Menelaus. Second, the drama takes place within the family unit, and third the shift from female riot to masculine reason parallels the little boy's separation from his mother and identification with his father.

But the Oedipus complex is never fully resolved. Repressed instincts, such as aggression towards the father, threaten to return. In *The Oresteia*, though, it is not the father who may erupt into the present but the mother. Clytemnestra could be seen as a substitute for the father because of her masculine qualities and hence when Orestes kills her he is, in a sense killing Agamemnon, his father. But the very fact that he is stabbing Clytemnestra also suggests he desires to penetrate his mother. Be that as it may, the key point is that Clytemnestra's murder is not dealt with properly because her killer goes unpunished. Her corpse props up civilization, but her soul cries out for justice and no one hears. This creates the potential for her unquiet ghost to rise and seek vengeance, the dramatic equivalent of the return of the repressed in psychoanalysis.

Oedipal desires and Clytemnestra's restless spirit put a strain on the underlying sacrificial structure of *The Oresteia*. The former, for example, symbolize degeneration, the loss of fertility which sacrifice is intended to secure. There are a number of references in the trilogy to the failure of sacrifice. Priam, the king of Troy, 'pours libations/To lubricate the favours of the heavens in vain',[37] while Agamemnon's sacrifice of Iphigenia is 'A sacrifice that cannot be eaten/A sacrifice that poisons the heart.'[38] Such misgivings about the efficacy of sacrifice, which are also found in *Oedipus the King*,[39] highlight the main argument, which is that the straightforward sacrifice of the Furies and the more problematic 'sacrifice' of Clytemnestra neither bring about the end of savagery nor the beginning of civilization. Right at the very start of our journey, we find that sacrifice is flawed, that it cannot bring about the desired end. This has implications for our understanding of the term which, in the fullest sense of the term, is way of ordering and making sense of ourselves, of our relation to others, of life and death and of our connection to both nature and the heavens. So, when sacrifice falters, the cosmos cracks. Where there were answers, there are now questions. The failure of sacrifice gives rise to the birth of philosophy already evident in those thoughts about the nature of life that we find scattered throughout tragedy: 'we use what we love dearly to buy what we loath'.[40] And yet sacrifice does not disappear; its presence continues to be felt in tragedy and comedy right up to the present. It no longer embraces all of life, nor expresses our relation to the circumambient universe, yet we do not seem to be able to do without it.

Old Comedy

Aristophanes wrote about forty plays of which eleven survive. There were competitions for the best comedies just as there were for the best tragedies. The Lenaea was originally intended only for comedies; tragedies were introduced around 430 BCE. The first three days of the City Dionysia were devoted to tragedies and their accompanying satyr plays; on the fourth and final day single comedies by five playwrights were performed. The rivalry between competitors could be intense. Aristophanes dismissed Cratinus (519–422 BCE), his elder contemporary who was victorious six times at the City Dionysia, as an incontinent, drunken has-been, while he himself was accused of plagiarism.

Both men wrote what is known as Old Comedy.[41] The only examples we have of this genre are Aristophanes' surviving plays. Of the other writers of Old Comedy, Cratinus, Eupolis (446–411 BCE) and Hermippus (dates unknown) only fragments remain. Old Comedy differs from tragedy in terms of plot, character, subject matter, representation, language and production values. In tragedy the tightly organized plot mimics the inevitability of fate. What had to happen, happened; nothing could be otherwise.

This is not the case in comedy where the plot structure is much looser and where the general impression is of a chaotic rather than an ordered universe. Similarly while part of the meaning of tragedy lies in the fixed nature of the heroes which determines their actions, that of comedy lies in the fluid nature of the heroes which enables them to adapt to situations and improvise their way out of trouble. Of course both the tragic and the comic protagonist are subject to misfortune but it is of a different kind and they deal with it in different ways.

The subject matter of tragedy is largely based on myth – that of Old Comedy on current events. One of Aristophanes' frequent targets was the statesman Cleon (died 422 BCE), whom he saw as a warmonger and a demagogue. Aristophanes' plays were considered to be such an accurate reflection of contemporary life that when Plato was asked by the tyrant Dionysius of Syracuse (432–367 BCE) to explain the Athenian system of governance the philosopher responded by sending him Aristophanes' complete works.

Although tragedy deals with myth, it presents it in a fairly realistic manner. The characters are psychologically consistent and there is a respect for the physical laws of nature. This is not the case in Old Comedy which is characterized by magic and fantasy and where characters behave in a haphazard fashion. Similarly, where tragedy seeks to maintain the dramatic illusion, Old Comedy constantly breaks it with appeals and addresses to the audience.

Tragedy is written in a high style. Old Comedy spans a range of styles from the colloquial to the artificial. It is bawdy, rude and revels in bodily functions. It parodies the metre[42] and sentiments of tragedy and uses its noble idioms for the most ignoble subjects to hilarious effect. This does not mean that Old Comedy lacks seriousness. On the contrary, Aristophanes aimed to make his audience think critically about their society, in particular about the deceptive art of political rhetoric: 'He's taught you all their tricks, and now you *never* let them cheat you,' he writes of himself in *The Acharnians* (425), adding that he will 'carry on impeaching/Every abuse he sees, and give much valuable teaching,/Making you [the audience] wiser, happier men'.[43]

Old Comedy was more expensive to stage than tragedy, partly because the chorus of twenty-four members was nearly double that of tragedy and partly because it had to be more lavishly costumed. Fantasy choruses of wasps, frogs and clouds abounded. The chorus in Aristophanes' *The Birds* (414 BCE), for example, were required to represent twenty-three different species of fowl. Money didn't just go on costumes; it was also spent on training the chorus and choreographing their every move so as to create an arresting display. Spectacle, indeed, was a strong element of Old Comedy and therefore more use was made of props, stage machinery and special effects than was the case in tragedy.

These differences, though, should not make us overlook the fundamental similarity between tragedy and Old Comedy, namely that they both stem from sacrificial ritual. Moreover, as we shall see, Old Comedy is in continuous dialogue with tragedy and, by the time we get to Menander, comedy has taken on some of the features of tragedy.

Aristophanes (c. 445 BCE–c. 383 BCE), *Women at the Thesmophoria* (411 BCE)

The connection between ritual and Old Comedy is obvious in Aristophanes' *Women at the Thesmophoria* because the Thesmophoria was a religious festival in honour of Demeter, goddess of agriculture, and her daughter Persephone, goddess of the corn.[44] It took place in autumn before the sowing of the winter seed. It lasted three days and was attended only by married women. Thesmophoria derives from *thesmoi*, or laws which govern the working of the land.[45]

Both the myth and the name make clear the festival's connection with fertility. Persephone was kidnapped by Hades, the god of the underworld. Consequently her mother forbade the earth to produce any food until her daughter was found. Zeus could not allow humans to starve and so he negotiated with Hades that Persephone be permitted to return to the upper world for six months of the year thus ensuring that humans will be fed.[46] The story of Demeter and Persephone was at the heart of the Thesmophoria. The action takes place at the temple of Demeter and the first words of the chorus leader are: 'Silence, silence! Pray you to Demeter and the Divine Maiden [Persephone].'[47] One of the rituals, moreover, involved digging up items that had been buried the previous year.[48]

Another ritual, according to a contemporary source, consisted of the women verbally abusing one another. This rather strange activity was a re-enactment of that part of the myth where Iambe momentarily lifts Demeter's grief by insulting Hades and relating crude tales; comedy provides comfort as well as crops. Iambe gave her name to the iambic, the metre in which comedy was written. The word 'iambic' itself comes from the Greek *iambizein*, which means to lampoon. Iambe's ridicule and satire derives from the invective found in phallic songs whose purpose was to ensure fertility by expelling evil influences. We find numerous examples of insults and abuse in *Women at the Thesmophoria*. The drama itself stems from Euripides' fear that the women who attend the festival are going to debate his downfall because he denigrates them in his tragedies. 'The things he says about us! Is there any crime he has not accused us of? Wherever there's a stage…there he is, coming out with his slanders.'[49]

Euripides' relative, Mnesilochus, offers to go to the Thesmophoria to speak in Euripides' defence, though he has to be disguised as a woman, which involves not only shaving his face but also burning off his pubic hair. Once there, Mnesilochus tries to placate the women by reminding them that there are far worse things that Euripides could say about them if he only knew what they really get up to. 'Why is it that we blame him for these things ... when all he's done is mention two or three of our little tricks. There are thousands of other things he *doesn't* know.'[50] A remark which initiates the agon or contest which is central to comedy and whose roots go back to the complex relation between life and death which lies at the heart of sacrifice.

The women are at first insulted, then outraged and finally incandescent at Mnesilochus' scandalous remarks. But before they can reply in kind Cleisthenes, a prominent Athenian gay man, enters and informs them that Euripides has sent a man dressed as a woman to spy on them. Suspicion immediately falls onto Mnesilochus and turns to certainty when Cleisthenes and Mica, one of the Athenian women, remove his clothing. He is then detained, guarded by Critylla, Mica's friend. This episode is followed by a parabasis, where the chorus leader addresses the audience on how women are unfairly perceived as 'a plague and a curse, the source of trouble and strife/And grief and war and sorrow and pain – everything dire in this life!'[51] Her remarks are endorsed by the rest of the chorus who claim that a woman can surpass any man the spectators care to mention.

So ends the first act of *Women at the Thesmophoria*. But what have we learnt? That the play contains two elements of ritual. The first is the insult and the second is the agon. The two are closely connected as invective is an integral part of conflict. But this is a play, not a ritual, which leaves us with the problem of how to interpret these elements. As we have seen abuse, insult and invective were intended to rid society of those things which might prevent a successful harvest but they do not appear to have that purpose here. Aristophanes' concern is with city, not country matters.

Having said that he does sometimes describe the role of the dramatist in terms that evoke the functions of ritual. In *The Wasps* (422 BCE), for example, Aristophanes claims he is a 'Champion' who 'sought to purge the land of grievous ills' with a view to 'sow[ing] a crop/Of new ideas'[52] but unfortunately he was not successful. The exchange of insults in *Women at the Thesmophoria* covers a range of social grievances from how men view women to how they prevent them from playing a full part in Athenian society. And yet these political issues are not entirely divorced from the concern with fertility that lies at the heart of sacrifice. Many of Mnesilochus' remarks about women reflect fears about their fidelity – about whether or not they are faithful to their husbands. Euripides, says Mnesilochus slyly, never mentions 'the woman who spread her skirt out wide to show her husband how nice it looked in the sunlight, while smuggling her boyfriend out underneath it'.[53]

This fear of female sexuality was central to *The Oresteia*. We saw how, in that play, the killing of Clytemnestra was, in part, an attempt to replace the principle of female fertility with that of male rationality. Clytemnestra was a danger because of her sexuality and her ability to transcend gender boundaries; she was both female and male. The same idea is present, but in a comic fashion, in *Women at the Thesmophoria*. Mnesilochus dressing as a woman and Cleisthenes' femininity are examples of Aristophanes playing with the categories of male and female. The anxiety about gender boundaries – which is a big part of comedy right up to the present day – is partly explained by the age-old dread that if sexuality falls into confusion through incest or same-sex desire, then the crops will fail.

But it may also express, however obscurely, a desire for a return to that androgynous state which Aristophanes described in the *Symposium*. It is characterized by a sense of oneness, for which Freud used the term 'oceanic feeling'.[54] He found its source in the infant's union with the mother, a state that reappears in love when 'the boundary between the ego and the object threatens to melt away'.[55] Whatever we may think of Freud's explanation it is at least worth noting that the dramatist and the psychoanalyst both recognize the existence of something fundamental in the human make-up, namely a deep desire to abolish the distance between self and other, self and world. From one angle, this is the instinct for life, because it means joining with another, embracing the outside; but from another angle it is the instinct for death because it means losing or surrendering the self.

The unsettling proximity between life and death finds expression in the intimate relation between tragedy and comedy. Euripides is threatened with death in *Women at the Thesmophoria* and so too is Mnesilochus. In addition, Mnesilochus, in a scene based on Euripides' *Telephus* (438 BCE),[56] snatches Mica's baby and grabs the sacrificial knife, ready to 'stain the altar with its bleeding veins'.[57] But this potential tragedy is instantly turned to comedy when Mnesilochus discovers that the 'baby' is in fact 'a full skin of wine complete with Persian booties',[58] a bundle that does credit to Mica's ingenuity if not her piety.

One of the most striking features of *Women at the Thesmophoria* is that it contains more allusions to Euripides' tragedies than any other of Aristophanes' plays.[59] The tragedy it most resembles is *The Bacchae* for in both a man infiltrates a ritual that is meant for women only. In the one he escapes, and in the other he is torn to pieces. The presence of tragedy in comedy and, indeed, comedy in tragedy is a legacy of their common origin in sacrificial ritual where the continuity or appearance of new life depended on the spilling of blood. No one has their throat cut in *Women at the Thesmophoria* but that doesn't mean there are no potential sacrificial victims. To Euripides, Mnesilochus and the 'baby', we can add 'the Scythian' who guards Mnesilochus in the second act.

He has no name and is known only by his country of origin. He is a 'barbarian', a term used by the ancient Greeks to signify anyone who was not Greek. The Scythian's status as an outsider is reflected in his grammatically weak and heavily accented language: 'you keep mouth shut!

I fetch da mat. Den I guard you'.[60] And it is his status as an outsider that
marks him as the true sacrificial victim of the play. The 'sacrifice' takes
the form of his being hoodwinked by Euripides. The playwright hires a
dancing girl to distract the Scythian from his guard duty. He promises
the Scythian that, if he pays one drachma, the girl will sleep with him. The
Scythian gives the money but she vanishes leaving him running round the
stage trying to find her. And when the chorus deliberately send him in
the wrong direction, crying 'good riddance',[61] his role as sacrificial victim
is confirmed.

But what does his 'sacrifice' achieve? Nothing less than the
reconciliation between Euripides and the women. He promises not to
say another bad word about them if they help him to rescue Mnesilochus
and they agree. Harmony is restored between the sexes. The fear of
ungoverned female desire is projected onto the lascivious Scythian and
vanishes with him. Uniting against the outsider restores the right relations
between men and women; reproduction is regulated and promiscuity is
banished.

This sacrificial aspect of the play is not self-evident. We can only find
it if we are attuned to what Mnesilochus says to the women and to how
his words relate to the Scythian. They alert us to worries about sexuality
which were rife in the *Oresteia*. But this does not mean we should overlook
the social dimension of *Women at the Thesmophoria*. Aristophanes is
clearly addressing tensions in the relations between men and women in
contemporary Athens. The problem is how to connect these two levels of
the play. My argument is that, since drama grew out of ritual, it is to some
extent shaped by it. Or, to put this another way, the structure of sacrifice
partly conditions how the social issues are played out, not just in *Women at
the Thesmophoria* but in tragedy and comedy generally. The social, we might
say, is filtered through the sacrificial, though this is an artificial distinction
since the sacrificial is itself social as we saw in the first chapter.

Semantics aside, I am not claiming that the sacrificial structure of
Women at the Thesmophoria is *the* key to understanding it. My point
is only that we need to acknowledge it and to relate it to other elements
of the play. Here again there is an obvious analogy with Freudian
psychoanalysis, one of whose axioms is that what happens in the early
stages of our development strongly influences our later behaviour. Self-
knowledge largely depends on the ability to connect past to present, and
the same is true of a society. It can never come to terms with the nature
of its institutions and characteristic forms of representation if it ignores
its artistic and cultural past. These force us to look beneath the surface of
its habitual forms of life where we may encounter surprising and possibly
disturbing truths about ourselves.

Returning to the play, we have said that sacrifice is the matrix in which
the action takes place. There are also numerous references to its associated
rituals: invocations to the gods, the selection of a victim and drinking and

dancing. One song refers directly to Dionysus, calling on 'The god of joy/The madcap boy' to lead them in 'their Bacchic frenzy'.[62] But there are important differences. For example, the Scythian is a sacrificial victim because he serves as a scapegoat for the disruptive effects of desire, but he is not treated with the reverence normally reserved for that role.

This also applies to Mnesilochus, one of the potential sacrificial victims in the play. In fact, what the chorus seek in deciding to burn him is 'vengeance...For your wrongs we shall repay you'.[63] We noted the close connection between the violence of sacrifice and the violence of revenge in our discussion of the *Oresteia*, and here we can make the further point that sacrifice is also seen as a form of punishment for wrongdoing. Mnesilochus has not only infiltrated the women's sacred mysteries; he has slandered them and snatched a 'baby'. He is therefore a 'criminal' as well as a potential sacrificial victim. The link between sacrificial victim and criminal is evident in public executions which provided both the spectacle of sacrifice and performed one of its functions, the expulsion of those who flout society's norms and break its laws.

'Spectacle' forms a bridge between ritual and drama. Among the elements included in the spectacle of Greek theatre were masks, phallic props, pictures hung to create scenery and a crane that gave the impression of a flying actor. Aristotle believed spectacle was the least important part of drama, particularly tragedy, whose main concern should be plot, that is the imitation of an action which has a beginning, a middle and an end. Nevertheless he thought that spectacle, like the other features of tragedy – plot, character, diction, thought and song – was a form of mimesis, a representation of reality. But, as Aristophanes demonstrates, theatre can be the art of illusion as much as the art of imitation, the art of improvisation as much as the art of faithful reproduction. In this context, spectacle is a display, even a flaunting, of the creative power of theatre – no longer a reflection of reality, but a revelling in its power to make it or bend it to our will.

It is this idea of spectacle that dominates the second act of *Women at the Thesmophoria* which centres on Euripides' various attempts to rescue Mnesilochus. Each of these attempts is based on an incident in one of Euripides' plays. For example, Euripides improvises a scene from his *Helen*[64] by pretending that he is the shipwrecked Menelaus arriving in Egypt and that Mnesilochus is Helen of Troy. They then both treat the guard, Critylla, as if she were Theonoe, the character who helps them escape from that country. Another example comes from Euripides' *Andromeda* (412 BCE). In myth, Andromeda was to be sacrificed to a sea monster in order to appease Poseidon.[65] She is, however, rescued by Perseus. There is no hero to rescue Euripides and Mnesilochus; they have to rely on their wits but the end result is the same: they avoid being killed. In general, comedy transforms a sword into a tickling stick and the community is cleansed by laughter, not bloodshed.

What, though, is the significance of Aristophanes' use of Euripides? There are several answers. First, it challenges the boundaries between tragedy and comedy in just the same way that Mnesilochus challenges the boundaries of gender by dressing as a woman. What is tragic may become comic and, conversely, what is comic may become tragic. Second, it demonstrates, in a comic fashion, the human powers of invention, improvisation and creativity. These show that we are not merely the playthings of the gods, but that we can control our own destiny. The idea that we can control our own destiny calls into question at least one of the functions of sacrifice, namely the scapegoat. If we are responsible for our own lives, then there is no need to find someone else to blame when things go wrong. Here is the most important point: that the artifice of theatre clashes with the rationale for sacrifice.

The idea of theatre and the idea of sacrifice stand in opposition to one another. It is true that they are both forms of spectacle but these spectacles mean different things. The spectacle of theatre stands for freedom and self-fashioning, the spectacle of sacrifice for obedience and subservience to the gods. To put this another way there is, in *Women at the Thesmophoria*, a clash between the religious and the secular view of the world. One result of that is to undermine the belief in the efficacy of sacrifice. We found a similar scepticism about sacrificial ritual in *The Oresteia* but for different reasons. There it was to do with the complex Oedipal structure of the play; in *Women at the Thesmophoria* it is to do with foregrounding the idea of theatre as a spectacle.

The radical implication of Aristophanes' use of Euripides is not just that drama but that all forms of spectacle can be reworked to produce quite different effects. Ritual and religious ceremony therefore have no greater authority than any other form of representation. They may be sanctioned by tradition, visually arresting, full of mystery and deeply embedded in the culture, but put any one of its elements in a different context and laughter rather than reverence might be the response.

On the other hand, we must reckon with the fairly common human need to feel that there is a power in the cosmos that cares for us. This power, whether it is god or some other entity, will watch over us if we worship it and keep its commandments. It offers safety and security in a harsh and dangerous world, and that is a very hard thing to resist. We desire love and protection as much as, if not more than, truth. We know that theatre is the art of making, but there is a part of us that wants to believe the illusion. Aristophanes may expose the mechanisms of ritual by foregrounding the art of theatre but *Women at the Thesmophoria* is still based round a sacrificial ceremony.

New Comedy

Like Aristophanes, Menander was a great admirer of Euripides and was fond of composing moral maxims, an activity not normally associated with comic poets. They must have been good though because Menander was quoted by, among others, Julius Caesar (110–44 BCE) and St Paul the Apostle (c. 5–c. 67).[66] But he is best known as the sole practitioner of Athenian New Comedy. Between Old Comedy and New Comedy come the innovations of Middle Comedy which include plots of deception and mistaken identity, the reduction of the role of the chorus and the cessation of political attacks on individuals and institutions.[67] From now on, comedy would have to find its subject matter in everyday life.

It found it in love. Love can be regarded as sublimated version of the sexuality found in sacrificial ritual. Marriage has replaced the orgy. The basic plot of New Comedy, lovers having to overcome obstacles, usually parents, in order to be together, is presented in a realistic manner. Everything takes place in a single location in real time. There are no visits to other worlds nor is the dramatic illusion broken as it is in Old Comedy. Similarly we do not find in New Comedy the sort of extravagant and exuberant language that we do in the Old.

The classics scholar N. J. Lowe maintains that many of these changes, such as the unity of place and time, were 'the direct result of the increased influence of tragedy'.[68] According to Aristotle, tragedy often depends on 'recognition', a move from ignorance to knowledge. Oedipus, for example, recognizes that he is the criminal for whom he searches while in Euripides' *Ion* (412 BCE) the eponymous hero eventually realizes that Creusa is his mother. Recognition is a key feature of New Comedy too because its plots often depend on disguise and mistaken identity. Indeed it is to Menander, says Lowe, 'that we owe the western comic tradition's reliance on ridiculously convoluted, coincidence-heavy, farcical plots centred on misunderstandings (especially of identity)'.[69] That is quite an achievement for a man who left only one more-or-less-complete play, *Dyskolos* (316 BCE), usually translated as *The Bad-Tempered Man*, the surviving seventeen of the hundred or so he wrote being like classic statues with missing parts.

New Comedy is also indebted to tragedy for its more realistic portrayal of character. But while Menander's characters are certainly more credible than those of Aristophanes' they are better described as types than as individuals. This is probably because Menander was influenced by Theophrastus (371–287 BCE) who is best known for *The Characters* (c. 286), a work which may have been written as an appendix to a treatise on how to write comedy. It contains thirty portraits with titles like 'The Chatterer', 'The Authoritarian', 'The Tiresome Man' and 'The Avaricious Man'. The claim that a person can be understood in terms of a single characteristic – the 'bad-tempered' man – hardly does justice to the complexity of human nature, but Theophrastus' portraits at least offer an explanation for why people behave the way they do and, to that extent, they mark the beginning of psychological 'realism'.

The fact that New Comedy has acquired some of the features of tragedy underlines, yet again, the deep connection between the two genres.

The free-wheeling nature of Old Comedy, like the mobile sexualities of sacrificial ritual have been disciplined and codified, made into a set of rules that will govern the development of New Comedy until at least the eighteenth century. But does that mean that sacrifice has disappeared from New Comedy? Not at all. We can still see its basic pattern at work in *The Bad-Tempered Man*.

Menander (c. 341 BCE–c. 290 BCE), *The Bad-Tempered Man* (c. 316 BCE)

Knemon is the bad-tempered man of the title. He is so called because he is irritable and shuns all company. He talks to himself, he throws things at people when they appear on his land, he refuses to help them and wishes that he could turn people who annoy him into stone. Knemon has a daughter called The Girl with whom Sostratos, a rich young man, falls in love. Knemon wants his daughter to marry someone 'like himself'.[70] The Girl has a half-brother called Gorgias who at first suspects Sostratos' intentions but later is prepared to help him in his quest. Knemon, after being rescued from falling down a well, is happy for his daughter to marry Sostratos though that is the first he has heard of the matter.

This rather bald summary touches on some of the issues we have already covered. For example, there is a hint of incest in Knemon's desire that his daughter marries someone like himself and the fact that his daughter has no name is another, albeit minor, manifestation of the elision of the female that we noted in both *The Oresteia* and *Women at the Thesmophoria*. The play also echoes some of the themes that can be found in tragedy but in a more subdued form. Sostratos oscillates between believing that he controls his life and that the gods do and, like the tragic hero, Knemon gains a degree of self-knowledge. His remark that 'Troubles alone, it seems, can teach us'[71] echoes what the chorus say in *The Agamemnon* that 'The truth/ Has to be melted out of our stubborn lives/By suffering.'[72]

One of the ways in which *The Bad-Tempered Man* differs from tragedy and Old Comedy is that it has no chorus, at least not in the conventional sense. The chorus had many functions: it offered advice; it upheld the principle of hierarchy; it shaped how the audience viewed the central character and it provided a moral commentary on the action. It was, in short, an active participant in the drama. But in *The Bad-Tempered Man*, as in the rest of Menander's plays, its role has shrunk to providing entertainment in the interludes between the acts. Daos, Gorgias' slave, heralds the end of the first act with the words 'For I can see some worshippers of Pan/Approaching here, a bit the worse for drink;/It's not the time to bother them, I think.'[73] Daos gives us a picture of the chorus that is more like the old, riotous *kōmos* than the well-drilled unit audiences would marvel at in tragedy and comedy.

Moving the chorus to the margins of the drama revealed social divisions that had previously been concealed. Acting as the voice of the *polis* and positioned in the orchestra, the dancing area in front of the stage, the choruses of tragedy and Old Comedy projected the image of a cohesive society, no matter what befell characters in the play. But when the chorus cease to have a central role in the drama, unity is replaced by division. This is manifest, in *The Bad-Tempered Man*, in the difference between the rich and the poor, with the former coming from the city and the latter from the country. The opposition between city sophisticate and country bumpkin will be a constant in the development of comedy. It represents, in part, the weakening of man's ties with nature and the decay of those rituals through which he expressed his relationship to it. And it's worth noting that these divisions between rich and poor, country and city are also gendered. It is Sostratos who is rich and urbane and The Girl who is poor and rustic. Her reduced circumstances can, at a push, be seen as another example of the exclusion of the principle of female fertility that was at work in *The Oresteia*.

The division between rich and poor is touched on several times in *The Bad-Tempered Man*. One character notes that Knemon is simply one of many poor farmers who barely eke out a living from the thin soil, while Gorgias warns Sostratos not to 'despise us poor men'.[74] The problem of the play, then, is how to heal this division. The ritual of sacrifice creates unity through the killing or casting out of a scapegoat. Comedy does it through marriage. Sostratos weds The Girl. But he also does something which is very rare in the history of comedy, which is to step outside his social circle and work with those at the bottom of society. 'This', says Gorgias, 'is how a man's true nature is revealed, when though he's rich/He's prepared to lower himself to the level of the poor.'[75] His remark implies that there is such a thing as true identity but, if the history of tragedy and comedy tells us anything, it is that this identity is elusive to the point of non-existence.

The fact that marriage, rather than scapegoating, is the solution to social division in *The Bad-Tempered Man* may suggest a rupture between drama and ritual, but this is not the case. Much of the play's action stems from Sostratos' mother, another unnamed female, organizing a sacrifice to Pan, who speaks the prologue and whose shrine is visible on stage throughout. The purpose of her sacrifice is to ensure the dream she had about her son being fettered, that is married, 'turns out for the best'.[76] This suggests that sacrifice is linked to a belief in predestination and all that humans can do is to accept the determinations of the gods with good grace. But it's not the beliefs underpinning sacrifice that command the audience's attention; it's the difficulties the cook, Sikon, faces in preparing the feast such as getting a sheep to the shrine. What matters is the mundane, not the sacred. Knemon is well aware that a religious ceremony is often no more than an excuse for eating and drinking and having a good time. 'They bring their picnic hampers and their jars/Of wine not for the gods but for themselves/... they put on/The altar only ... the parts they cannot eat,/And guzzle down the rest themselves.'[77] We are reminded of Mica smuggling a wine skin in as a baby in *Women at the Thesmophoria*.

The preparations for sacrifice show, then, that New Comedy is still indebted to ritual for its humour and spectacle. But, one might object, isn't that humour evidence of scepticism towards the institution of sacrifice? If so, then *The Bad-Tempered Man* suggests that New Comedy, if it hasn't actually broken free from its beginnings in sacrifice, at least has developed a critical attitude towards it. The argument is persuasive only until we delve a little deeper into the play. New Comedy may rely on marriage to create social unity but marriage is nothing more than the socially approved and sanitized form of the ancient fertility festival. Moreover, it's not marriage alone that can heal divisions in *The Bad-Tempered Man*; a scapegoat is also required. The relation between the two is quite complex but what seems to happen is that, over the course of the play, the division between rich and poor gradually becomes the problem of how to rid Knemon of his misanthropy and incorporate him into society. A matter of economics, in other words, is turned into a matter of personality and, in the process, the whole question of inequality is sidelined.

Knemon fulfils the role of scapegoat because he is both inside and outside the community. One character says that while Knemon is 'sharp-tempered ... he's not/The only one, they're [poor farmers] nearly all like this'.[78] At the same time, Knemon himself wishes that he 'could take wings in high/And never meet the men who walked on earth'.[79] These two quotations, moreover, show the two sides of Knemon: his economic position and his psychological disposition – a man who, as Pan puts it in the prologue, is 'cross-grained to all'.[80] It is perhaps fitting, then, that Knemon suffers the fate of the sacrificial victim not once but twice. The first time is when he falls in the well and the second is when he is the object of a practical joke by two characters to whom he earlier refused to lend a bucket and a stewing pot for the sacrificial feast. This second sacrifice therefore has an element of revenge to it, a combination which we have already encountered in *The Oresteia*.

The first sacrifice may not seem like a sacrifice at all. How can falling down a well and being rescued possibly be regarded as an offering to the gods? There is no mention of any deity nor does it produce any discernible benefit. Well, there may be no mention of a deity but Knemon's symbolic death and rebirth comically recalls the death and rebirth of Dionysus or the year god. It is also reminiscent of Odysseus' descent into the underworld, by means of which he is able to find his way home. This was Freud's favourite episode in *The Odyssey* because it was an allegory of psychoanalysis. The patient visits his or her unconscious in order to learn the truth about themselves so that they are able to live a more rounded life. And this is precisely what happens to Knemon. The accident puts him in a wheelchair temporarily but it has benefitted him mentally because it makes him realize that he had been 'wrong'[81] to isolate himself from others. Finally, Sostratos has a semi-conscious wish to see his prospective father-in-law drown. He thought it was fun to watch, did nothing and, when pressed to help, 'nearly sent him to his death/Three times at least'.[82] His actions allude to the basic function of sacrifice, the removal of what is old to make way for what is new.

The problem with this first 'sacrifice' is that it doesn't work. Knemon may admit to having been mistaken in the past but he doesn't change. Moreover he claims that his way of life actually had some merit: 'if all men behaved like me,/Law courts would no longer exist.../... war would cease [and] all would live content with less'.[83] Perhaps so. But implicit in this defence is a rejection of law which, as we saw in *The Oresteia*, is the very basis of civilization. And that cannot be allowed to happen. The law must be maintained at all costs. There is therefore another 'sacrifice', one that humiliates Knemon, the comic form of sacrificial slaying, in order to integrate him into society. Getas and Sikon, the two characters who had earlier asked to borrow some utensils from Knemon, carry him out into the street while he is sleeping. When he wakes they pretend to see him for the first time and again request the use of various implements: pans, trays, tables and tripods. Having succeeded in thoroughly disorientating him, they then give him a brief lecture on how he should be more sociable. Finally they help him up, throw a garland round his neck and take him to the sacrificial celebrations next door.

But this sacrifice, like the first, is a failure. Knemon is content to 'endure the party'[84] but he doesn't enjoy it. He is there under duress, not by his own desire and so remains fundamentally apart from the others. *The Bad-Tempered Man* brings out an aspect of sacrifice that we have not so far considered – its coercive character. Everyone has to be involved. If not, then there is always the potential for someone to question the beliefs surrounding sacrifice and thus the authority of those who administer it. The key point, though, is that the two sacrifices in the play have failed either to change Knemon or to assimilate him into society or indeed to deal with the question of inequality. Marriage has also failed in its task of healing social divisions for *The Bad-Tempered Man* does not end with the union of Sostratos and The Girl. 'Tomorrow we shall hold the weddings'[85] says Sostratos, but tomorrow is after the play has finished. The happy ending is therefore forever delayed.

As in *The Oresteia* sacrifice, as a solution to social problems, is found wanting and so, too, is its civilized adjunct, marriage. But here's the crux: there doesn't seem to be any alternative way of conceptualizing society except through the medium of sacrifice. This is clear in *The Bad-Tempered Man* which has a sacrificial structure, the scapegoat, and which also takes the preparations for sacrifice as a good part of its subject matter. Sacrifice is at once the default mode of thinking and a deeply faulty mode of thought. It conditions how tragedy and comedy represent the world and deal with its problems.

But there is a crucial difference between sacrifice and tragedy and comedy. Sacrifice is based on the view that all meaning springs from divinity whereas tragedy and comedy are based on the view that, ultimately, humans must create their own meanings. Nevertheless, because of their roots in sacrifice, tragedy and comedy will, at least in the early stages of their development, aspire to the sort of completeness of meaning that only the gods can give. The problem for drama, in general, is that it is torn between its sacred inheritance and its secular mission. On the one hand it is bathed in the afterglow of spiritual truth and on the other it is committed to exploring concrete historical reality. But this is not a matter confined to drama. The Marxist revolutionary Leon Trotsky (1879–1940) hoped that revolution would turn the best of culture into the small change of daily life so that it would become expressive, harmonious and fulfilling. It did not.

4

Roman Drama

One of the problems in discussing Roman drama is that so little of it survives. We have the tragedies of Seneca (4 BCE–65 CE) and the comedies of Plautus (c. 254–c. 184 BCE) and Terence (c. 186–159 BCE) but that's all. Of the other playwrights of this period, from the middle of the Republic (509–27 BCE) to the end of the empire (27 BCE–476 CE), only fragments remain. Another problem stems from statements by the Roman poet Horace (65–8 BCE) which seem to imply that Roman literature was in thrall to its Greek original. 'Greece, now captive, took captive its wild conqueror and introduced the arts to rural Latium.'[1] An impression that is confirmed when we read Horace's advice to authors that they should 'study Greek models night and day'.[2] But he also said that they should win glory by 'venturing to abandon the footsteps of the Greeks and celebrate our own affairs'.[3] Despite being heavily reliant on Greek inspiration, the Romans did manage to produce a literature of their own. Their tragedies, for example, differed from the Greek version in not having a specific metre and in being more musical. We can do nothing about lost plays and there isn't the space to consider the nature of Roman drama in detail, but we can sketch a little of the history of Roman tragedy and comedy and the contexts in which they were performed. This approach also enables us to better assess what Roman drama contributes to our understanding of sacrifice, the main focus of this book.

Origins and Overview

Roman drama emerged from the festival of *Liberalia*. The name is a combination of Liber, a god of wine, fertility and freedom and his consort Libera, a fertility goddess. The *Liberalia* itself was a celebration of a boy's entry into manhood, in psychoanalytic terms the successful resolution of the Oedipus complex. The celebrations included a sacrifice, a procession, ribald songs to ward off evil spirits, the wearing of masks and the carrying of a phallus to ensure healthy crops. The Roman historian Livy (59 BCE–17 CE) gives the date of 364 BCE for the appearance of theatrical shows saying they were instituted 'to appease the wrath of the Gods',[4] a clear link with sacrificial ritual. But the shows which Livy mentions – basically dancing to a flute – cannot be described as plays in our sense of the term. Livius Andronicus (283–200 BCE) is generally credited with scripting the first play with a plot, an adaptation of a Greek tragedy, in 240 BCE. It was part of the celebrations of Rome's victory in the war with Carthage, known as the first Punic War (264–41 BCE), an example of how Roman drama worked in tandem with triumphal processions to promote civic identity and social unity.

Plays were mostly performed as part of the official *ludi*, that is, shows which accompanied religious festivals in honour of deities including those responsible for fertility like Flora, Magna Mater (Great Mother) and Ceres.[5] The connection between drama and ritual was, initially at least, as strong in Rome as it had been in Athens. According to A. J. Boyle, plays, or *ludi scaenici*, 'were technically a religious ceremony performed in homage to the respective deity and subject to religious rules governing their completion'.[6] They began with a sacrifice and a procession from the temple to the theatre where a special chair, decked with emblems of the relevant god, was placed in position of honour so that he or she could view the stage.

The Games

Since Roman drama was only one part of the *ludi* accompanying religious festivals, it did not have the same status or significance that Greek drama had. It took, for example, nearly two hundred years for Rome to acquire its first permanent theatre, built by the Roman general Pompey (106–48 BCE) in 55 BCE. It was also the case that some tragedies, like those of Seneca, were not meant for public performances but for reading or recital at private gatherings. The meaning of those plays which were staged for a wider audience came not just from the works themselves but from their relation to the other forms of entertainment. Initially these included boxing, tight-rope walking, chariot races and animal hunts, but, during the course of Rome's passage from the Republic to the empire, they developed into the huge spectacles we know as the Games.[7]

During the Republic, the Games were sponsored by candidates seeking office. They aimed to win more votes than their rivals by staging increasingly lavish displays which the Roman orator and philosopher Cicero (106–43 BCE) dismissed as mere bribery: proof of wealth, not worth. The emperors used the Games to celebrate victories, to commemorate the achievements of their families, to legitimate their rule and to amplify their authority. In the Republican period, the Games were a mixture of chariot races, naval battles, gladiatorial combats, plays, water ballets, executions, animal hunts and the distribution of food to spectators. It was a similar story in the empire. Augustus (63 BCE–14 CE), the first Roman Emperor, built Rome's largest theatre, the Theatre of Marcellus, and he also standardized the shows themselves. There were hunts in the morning, executions at midday and gladiatorial combats in the afternoon.

The Games, like tragedy and comedy, have their ancestry in ritual. Animal hunts re-enacted the search for food which, according to Burkert, evolved into the ceremony of sacrifice, while distributing food among members of the audience recalled the sharing of the sacrificial meal. The gladiatorial combats grew out of funeral games to commemorate the dead, in Freudian terms, the primal father. The Romans took the custom from the Etruscans who believed that unless they were appeased by blood, the souls of the departed would return, which again Freud would see as a ritualistic expression of the unconscious fear of the murdered father rising up to take his revenge. The executions of criminals and Christians served the sacrificial purpose of ridding society of those who threatened its beliefs, values and institutions. Spectacle was a key feature of these executions, just as it was in sacrifice. Victims often suffered the fate of mythological characters. 'Frequently', says the Christian apologist Tertullian (160–225 CE), 'criminals act the parts of the gods' and so the audience see 'Attis being castrated and Hercules burned alive'.[8] The Roman poet Martial (40–102 CE), best known for his twelve books of *Epigrams*, was less troubled by the cruelty of such spectacles than by their fidelity to myth, complaining that one victim, who was bound like Prometheus, should have had his liver torn out by an eagle instead of being ripped to pieces by a bear.

This, then, was the context in which the Roman public, a considerably more diverse body than the Athenian one, saw their plays. The displays in the arena led to greater emphasis being placed on the visual element of drama, evident in the design of theatres, the scenery, the special effects and the fondness for 'structuring the dramatic action around moments of high spectacle'.[9] But no matter how grand the theatre, or imposing the scenery, or breathtaking the special effects, neither tragedy nor comedy could compete with what could be seen at the Games. Consequently, from about 27 BCE, interest in the drama declined, a process accelerated by the growing influence of Christianity in the empire after the conversion of the Emperor Constantine (c. 272–c. 337 CE) in or about 312 CE.[10] The church followed in the footsteps of some Roman commentators who found both the Games and plays to be base and corrupting. Seneca declared that mixing with crowds made him 'greedy', 'dissolute' and 'cruel' while author Tertullian said that what goes on in the theatre 'is not worthy to be seen'.[11]

Although the Games have clear parallels with sacrificial ritual, it would be wrong to understand them solely in those terms. For one thing they were not always performed as an accompaniment of religious festivals. The emperors added Games to the calendar for their benefit, not for the worship of the gods. They were both means of self-aggrandizement and a form of social control. The arena provided an opportunity for the audience to express their desires and their frustrations in an approved fashion. In other words, the Games had a political as well as a religious purpose. But what really prevents us from viewing them as a type of sacrifice is their nature as spectacle. Spectacle is an important part of sacrificial ritual. It heightens the solemnity of the occasion and invests the act of killing with a religious significance. But in the Games sacrifice and spectacle have come apart.

Such traces of sacrifice that we can find in the slaying of animals, the executions and the distribution of food are completely overwhelmed by the sheer scale of the presentation. It is the exhibition itself, rather than any ritual purpose, that commands attention. Furthermore the Games, unlike ritual, have no narrative. The various acts form a sequence but not a story; hence there is no framework for making sense of the parade of human and animal deaths. It is true that the Games have certain ritualistic elements such as processions, prayers and songs, but these are merely perfunctory, making the killing nothing more than a sadistic form of entertainment. The functions of ritual, fertility or maintaining good relations with the divinity have all but disappeared while its actions have been exaggerated and caricatured. Spectacle, we might say, is ritual emptied of meaning.

Roman Tragedy

As already noted, Livius Andronicus was the first recognized Roman dramatist. Only a few scattered lines of his plays remain but they suggest that he wrote about Rome's Trojan lineage[12] and that his key themes were love, lust, rage and madness. Gnaeus Naevius (270–201 BCE) is the next important figure in the development of Roman tragedy. He was responsible for introducing the *fabula praetextae*, that is, plays based on Roman history in contrast to *fabula crepidata*, that is, plays based on myth. The fact that Romans produced history plays, not all of which were tragic, is another difference between them and the Greeks whose tragedies mostly avoided references to real events. A further difference between Rome and Greece is that most Roman playwrights wrote both tragedies and comedies. Gnaeus, apparently, was more famed for his ability to make audiences laugh rather than cry. His successor was Quintus Ennius (239–169 BCE) often regarded as 'the father of Roman poetry'. Again, given the paucity of evidence, we have to be cautious, but the main themes of his tragedies, family, power and honour are typical of the genre.[13] Ennius' main work, however, was *Annales*, an epic poem in eighteen books covering the history of Rome from the fall of Troy in 1184 BCE to the censorship of Cato the elder[14] (234–149 BCE) in 184 BCE.

The interest of these writers in history can be looked at in terms of sacrifice and in terms of the immediate context of writing. The German anthropologist A. E. Jensen (1899–1965) argued that sacrifice is the re-enactment of a creation myth, the killing of a deity whose death created human beings and whose dismembered body provided their food.[15] Sacrificial ritual thus affirms a society's sense of itself by replaying the story of how it came into being. Roman tragedy worked in a similar way, reinforcing the city's identity by constantly revisiting its Trojan beginnings. But the preoccupation with Rome's Trojan origins was also prompted by a second-century crisis in what it meant to be Roman. The conquest of the East brought in slaves, wealth and unheard of luxuries which threatened to undermine the city's traditional values of austerity, simplicity and service. To a certain extent tragedy was an attempt to uphold these values, partly through an exploration of Rome's past and partly by placing such virtues as courage, patriotism, self-sacrifice and ancestry at the heart of the action – the plays serving as a warning to the aristocracy of what lay in store if they failed in their duties or responsibilities: upheaval, confusion and anarchy.

The theatre, at the end of the Republic, was a lively expression of Roman political life. The audience were intensely involved in plays, responding fully to the action on stage by cheering, hissing, laughing and weeping. This changed at the beginning of the empire. Augustus reorganized the theatre and its audience. The buildings were more grand and scenery was more elaborate. There were three different kinds: columns and statues for tragedy, private buildings with balconies for comedy and landscapes for satyr plays. The rules for performance were codified. Tragedy should consist of five acts, there should be no more than three actors and there should be no *deus ex machina*. Augustus insisted on certain dress requirements and stipulated that seating should be according to rank. He also implemented the *infamia* laws for actors which basically meant they did not enjoy the privileges of a Roman citizen and so could be subjected to summary punishments and even execution.

According to Boyle, the effect of these various reforms was to 'diversify, trivialise and spectacularise the dramatic repertoire, marginalising tragedy itself'.[16] What were regarded as 'low' forms of entertainment, Atellan farce, mime and the new art of pantomime took its place. Pantomime was extremely popular. It appeared in 22 CE and consisted of a masked performer who, accompanied by music, used dance and gesture to interpret a mythological theme in either a comic or a tragic mode. The position of tragedy did not improve under the rule of the second emperor of Rome, Tiberius (42 BCE–37 CE), who had an author executed simply because he criticized Agamemnon in a tragedy – criticism which Tiberius took as being aimed at him. Tiberius was not fond of theatre and in 23 CE issued decrees of banishment against actors and pantomimes.

Actors returned to Rome when Caligula (12–41 CE) became emperor in 37 CE. He was a devotee of the theatre and enjoyed playing the parts of gods and women. His performances fused together drama and the Games since they included chariot racing and gladiatorial combat as well as tragedy. They were not, however, intended for the public stage; instead they were acted out in the imperial palace. But Caligula did encourage attendance at the theatre by visiting it himself and by relaxing some of Augustus' strictures on dress and seating. The atmosphere was, though, oppressive. Caligula's habit of having authors or even audience members thrown into the arena for perceived slights was not conducive to the writing of good tragedy or indeed comedy.

Nero (37–68 CE), the first emperor to persecute the Christians, shared Caligula's love of theatre, singing, acting, playing the lyre and driving chariots at first in private but later in public venues. Nero is infamous for the murder of his mother Agrippina (15–59 CE) and, according to contemporary sources, paraded his crime on the stage by acting the role of Orestes in a mask that resembled his own face thus confounding the distinction between reality and illusion, which Boyle finds to be characteristic not just of Roman drama but Roman society itself. He claims tragedy and comedy developed in a culture that was theatrical from its very outset and that 'public celebrations, sacrifice, divination, communal prayer, political and military oration, legal trials and executions, marriage, funerals, religious and triumphal processions and even a magistrate's movements through the city streets involved self-conscious (re-)enactment of a social script'.[17]

Seneca (4 BCE–65 CE), *The Trojan women* (c. 54 CE)

Lucius Annaeus Seneca was a Stoic philosopher, dramatist and statesman. He was also a tutor and later advisor to Nero, but his closeness to the emperor did not save him when he was implicated in the Pisonian Conspiracy.[18] The basic tenet of Stoicism is that we should control our emotions; otherwise we will not be able to discover the truth about the divine and human worlds. What's more, being able to control our emotions means we can meet what happens to us in life with equanimity or tragic resignation. As Seneca puts it in one of his letters, we must 'bear up bravely under all that fortune sends us and bring our wills into tune with nature's'.[19] His tragedies were greatly admired in the Renaissance for their moral lessons and observations about life. Andromache's remark in *The Trojan Women* that 'the only comfort in great sorrow [is]/Freedom from fear'[20] is echoed in Edgar's observation in *King Lear* that 'The lowest and most dejected thing of fortune/Stands still in esperance, lives not in fear.'[21]

Most scholars describe Seneca's *The Trojan Women* (54 CE) as conflating parts of Euripides' *Trojan Women* (415 BCE) with Euripides' *Hecuba* (424 BCE). The Greek version was part of a trilogy[22] but Seneca's play stands alone, though it does belong to that tradition of plays which dwell on the Trojan origins of Roman history. It tells the tale of Hecuba, widow of Priam, king of Troy, and Andromache, widow of Hector. Hecuba laments the fall of Troy and the death of her husband and urges the chorus to weep for what has befallen the city. Andromache learns that the Greeks want to kill her son, Astyanax, to prevent him for raising an army against them in future years. Hecuba, too, finds that she must lose her remaining child, Polyxena, who is to be killed to appease the ghost of Achilles. There is a debate between Agamemnon and Pyrrhus, Achilles' son, about the necessity of particularly Polyxena's death which is resolved by Calchas, 'the interpreter/Of heaven's will'.[23] He it is who insists that Polyxena should die and he it is who demands that Astyanax must suffer the same fate. The play contains a number of themes familiar from Greek tragedy, for example, that the gods must be honoured and that nothing is certain in this life. It also picks up the discussion, found in *The Oresteia*, about whether humans have free will or whether they are ruled by fate.

But *The Trojan Women* also marks a departure from the conventions of Greek tragedy. In the first place it is divided into five acts and in the second there is no central protagonist. The focus shifts from Hecuba to Agamemnon and Pyrrhus and then to Andromache and then to Helen, Hecuba and Andromache before finishing with the messenger's report of the deaths of Astyanax and Polyxena – an action, incidentally, which recalls the announcement of the death of the deity in the myth of the year god. The messenger's account also shows the play still adheres to the Greek tradition of describing violence rather than it being enacted on stage. A third difference is that Ulysses utters what may be the first aside in the history of tragedy. Andromache has hidden Astyanax in her husband's tomb (a move which ironically anticipates his death), in the hope of convincing Ulysses that he is dead, but Ulysses does not believe her. 'But wait. Ulysses may convince the Greeks;/What is convincing him?'[24] Addressing the audience has, typically, been a feature of comedy but now it appears in tragedy. The fact that Ulysses is trying to locate Andromache's son in order that he can be sacrificed associates the technique of aside with the villain. And, indeed, the villains of Renaissance tragedy often take the audience into their confidence making them complicit with their schemes. What's more they sometimes do so in a comic fashion which again underlines the close relationship between tragedy and comedy, death and life.

A fourth difference is harder to express. It comes from Andromache's words about the imminent killing of her son. 'A scene more tragic/Than our great Hector's death these walls must watch.'[25] They suggest a theatrical self-consciousness about tragedy both as a genre and as part of the human condition which is rare if not completely absent from Greek tragedy. It introduces a note of artifice into Andromache's affliction, as if she sees herself playing the part of a woman who is suffering rather than actually being the woman suffering. This means that there is a slight diminution in the intensity of Andromache's grief. Her self-consciousness of tragedy as part of the human condition, however, points to the possibility of transcending pain and misery because, if we are aware of them, if we can reflect on them, then we must have achieved some emotional distance from them. Does Andromache's observation therefore mark the moment when

tragedy starts its centuries' long decline if, that is, we judge it in terms
of a character getting the better of sorrow rather than sorrow getting the
better of the character? That would be too much to claim; but, equally, we
should not let her exclamation pass without pause. Especially when we
align it with a question the chorus ask, namely 'What is misfortune but
comparison?'[26] This, too, lessens the impact of tragedy for it makes it more
a matter of relation rather than an absolute loss. No one's life can be truly
tragic if there is always someone who is rendered more wretched than we.

But what about sacrifice? Can we find any trace of it in *The Trojan
Women*? Most certainly. The play has a very clear sacrificial structure
since it builds up to the deaths of Astyanax and Polyxena, the high point
of the drama. The Greeks leave their ships and take their place on rocks,
high ground, or even sit in trees to watch the boy thrown from Troy's one
remaining tower and the girl to be slain on Achilles' tomb. The gods are
asked to accept the 'sacrifice'[27] which is described as a piece of 'theatre'[28]
to the extent that it arouses an array of emotions in the audience from
admiration to sorrow. It is clear, then, that the play has a sacrificial structure,
but it is equally clear that this structure does not function properly.

For example, sacrifice is partly about the renewal of life but *The Trojan
Women* is dominated by death. It starts and finishes with death; Hecuba
and Andromache both pray for death and hope 'there is nothing after
death'.[29] The Greeks aim to extinguish fully the life of Troy. That is why
they are determined to kill Astyanax. The imagery used to describe how
he might return and punish them is redolent of the natural world. He is
a 'young calf' and 'a young sapling'[30] so, in killing him, the Greeks are
destroying the life cycle. With his death Troy, and by implication nature,
comes to an end. Nor can we really say that the Greeks embody the
spirit of new life. They are exhausted by their struggle and weakened
by divisions in their ranks. In this devastated environment, only the
dead return. Achilles and Hector rise from their graves confounding the
distinction between life and death. The two appear indistinguishable as
they do in Polyxena who is to be sacrificed dressed as a bride on Achilles'
tomb – an image that captures the disturbingly intimate connection
between the shedding of blood and new birth.

One of the main functions of sacrificial ritual is to order the relation
between life and death, to present them as separate yet dependent on each
other. Hence they are organized into a 'narrative' sequence in which the
slaying of the sacrificial victim is seen to 'cause' a particular 'effect' such as
the growth of the crops or the ripening of the vine. In *The Golden Bough*,
Frazer explained the killing of the King of the Wood as means of preserving
nature's fertility and there is a faint echo of this in the detailed description
of the murder of Priam. Pyrrhus clutched the king's hair at the altar and
'Forced the head back and drove the foul blade deep/Into the old man's
throat.'[31] But despite the killing being performed on an altar this is not

a sacrifice, but an act of vengeance. The Greeks sack Troy because Paris
eloped with Helen, the wife of Menelaus, and devastation, not regeneration,
is the consequence.

The violence of vengeance is confused with the violence of sacrifice in
The Trojan Women. The former is characterized by excess, the latter by
restraint. The confusion between the two is illustrated by the demand for
the 'sacrifices' of Astyanax and Polyxena. These 'sacrifices' are deemed
necessary for the Greek fleet to leave Troy but Agamemnon sees them as
further acts of vengeance when 'vengeance enough, and more/Has been
exacted'.[32] The question of whether the deaths in the play can be considered
as sacrifice or vengeance is further complicated by Astyanax not waiting to
be pushed from the tower but leaping from it. By seizing the initiative for his
own death he disrupts the sacrificial ritual rendering its outcome uncertain,
as does Polyxena by the courage with which she meets the sword. The
blood of both victims simply disappears into the ground and the suggestion
is that the earth itself has become one huge tomb from which only ghosts
will come back to demand yet more deaths.

The disappearance of fertility in *The Trojan Women* cannot be divorced
from the treatment of Hecuba and Andromache. We saw in the previous
chapter that the death of Clytemnestra was analogous to the suppression of
female goddesses of fertility. A similar process is at work in this play. The
repression of Hecuba and Andromache is at the same time the repression of
the female principle of generation. As in *The Oresteia*, the future of society
is shown to depend on the subjugation of women for the Greeks deprive
Hecuba and Andromache of everything that gave them a life and an identity:
home, husband and children. They are, in effect, turned into ghosts. Coupled
with the actual killings in the play, this symbolic slaughter means the Greeks
can return home and have a life free from the fear of Trojan reprisals.

To that extent, we can argue that *The Trojan Women* does have a
sacrificial structure; the violence has removed any threat to Greek security.
But, against that, we have to set the following: the conflation of sacrifice and
vengeance, the merging of life and death, the sabotaging of the sacrificial
ritual and the weariness and fractiousness of the Greeks themselves. The
most we can say, therefore, is that sacrifice in *The Trojan Women* is highly
problematic. But that is not all. There is a profound irony about this play
which can only be mentioned here. It is, as I have said, drenched in death.
One could almost say that it is about genocide. Yet what is most striking is
that death will not come to the very characters who long for it most, Hecuba
and Andromache. 'I have desired you' (meaning death), says Hecuba, 'and
you have not come.'[33] This condition of longing for death without being
able to die is one we shall encounter again in the work of Samuel Beckett
(1906–1989) though death does not appear in his work as it does here, as a
lover who denies the fulfilment that lovers can give. Death withholds itself
while at the same time being all pervasive. But death, by suspending itself,

at least for Hecuba and Andromache, is no longer death. It does not destroy them but instead condemns them to a living death, stripped of all that made them what they were.

Roman Comedy

There were two basic types of Roman comedy, the *fabula palliata* and the *fabula togata*. The *fabula palliata* were mostly based on plots and characters from Greek New Comedy while the *fabula togata*, or comedy in Roman dress, which eventually superseded the *palliata*, dealt with lower class life in Rome or in nearby country towns. But what were their beginnings?

Horace finds the origins of Roman comedy in harvest festivals. He claims that during the sacrificial ceremony farmers would utter rude and abusive jests in alternate verses called *Fescennina licentia*, the name possibly deriving from the Etruscan town of Fescennium. Since they were thought to ward off witchcraft, these verses correspond to the invective which was part of the phallic songs used in the worship of Dionysus. The purpose of both was to promote fertility by scaring away evil spirits. That's why the *Fescennina licentia* were also performed at weddings. The more ribald the verses, the more children the couple would have. The dramatic quality of the verses lay in their claim and counterclaim and in the gestures that produced them.

Livy states that drama began as means of appeasing the wrath of the gods who had visited a plague on Rome. Performers were recruited from Etruria to drive it away by dancing, in an improvised fashion, to the flute. With the addition of action and dialogue this became known as *histriones*, from *ister*, the Etruscan word for performer. It is also the root of the English word 'histrionic', used to describe someone who is behaving in an exaggerated or affected manner. 'Hypocrite', incidentally, is derived from *hypokritēs*, the Greek term for, first, an 'answerer' and later an 'actor'.[34] *Histriones* developed into the *satura*, which comes from the phrase *lanx satura* meaning a platter filled with mixed foods. Consisting of song, dance and dialogue, the *satura* were more structured than the Fescennine verses. There is, though, some doubt about the existence of the *satura*, despite Livy's testimony.[35]

The next stage in the development of comedy was, according to Livy, the introduction of a plot, evident in Livius Andronicus' adaptation of a Greek tragedy and a Greek comedy in 240 BCE. Finally, there was a return to the improvised 'drama' of the Fescennine verses in the form of *exodia* or afterpieces. These were attached to tragedy and to the *fabula Atellana* which, of all the forms we have mentioned, most resembles our idea of comedy. They were named after the town of Atella and were extremely popular. The titles of the plays were often derived from festivals[36] and the plays themselves depicted life in the country or small town. What little is known about the plots comes from the casual references in the work of writers such as Livy for the plays themselves have not survived. They apparently involved cheating, trickery, farcical situations and a good deal of obscenity. Music and song played an important part in the *Atellana* but their most interesting feature was the cast of stock characters: Maccus, the fool or clown; Bucco, the glutton or braggart; Pappus, the foolish old man; and Dossennus, the swindler or cunning hunchback. The lovers, who are the dominant forces of new comedy, have yet to make their appearance in the Roman version of the genre.

Yet another precursor of Roman comedy was the Italian mime which reached the capital in about 211 BCE. Despite its name, mime was a noisy, boisterous affair. It was performed as part of the celebrations in honour of Flora, the goddess of spring. Consisting of two or three persons, male and female, mime was more of a sketch than a complete story. Generally, it had an urban setting and adultery was a key theme, the cuckolded husband being the figure of fun. Mime's explicit nature – sexual intercourse sometimes took place on stage – meant it was condemned by Christians. One contemporary defined it as 'an imitation of speech and action without reverence, the lascivious imitation of shameful deeds and words'.[37] Such moral outrage did not, however, stop mime from being the most popular form of comedy throughout the empire.

Horace and Livy were writing in the reign of Augustus, centuries after the events they described had taken place. Since their sources were likely to be patchy and possibly corrupt we cannot be sure how accurate their accounts of the beginnings of Roman comedy really are. What lends their remarks a degree of truth is that much of what they say accords with what we know of the roots of Greek comedy: in both we find song, dance, abuse, ribaldry, trickery, obscenity and a connection with festivals. Nor should we forget that Roman New Comedy, like its Greek counterpart, is partly shaped by tragedy, particularly the work of Euripides who provides it with its love interest, its theme of mistaken identity and its dependence on trickery. Whether or not all these are really derived from Euripides is debatable,[38] but there is no doubt that Roman New Comedy touches on themes that are familiar from tragedy. In Plautus' *The Rope*, for example, Palaestra complains about her treatment by the gods. What has she done to deserve the fate of being washed up on a foreign shore, completely destitute?

Although both Greek and Roman New Comedy are centred on the city state and rely on stock characters such as the young lovers, the strait-laced father and the wily slave, there are also some differences between the two.[39] Roman New Comedy, or *fabula palliata*, was influenced by the *Fescennina licentia* and the Saturnalia held in honour of Saturn, another agricultural deity. It took place in December and consisted of a sacrifice, a banquet, endless partying and the overturning of social norms; masters, for example, served their slaves. Both these influences are a reminder of the drama's origins in ritual but Roman New Comedy also had a clear social function, namely to ensure the stability of the social hierarchy by discouraging marriage outside one's status group. The young man defies his father by falling in love with an apparently unsuitable girl but this conflict between private passion and public duty is resolved by the girl being found to be a suitable marriage partner after all. The demand that one should marry within the group is the very opposite to the taboo, discussed in Chapter 1, against having sexual relations with anyone from the same tribe. To do so was seen as a form of incest and, indeed, incest seems to be an ingredient of Roman New Comedy to the extent that the typical plot requires that marriage be confined to members of the same social strata.

Plautus (c. 254–184 BCE), *The Rope* (c. 211 BCE)

Beyond the fact that Plautus was an actor, then a merchant shipper and finally a playwright, little is known about his life. His real name was Titus and he was given the nickname 'Plautus' because he was broad-footed, a defect that made him perfect for the part of the clown in Atellan farces. Plautus' comedies are the earliest complete works of Latin literature that we possess and they were highly regarded by his contemporaries. Most were adaptations of Greek New Comedies but we have no record of the originals. Plautus' own contribution to New Comedy is his portrayal of slaves; irrepressible and endlessly resourceful they have a spontaneity that is often lacking in the stock characters.

Like all New Comedy, *The Rope* is a variation or even an improvisation on the standard plot of the genre. Hence we have the young man Plesidippus who loves Palaestra. The obstacle to their union is not her father, Daemones, but Labrax, a pimp who bought Palaestra from a pirate who stole her from her parents when she was a child. Plesidippus buys her from Labrax but he reneges on the deal and, on the prompting of his friend, the rascally Charmides, plans to take Palaestra and her companion Ampelisca to Sicily where they will work in a brothel. But their scheme is foiled by the god Arcturus, 'most formidable of all the constellations'[40] who shipwrecks them causing Labrax to lose the trunk containing all his money.

They come ashore near the cottage of Daemones and the girls take refuge in the temple of Venus. Labrax tries to recapture them but is prevented from doing so by both Daemones and Trachalio, Plessidipus' slave. While out fishing, Gripus, one of Daemones' slaves, finds Labrax's trunk which also contains proof of Palaestra's identity. Consequently she is reunited with her parents and will marry Plessidipus with her father's blessing. Meanwhile Trachalio earns his freedom and will marry Ampelisca and the play concludes with Labrax being invited to dinner by Daemones.

The basic plot of New Comedy has its roots in sacrificial ritual. The conflict between the lovers and the older figures who oppose their union is the dramatic equivalent of the fight between winter and spring. The eventual marriage of the young couple is the socially acceptable version of ancient fertility rites. But in *The Rope* Plesidippus and Palaestra do not get married; we are merely given to understand that this event will take place sometime in the future. Similarly Labrax, the person who seeks to prevent their union, is not defeated but sits down to supper with the man whose daughter he wanted to pimp. This is in keeping with comedy's function of reconciliation and it is also a faint echo of the feasting that followed the sacrifice part of whose aim was to reinforce the social bond. However, as is suggested below, Daemones' and Labrax's sharing of food also signifies the corruption of sexuality, the celebration of which was an essential part of the festivities.

Money is an important theme in *The Rope* just as it was in *The Bad-Tempered Man*. There the spotlight was on the division between the rich and the poor and *The Rope* also draws attention to the gap between the two. 'A poor man's life is a sad man's life',[41] sing the Fishermen as they come up from the sea. They only appear once in the play but their song helps explain why Gripus, himself a fisherman slave, is so keen to make as much money as he can from the recovery of Labrax's trunk. *The Rope*, though, goes much further than *The Bad-Tempered Man* in its portrayal of the effects of money on human interaction.

It is seen as a malign force because it destroys human freedom by turning people into goods that can be bought and sold. Labrax believes that Palaestra and Ampelisca are his to do with as he pleases because he 'paid good money to their owners for the two of them'.[42] Trachalio responds by telling Labrax that he is not going to let him 'keep free children stolen from their parents and work them to death for [his] filthy profit'.[43] Money is also corrosive of law, custom, religion, freedom and ethics. Labrax, for example, shows no respect for the Temple of Venus when Palaestra and Ampelisca seek refuge there. 'They're clinging to the statue of Venus', Trachalio tells Daemones, 'and a wicked fellow [Labrax] is trying to abduct them'.[44] But money also enables at least some of these values to be realized. For instance it liberates as well as enslaves. In exchange for a thousand 'smackers'[45] from Labrax's treasure, Daemones will release Gripus from his bondage.

Since money undermines society's time-honoured traditions and, more fundamentally, converts sexuality, a principle of fertility, into a business proposition, it must be removed. Labrax stands for the evils of money. Hence he is threatened with prison, violence and execution. These represent the symbolic sacrifice of the scapegoat. On the other hand his financial approach to human affairs is sanctioned by Daemones inviting him to dinner. This represents not the return of new life which follows the sacrifice of a scapegoat, but the renewal of the very thing which saps its energies. In short, there is no sacrifice in the play, only a gesture towards performing it. The very thing that could potentially destroy society, money, is the very thing on which it is starting to depend.

Another way of putting this is to say that money is beginning to usurp sacrifice as a form of exchange. Instead of bargaining with the gods, humans bargain with each other. This represents the first step to taking responsibility for their own lives rather than relying on the gods, a shift which has huge implications for understanding sacrifice. Very briefly, cleaving to sacrifice retards the development of autonomy, but once sacrifice is relinquished – if indeed it ever really is – then two problems appear. First, humans have to accept that they and they alone are responsible, not just for themselves but for others too, and second they face the task of making life significant in a godless and expanding universe that is indifferent to their plight. The point to note here, though, is that the change of focus from the divine to the human means that the idea of exchange has to be rethought.

Previously it was a hugely unequal relationship with humans having to flatter, cajole and praise the gods if they were to win their protection and favour. But now the relationship – potentially at least – is more equal because humans are dealing with each other. *The Rope* foregrounds a whole series of question about exchange in its attempt to rethink the idea in a more secular form. Is it a simple act of reciprocity as when Ampelisca says she is getting the water for the priestess because she was kind to her and Palaestra when they were castaways? Is it desirable to give without asking for anything in return? Ampelisca thinks so; Sceparnio, another of Daemones' slaves, disagrees. 'I don't expect nothing for nothing.'[46]

The debate about exchange, which becomes more complex when the effects of money are taken into account, cannot be divorced from the portrayal of sacrifice. Traditional forms of sacrifice are mentioned but not performed. Daemones, for example, issues orders for a 'thank-offering' to the household gods 'to celebrate/The increase in our family'[47] but, like the marriage, it doesn't occur within the time frame of the play. What's more, the ceremonial language and solemn purpose of sacrifice are parodied in an exchange between Daemones and Trachalio. 'Sir', says the latter, 'I implore and abjure you, as you hope for a bounteous harvest of laserwort and asafoetida … or alternatively a satisfactory season of silphium seed, that you will not disdain to hearken to my prayer' to which Daemones' response is 'have the goodness to tell me what the devil you are shouting about'.[48]

If sacrifice has been reduced to a joke, what does that say about fertility? At best it is deferred, as in the case of the Plesidippus' and Palaestra's wedding; at worst nothing will grow. We are not just talking about the act of generation here but also about the ability of society to renew itself and prosper. One indication that fertility is in decline in the play is the condition of Venus' temple. There is no suggestion that anyone actually worships there and it can't even act as a safe refuge. Its diminished status is reflected in the character of the priestess, Ptolemocratia, who is described as 'a nice old lady',[49] a phrase that doesn't quite do justice to her vocation as a servant of the goddess of love. But that is the point. Love and indeed sexuality are no longer matters of ritual; they are matters of money. Labrax's status as a pimp, his desire to make a profit, has stripped sexuality of its sacred character, transforming it from an act believed to encourage the fecundity of nature to a mere business transaction.

This malfunction of the sexual instinct is also apparent in the spectre of incest lurking in *The Rope*, as it did in *The Bad-Tempered Man*. Daemones – whose name is uncomfortably close to demon – is sexually attracted to Palaestra and Ampelisca, 'the prettiest pair you ever saw.[50] In his defence he doesn't know that Palaestra is his daughter but then that is just another way of saying that incestuous desire is always unconscious. The big recognition scene where Daemones realizes that Palaestra is his daughter also carries a hint of incest because it prioritizes family relations above social ones. They are the focus of interest; they command the attention.

It could be argued that family relations are the basis of social ones and that they must therefore be clarified if society is not to be undermined by mothers sleeping with their sons or fathers with their daughters. But, in *The Rope* at least, Daemones' recognition that one of the girls to whom he is attracted is his daughter does not lead to a strengthening of social relations but to their weakening. His intention to marry Palaestra to 'a fine young man,/From a fine old family, an Athenian family,/My own, in fact'[51] merely relocates the incestuous desire to another part of the family.

Even if we discount the issues of incest, it is still the case that family unity is brought about at the expense of social cohesion. Community, which sacrifice always seeks to affirm, seems to have all but disappeared. *The Rope* depicts not so much a society as a collection of disparate individuals brought together by a shipwreck. And, although there are references to morality, the main relationship between all of them seems to be monetary. This is best shown by two episodes in the play which parallel one another in highlighting questions of ownership. The first is the argument between Trachalio and Labrax over whether Palaestra and Ampelisca are autonomous agents or pieces of property, and the second is the argument between Trachalio, Gripus, Daemones and Labrax over who owns the latter's trunk. It is this section that gives the play its title for at one stage we see Trachalio and Gripus having a tug of war over the portmanteau, as it's also called.

The exploration of ownership, exchange and what bearing they have on morality as it is embodied in custom, law and religion is partly an attempt to reconcile ethical and financial behaviour. It is here that sacrifice becomes important since it acts as a bridge between the two. Essentially, sacrifice becomes an individual matter understood as the relation between cash and conscience. When Gripus says to Daemones, 'No wonder you're poor; you're too bloody honest',[52] his master replies, 'It may be worth our while to lose that gain/Whose loss may be more profit than the keeping.'[53] In other words it is better to sacrifice the chance of riches if it involves sharp practice or deceit. Integrity should trump wealth.

But this praiseworthy principle is instantly undercut by Gripus'
observation that 'actors in comedies spouting that sort of stuff, telling
people how to behave' doesn't make the audience behave any the better
'after they get home'.[54] His remark suggests that Daemones is playing
to the gallery, he is not being sincere, he is merely paying lip service to
the conventional idea that comedy should improve how people act. In
addition Daemones' acceptance of Labrax amounts to an endorsement of
the latter's desire to make a profit at all costs. In other words, the kind of
sacrifice espoused by Daemones may, in this context, be no more than a
matter of form.

There are thus two forms of sacrifice in *The Rope*, both of them flawed.
The first is the half-hearted attempt to create a scapegoat out of Labrax.
Part of his humiliation is linked to the return of Palaestra to her father. In
ritual, the return of the god is a sign of new life but here 'return' carries
the taint of incest. The second form of sacrifice is self-sacrifice, which
is compromised by an apparent lack of sincerity and by an association
with the very principle it renounces. This new and sketchy conception
of sacrifice, suppressing immediate desires in the hope of greater gain, is
very much at odds with the traditional meanings of the term, purging,
community, renewal and so forth. In many ways it represents a dilution
of sacrifice, a weakening of its powers to at least confront if not explain
the great mysteries of life and death and the connection between them. But
therein, perhaps, lies the very reason why these old ideas of sacrifice not
only survive in the drama but continue to shape it.

5

Medieval Drama

Although we encounter some of the same problems with Medieval drama that we did with Greek and Roman drama, for example, having to draw conclusions from only a small number of surviving plays, we also encounter new ones. The first being that Medieval drama appears to be quite different from that which preceded it. One of the consequences of the fall of Rome in 476 CE was the disappearance, from Western Europe, of the cultural heritage of the ancient world. Hence the use of the term 'dark ages' to describe the time between the late fifth and the late tenth centuries.[1] When, eventually, plays began to be performed again, there were no tragedies or comedies in the sense that we have been using the terms.[2] This was partly because authors had lost touch with classical traditions and therefore had to rely for inspiration on festivals and folk plays, but mainly because the Christian message of salvation negated, to some extent, the idea of tragedy.

The second problem we encounter is that of terminology. The rupture with the ancient world meant the loss of a body of dramatic theory and knowledge and, indeed, vocabulary with which to describe, classify and comprehend the many types of performance found during this period. The clergy, who were largely hostile to all forms of merrymaking, use the terms *ludi* and *speculata* to condemn a whole range of activities from singing and dancing to acting. Nor are the words *ludi* and *speculata* themselves very precise. As William Tydeman points out, *ludus* signified 'both a game and a stage play' while *spectaculum* 'could indicate no more than something to look at, such as a sporting contest, though a stage play is not ruled out'.[3]

A further difficulty is how to distinguish drama from revels, rituals and folk plays. Take the summer celebrations. They began on May Day with everyone going into the woods and meadows 'to rejoice their spirit with the beauty and savour of sweet flowers and with the harmony of birds'[4] but the eating, drinking, dancing, games and festivities of all kinds would carry on for the next two months. A mock king and queen were also crowned and they presided over theatrical and musical entertainments accompanied by their own guards and soldiers. Given that all these activities overlapped with one another it is hard to separate them out and say that this one is 'ritual' and that one is 'drama'. The coronation of the mock king and queen, for example, qualifies as ritual because of its associations with the ceremony of removing an old king who could no longer guarantee the fertility of the land with a young one who could, but it also qualifies as drama because the persons who played the mock king and queen were acting a part, one that required costumes, props and the audience's acceptance of their roles.

The Survival of Ritual

While it is true that drama effectively disappeared with the collapse of the Roman Empire, rituals and revels of all sorts did not. These fed into the largely improvised and very popular folk plays. At the centre of each was a death and a resurrection. For example, in the mumming play[5] the *Hero-Combat* 'King George' is challenged to a fight by the Turkish knight. George kills the knight who is then brought back to life by the doctor, a comic figure. The piece concludes with the *quête*,[6] a procession of characters who collect money for the performance. One of these characters, Little Devil Doubt, carries a broom, a symbol of cleanliness. Shakespeare has Puck do the same at the end of *A Midsummer Night's Dream* (1595), an example of continuity between folk drama and plays proper.

A slight variation on death and resurrection can be found in the Robin Hood plays which were characterized by combat and the celebration of fertility. The combat, a version of the struggle between winter and spring, took place between Robin and various others such as a knight and a potter. Robin's connection with fertility rites partly comes from his association with the May Day celebrations and partly from the sexual explicitness of the plays themselves.[7] As an anti-authoritarian figure, Robin also represents the anarchic spirit found particularly in Old Comedy. He was the summer equivalent of the Lord of Misrule who presided over the Christmastide revels. Robin's subversive character was sometimes all too real. One performance at Willenhall Fair in 1498 ended in a riot which cost lives.[8]

The mumming plays, the Robin Hood plays and other ritual-like performances were the context in which Medieval drama evolved. What we know of the various revels, festivals and celebrations derives chiefly from the denunciations of clerics who maintained that they encouraged much evil, especially lechery and pride. And yet what was the Church if not a form of politically authorized ritual? Sacrifice was as much at the heart of the Christian religion as it had been of the pagan ones, though no doubt the clerics would counter that the bread and wine was nourishment for the soul rather than the body. I use the word 'pagan' because it captures better than the word 'secular' the idea of what was at stake in the opposition between the Church and popular pleasures.

The historian Ronald Hutton argues that many of these customs were not pagan at all[9] and that 'only a few folk rituals can be traced back beyond the Christian era with any certainty'.[10] But there is some room for disagreement here. The *quête*, for example, seems to be related to the *kōmos*.[11] This noisy and drunken procession was part of the worship of Dionysus and a version of it was used at the end of Aristophanes plays as the characters disappeared off stage. In particular the hero was often accompanied by a mysterious woman who, along with the other characters in the procession, had no real connection with the action. All this is very similar to the *quête*. It marks the end of the play; a character often referred to as 'The Woman' is a prominent figure and she, like the rest of those who appear in the *quête*, has no link with the drama.[12] Moreover, the behaviour of the *quête* was every bit as uproarious as the behaviour of the *kōmos*. Alan Brody claims that in the celebration of the *quête* 'we find the remains of the primitive celebration analogous to the *kōmos* of the Phallic Song'.[13]

It is true, as Hutton says, that English folk rituals bear little resemblance to those of ancient Greece. But that only applies if we look at stories rather than the underlying structure. For at the heart of ancient and Medieval festivals lie the same ideas of death and resurrection, combat and celebration of new life. The desire to use narrative performance to make sense of the relation between being and non-being is what justifies us in seeing continuities between the pagan and Christian eras. It is easy to account for difference; it's much harder to explain why things remain the same or very similar.

What is not in doubt is that folk plays preceded and outnumbered all types of religious drama. The year 970 CE is the generally agreed date for the beginning of Latin liturgical drama but it wasn't for another two centuries that vernacular pieces in Anglo-Norman began to appear and then a further two hundred years went by before the first texts in English emerged. These are the Cycle plays, the miracle and morality plays which were regularly performed until about 1580, just a few years before, *Henry VI Part 1* (c. 1591), thought to be Shakespeare's first work.[14] It used to be assumed that Latin liturgical drama was the biggest influence on these plays but recent scholarship suggests that it is folk drama which is more responsible for their broad characterization, earthy humour and vivid idioms.[15]

The Mass, the *Visitatio* and Paganism

The aim of Church drama was to promote Christian doctrine. The Church was originally hostile to drama and the rituals from which it sprang. It was seen as a pagan falsehood and a distraction from the serious business of saving one's soul. That's why the Church had effectively banned drama in Western Europe by the sixth century. By the end of the fourteenth century, however, it saw drama as a useful tool for conveying the truths of scripture. How had this change come about? There are a number of reasons but two stand out.[16]

First, the church realized that it would never be able to suppress the drama completely. Much better to use it to disseminate Christian doctrine than to persist with fruitless efforts to ban it. Second, and most important, drama was an inherent part of the Christian liturgy, and this was nowhere more evident than in the celebration of the Eucharist, or Mass, as it is more familiarly known.[17] The Mass is central to Christian worship because it commemorates the Last Supper, but sharing a meal had always been a significant feature of religious ritual, going back as it does to the consumption of the god sacrificed in animal form. Eating the body of Christ and drinking his blood echoes the ancient practice of taking the god into oneself and of binding the community together. The Mass and the sacrificial meal, though belonging to different belief systems, are also both highly spectacular. Peter MacDonald claims that between the eighth and the eleventh centuries,[18] the Mass 'ceased to be a communal service and became the means by which the priest made God really and truly present in the consecrated bread and wine so that the faithful could adore and worship him'.[19] It became, in short, a piece of theatre. The elaborate dress, the Latin speech, the elevation of the host, the bell ringing, the incense, all made the Mass a highly charged performance.

It should therefore come as no surprise to learn of the introduction of liturgical drama in 970 CE. The *Visitatio Sepulchri* or Visit to the Sepulchre is generally regarded as marking the rebirth of Western drama after the fall of Rome. It is mentioned in *Regularis Concordia* (970 CE), a list of agreed rules for members of the Benedictine order, drawn up on the initiative of the saintly Bishop of Winchester, Æthelwold (c. 904–984 CE).[20] The 'script' of the *Visitatio* stipulates that four brethren shall play the parts of the Virgin Mary, Mary Magdalene, Mary, the sister of Lazarus and the angel in the tomb. The angel asks whom they seek; they reply Jesus of Nazareth and he tells them that Jesus is not there but has risen and that the women should spread the news of his resurrection.

A great many words have been expended on whether the *Visitatio* is really the first example of Western drama for five hundred years or even whether it qualifies as drama at all. William Tydeman has noted that there are passages of pseudo drama to be found, for example, in the *Book of Cerne* (820–840 CE), among which is the liturgical drama the *Harrowing of Hell*.[21] But, says Tydeman, these can all be discounted because 'there is not the slightest hint that they were ever presented before an audience'.[22] O. B. Hardison Jr. argues that the *Visitatio* cannot be considered as drama because the idea of acting was alien to the Medieval mind, while others, such as Katie Normington, disagree arguing that the use of costumes and stage directions indicate that it was indeed a piece of theatre.[23]

Whatever significance the *Visitatio* has in the history of theatre, it is also important because it echoes ancient rituals which celebrate the return of new life. The risen Christ is another manifestation of the year god, discussed in Chapter 2. Moreover, Jesus shares many traits with Dionysus. Both had a mortal mother and an immortal father, both were associated with wine,[24] both were itinerant charismatics who acquired a cult following and both, according to Barbara Ehrenreich, held out the promise of eternal life.[25] These parallels testify to the fact that Christianity, like paganism, is a deeply felt expression of the profound connection between life and death. At the heart of each is the sacrifice of a god-like figure whose death opens the way to new life. But there are differences. Christ did not induce frenzy in his followers and Dionysus did not raise anyone from the dead. More generally Christ, in contrast to his pagan counterparts, chose the role of sacrificial victim, though he also asked for that responsibility to be taken away from him,[26] a request which suggests that his sacrifice was as much destiny as choice.

Like pagan sacrifice, the killing of Christ serves to purge a community of sin and evil. But there is an important difference. Christ's death was about saving souls, whereas the death of the sacrificial victims was about the renewal of nature. The cross establishes a new order, one that transcends nature because its focus is the heavenly beyond, not the earthly here and now. As Jesus advises in The Sermon on the Mount, we should take no thought of how we will eat, drink or be clothed instead we should 'seek the kingdom of God and his righteousness [and then] all these things shall be added unto you'.[27]

Christian Drama and the Cycle Plays

Marion Jones identifies four types of Christian drama, plays based on events of the Old or New Testaments, 'plays about the lives of saints, plays about miraculous happenings and plays expounding points of moral doctrine'.[28] Most surviving English drama from this period belongs to the first type which is variously referred to as mystery or Cycle plays.

As Janette Dillon points out, the phrase 'mystery play' only came into existence in the eighteenth century. The word 'mystery', which is thought to derive from the Latin *min[ni]sterium*, meaning trade or occupation, may refer to the fact that plays were usually put on by craft guilds, that is organizations of tradesman, carpenters, smiths and tile makers and so on, but then not all plays were paid for by the guilds.[29] The term may therefore refer to the various Christian mysteries such as the nature of God, the Virgin Birth, and the Resurrection and so on but again we have to remember that 'mystery' was not used by Medieval dramatists themselves.

'Miracle Plays' commonly signifies plays about saints' lives and miraculous happenings but this term is also misleading because contemporaries used it to describe plays on any religious subject.[30] You might think the Church would approve of such productions because of their educational value and because they were performed by clerics, but you would be wrong. Robert Grosseteste (1175–1253), bishop of Lincoln (1236–1244), demanded that they be stamped out, on the grounds that they were acted by minor clerics whose performances lacked official approval and whose leanings were more to sensationalism than sacred truth.

'Morality plays' have been defined as 'the dramatization of a spiritual crisis in the life of a representative of mankind whose spiritual struggle is portrayed as a conflict between personified abstractions representing good and evil'.[31] The use of allegory or personified abstractions is one way in which morality plays differ from Cycle plays and miracle plays. Another is that they are not based on biblical incidents. Their focus is not on the Old or New Testament but on the battles the Christian faces if he or she is to go to heaven rather than hell. The term 'morality play', like that of 'mystery play', was also coined in the eighteenth century. 'Interlude' or 'stage play' were the more common expressions at the time with interlude eventually coming to mean short dramatic pieces performed indoors by small groups of professional players.

The Cycle plays generally took place on the Feast of Corpus Christi which gave thanks for Christ's sacrifice and for the gift of his body and blood in the Eucharist. The Feast was instituted in 1311 and was quite different from others such as Christmas and Easter. They were primarily commemorations of the events they celebrated but Corpus Christi was separated from the occasion which gave rise to it. This was because the Easter schedule was felt to be too crowded and also because it was hard to celebrate the meaning of the Eucharist when the memory of it was tainted by Christ's arrest and execution.

The new date, between 23rd of May and the 24th of June depending on when Easter fell, was free from any such associations and so the Eucharist, and what it meant for man's salvation, could be remembered with unalloyed joy. The change of date was also an opportunity to exploit the theatrical nature of the Mass. Divorcing it from its origins meant it was free to be developed as a spectacle. Consequently the Procession of the Blessed Sacrament became the dominant feature of the Feast of Corpus Christi. At the front would be the clergy, bearing aloft the pyx which contained the Host and, behind them, the aldermen and then, decked in their characteristic livery, the guilds. The Procession was also, therefore, an expression of civic identity, the order of the parade a reflection of the city's complex and not always harmonious hierarchy. In York's 1419 Corpus Christi Procession, members of the Carpenters' and Cobblers' guilds attacked the members of the Skinners' guild with clubs and axes.

It was the guilds who were responsible for the production of the Cycle plays, providing actors, costumes, properties and often finance. The York Cycle, the oldest and best preserved of the surviving Cycles, began at

4:30 a.m. and finished around midnight. It consisted of more than thirty plays or 'pageants', each one performed on a wagon that moved from station to station round the city. So, for example, the first pageant, 'The Fall of the Angels', would be performed at the first station and, when it was finished, the wagon would move to the second station where it would be performed for a new audience. In the meantime the second pageant, 'The Fall of Man' would be performed at the first station and so on until all the pageants had been performed at all the stations in the city.

Like the other surviving Cycles, the York one focused on the Fall and Redemption of man. The key episodes were the Creation of the world, the sin of Adam and humanity's Salvation through the Incarnation, the Passion, and the Resurrection of Christ. All the other plays in the Cycle reflected and reinforced this basic theme of humanity's descent into sin and death before Christ's sacrifice redeemed it – if it so chose. And so we find that 'The Fall of Lucifer' parallels 'The Fall of Man'; that 'Moses and Pharaoh' parallels 'Christ before Herod'; that 'The Slaughter of the Innocents' parallels 'The Crucifixion' and so on. In addition, all the extant Cycles present a play about the Second Coming and the Day of Judgement.

The Cycle Plays do have some themes in common with Greek and Roman drama. Power, obedience and rebellion are as much a feature of the Christian plays as the classical ones. Satan's rebellion against God also has a faintly Oedipal character. Satan certainly wants to be 'like unto him that is highest on height'[32] but there is no rivalry over a mother figure. The portrayal of women in the Cycle plays has some similarities to the portrayal of women in Greek and Roman drama; that is, they are seen as a threat to male power and therefore need to be controlled. Eve disobeys God and brings Paradise on earth to an end. Noah's wife is also defiant. Both also are connected to sexuality and fertility but not as obviously as in the case of Clytemnestra. Eve is punished because she and Adam become aware of sexual difference while Noah's wife is a character in a story with a basic sacrificial structure. God gets rid of wickedness by destroying all living things except those abroad the ark who must, when the rains have stopped, repopulate the world.

Christian Drama: Tragedy and Comedy

If there are some affinities between the Cycle plays and Greek and Roman drama then are they tragedy or comedy? It is difficult to see the Cycle plays as tragedy. In the first place, Christianity's claim that king and commoner were equal before God undermined the principle that only the high-born were fit subjects for tragedy. In the second place, Christianity replaced the idea of tragic fate with that of individual choice. Humans were no longer the playthings of the gods; they had free will. What's more, Christ's death gave suffering a meaning. To endure torment and privation in Christ's name was to participate in his agony on the cross. It was also a form of cleansing and spiritual growth and finally a guarantee of eternal joy and bliss. If belief in Christ could wipe away tears, right wrongs and help us triumph over death then grief, pain and sorrow lose something of their power. Christianity gives hope, and that makes it the enemy of tragedy.

Such, at any rate, is the conventional account of the impact of Christianity on the tragic vision. But if we look more closely, we can see that it is not so much the opposite of tragedy as a continuation and development of it. The claim that the hero of classical tragedy merely acts out a role assigned to him or her by the gods conveniently overlooks the fierce debates about fate and free will in plays such as *The Oresteia*, debates which are at least touched on in some of the Cycle plays; for example, in 'Joseph's Trouble about Mary' Joseph struggles with Mary's pregnancy. Is it the result of a moral lapse or fulfilment of the prophecy that 'A maiden clean should bear a child'?[33] More generally Christianity was riven, for centuries, by the question of whether humans are saved by grace or by their own efforts. The dust we breathe carries the atoms of those burned for their adherence to one side of this issue or the other.

The notion of the tragic flaw also resurfaces in Christianity as the doctrine of original sin but with one important proviso. Belief in Christ means the Christian can escape the consequences of Adam's curse, but there is no reprieve for the tragic hero whose defect of nature condemns him or her to ruin, humiliation and death. That death, though, is what heralds new life. And here is where we find the key resemblance between the Cycle plays and Greek tragedy. For they both follow the same basic trajectory, defiance of a deity, punishment and then a new start. But there's a difference. Christ's death upon the cross cleanses humankind of original sin and brings about a state of spiritual purity. The sacrifice of Oedipus rids Thebes of incest and revitalizes the instincts which are then indulged in the satyr play.

It is in such revels that we find the source of comedy. The Cycle plays are comic to the extent that Christ's death inaugurates a new beginning for humanity but only in spiritual terms. The body is not to be celebrated as it is in Aristophanes but to be chastised. Feasting, sexual activity, fine clothes and material comfort may have signified nature's return in ancient Greece but, in the Christian view, these things are to be shunned because they make a person care more for the passing pleasures of this world than the eternal bliss of the next. Attachment to fleshy indulgence and sweet sensation is spiritual death. There can be no new life for those who ignore Christ's offer or fail to take it up. There will be no welcome for them in heaven, but there will be a fine blaze awaiting them in hell.

Should we not, then, use the word 'comedy' in relation to the Cycle plays? David Mills is happy to deploy it. He claims that the action of these works 'is inevitably comic in that it realises an ultimate divine justice which precludes tragedy'.[34] But the avoidance of tragedy is no guarantee of comedy. Indeed, tragedy is required for comedy in the sense that we are using the terms, that is 'death' and 'new life'. Perhaps 'humour' is a more accurate word to apply to the Cycle plays. One source of humour is man's helplessness in the face of the divine, though that could also be a potential source of tragedy.

There is also humour in portraits like that of Noah's wife in The York Cycle. Her objections to what she considers to be her husband's hare-brained scheme of building an ark are of a decidedly practical nature. Why on earth is he messing around with that when there are so many jobs that need doing round the house?[35] Such characters are funny. Their lack of inner life means they possess that mechanistic element which Bergson regarded as essential to comedy,[36] but their primary purpose was to reinforce the teaching of scripture – in the case of Noah's wife the need for obedience to one's husband and ultimately to God.

We can argue endlessly over which are the best words to use. But, broadly speaking, the Cycle plays are a blend of tragedy and comedy where tragedy is understood as Christ's self-sacrifice and comedy is understood as the possibility of a new spiritual life based on the rejection of the body. But why do we find these mixed together in the Cycle plays but separate in Greek and Roman tragedy? There are several answers. The first is that Medieval dramatists were largely ignorant of ancient literature and its generic divisions. The second is the rise of Christianity. The fusion of genres may well have been modelled on Christ's dual nature. If Jesus can combine human and divine in one person then drama can follow his example, though at a much lower level, by combining laughter and tears.

The third answer follows from the second but is more complex. Basically, drama's ritualistic character is more evident when its subject matter is religious than when its subject matter is secular. This is because the relation between ritual and religion is closer than the relation between ritual and secular life. Consequently we find a clearer demarcation between tragedy and comedy in Greek and Roman drama, where the subject matter is primarily secular, than we do in the Cycle dramas, where the subject matter is primarily religious. But why is there a close relation between ritual and religion? They are both based on belief in a supernatural power and central to that belief is the idea that sacrifice is necessary for cleansing and the creation of new life. The difference is that organized religion has a more sophisticated account of this process than is found in earlier ritual forms. Nevertheless, the connection between ritual and religion – in this case Christianity – is a factor in why we find the two parts of sacrifice, death and new life, or to use the language of drama, tragedy and comedy, side by side in the Cycle plays.

Anonymous, *Everyman*

Everyman is one of five surviving English morality plays.[37] But it isn't originally English. It was a translation of the Dutch play *Elckerlijc* which was written in the 1490s. *Everyman* was published in England between 1510 and 1519, an indication that drama was now establishing itself across Europe.[38] In its central figure, who represents all mankind, and in its offer of ethical instruction through allegorical figures, *Everyman* is similar to the other moralities. But it differs from them in not portraying the usual conflict between Vice and Virtue or between good and bad angels as they struggle for the soul of the protagonist. Pamela King says *Everyman* 'reverses the accepted morality play focus on defining evil … and concentrates on defining the good'.[39] The absence of wicked figures, who were often the source of humour, makes *Everyman* the most serious of the moralities, its grim message unrelieved by laughter. And that message, stated at the beginning and the end of the play, is first that our lives are transitory and second that we must do good deeds if we are to avoid eternal damnation.

All the action leads up to Everyman's death, for which he must prepare thoroughly. Naturally afraid of the journey he must make, he seeks friends and family to accompany him. But Fellowship, Kindred, Cousin and, most of all, Goods refuse. Everyman's realization that he has put his trust in the wrong people approximates to the self-knowledge that the tragic hero gains through his or her suffering. His abandonment by his false companions is balanced by his finding true companions in Good Deeds, Knowledge and Confession with the later addition of Beauty, Discretion, Strength and Five Wits. But, as Everyman approaches his end, these last four desert him just as did Fellowship, Kindred, Cousin and Goods. Only Good Deeds accompanies him into his grave. Knowledge stays to see where Everyman will go, heaven or hell, and Confession departs after Everyman has done his penance, there being no further need of him.

The play has a number of characteristics that belong to ritual. There is a clear demarcation between the sacred and the secular, it depends upon religious belief, the richly patterned action negotiates a rite of passage, and there is a feeling of awe and dread in relation to a divine power. The demarcation between the sacred and the secular is very clear. It can be summed up in whether Everyman should choose Goods or Good Deeds. The former belong to the world, the latter give him access to heaven. It is self-evident that the play is based on Christian belief. There are references to the crucifixion and the sacrament of penance. The play deals with the rite of passage from life to death and does so in a symmetrical fashion since Everyman is twice forsaken. And he certainly feels dread in the face of divine judgement unless he mends his ways.

Everyman is like a sacrificial victim because these various rituals help to set him apart from the human community for which he stands and prepare him for death. But how will his death help this community? As its representative, what happens to him also happens to the community. So when Everyman enters Confession's 'cleansing river'[40] the 'spots of vice'[41] that are washed from him are also, symbolically, washed from the community. Similarly when he is being whipped, Everyman functions as the scapegoat for the sins of the community. He is punished on their behalf. Being scourged also makes him like Christ. He even sounds like him. Everyman's cry 'all hath forsaken me'[42] echoes Christ's 'My God, my God, why hast thou forsaken me?'[43] while his final words 'Into thy hands Lord, my soul I commend'[44] are reminiscent of Christ's 'Father, into thy hands I commend my spirit.'[45] As a Christ-like figure, Everyman re-enacts Christ's sacrifice which 'would every man redeem/Which Adam forfeited by his disobedience'.[46]

The play does introduce a new meaning of sacrifice. In Greek and Roman drama the focus is mostly on the scapegoat. He, she, or it is sacrificed on behalf of the community. But in *Everyman* we are introduced to the idea of self-sacrifice. This is inspired by Christ's sacrifice of himself for mankind. In the play it takes the form of Everyman giving up his goods for good deeds. He renounces earthly pleasures in order to gain heavenly ones. We can certainly question the ethics of this form of sacrifice. If we do good in order to benefit ourselves, then are we really doing good? Here we are brought back to the relation between sacrifice and exchange. The basic question is this: Does one side get more than the other? Is a slaughtered ox the same value as a full harvest? Is the death of Christ really able to redeem every human sin, great and small, from the beginning to the end of time?

In short, does an excess lie at the heart of sacrifice? Is the victim's death worth more or less than what is received in exchange for it? Christ's sacrifice seems like a pure gift because it was unsolicited but God's words in *Everyman* present a different picture. 'My law, that I showed when I for them died,/They forget clean, and shedding of my blood red.../To get them life I suffered to be dead.../And now I see the people do clean forsake me.'[47] Clearly God expects humans to repay him for sacrificing himself on their behalf. His annoyance that they have not done so is apparent a few lines later. 'They thank me not for the pleasure that I to them meant/Nor yet for their being that I to them lent.'[48] Consequently he decides to frighten the human race, in the form of Everyman, with death.

That, though, is not as important for our purposes as the fact that God conceives of sacrifice not so much as an excess but as an exchange, a transaction one, moreover, that is symbolized by a ledger. God's relationship with man is consistently cast in terms of 'accounts', 'reckonings' and 'counting books'. In Plautus' *The Rope* the exchange of money stands in opposition to the exchange of sacrifice, but in *Everyman*, money and sacrifice are fused together. This partly reflects the growing importance of commerce in the late Medieval period evident in the growth of towns. With the ending of Viking raids in the tenth century, trade was able to prosper and finance played a greater role in the development of the economy.

But the key point, for our purposes, is that the language of money has become central to the concept of sacrifice. This means that is harder to tell the difference between material and spiritual values. The opposition on which *Everyman* is based, that the things of this world are bad and the things of the next world are good, becomes decidedly shaky. Worse, God has become a merchant whose only concern is to balance his books. The otherness of divinity has diminished; its sheer mystery shrunk to a quill, a pot of ink and a column of figures. In the process, sacrifice has been transformed from being primarily a relation with the supernatural to being primarily a relation with the self. Yes, Everyman is aware of the existence of God and the demands God makes of him but his relationship to him is rendered in a largely financial idiom.

And that makes Everyman's sacrifice different from that performed in ancient ritual. There the group gave the deity something material, for example, an ox, and he or she gave them something material in return, for example, a good harvest. But Everyman is acting as individual, not as a member of a community. Moreover, he is not offering anything material to God, nor is God offering anything material to him. Everyman is simply having to pay off his debt to God, to present the Almighty with a clean set of accounts. Meanwhile, the treasure that God gives is not worldly wealth but spiritual bliss.

We have said that *Everyman* marks a change in our understanding of sacrifice. Its link with money has weakened its connection with the supernatural world. What's more, there's a new emphasis on sacrificing for the self rather than sacrifice for the community. But the play invites us to consider one further aspect of sacrifice, what I would call its existential quality. To understand this we have to appreciate that one of the main functions of sacrifice is to make sense of the relation between life and death. It was able to do this because it relied on a mythology or a theology that explained how the natural world was connected to the supernatural world. But because the identification between money and sacrifice has weakened that connection, the relation between life and death is no longer so clear. We can see this in *Everyman*'s realization of his own mortality.

The play opens with Messenger reminding the audience of the transitoriness of life followed by God sending Death to Everyman. From that moment, the action is focused on how Everyman deals with his imminent demise. What requires explanation is this extraordinary emphasis on death. The conventional Christian account, that death was introduced into the world by the sin of Adam, that Christ's death redeemed mankind and that, by accepting his love, it was able to join him in heaven, does not really defuse the threat of death in the play. It defies all attempts to rationalize it; this is what makes it so terrifying. And far from banishing the horror of death the Christian faith only serves to heighten it. For it is God who has sent Death to Everyman, it is God who makes death so terrifying because of the pains that could lie beyond it.

This portrayal of death is bound up with a new conception of time. In the ancient world, awareness of it was tied to the seasons and so time was largely cyclical – which meant that nothing could ever really be lost. Such a view of time mitigates the fact of death. It seems less traumatic in a world where every death means a new birth. But this changes with Christianity.

Time becomes linear. There is therefore no guarantee that what is lost will ever be restored. And time has only one end point to which it moves ever more swiftly. 'Your time draweth fast,'[49] Confession tells Everyman. It is the consciousness of possible irreparable loss and the speed with which time passes that makes death more terrifying in Christianity than it perhaps was in sacrificial ritual.

Another reason why death may be harder to bear in Christianity is that, as *Everyman* suggests, it must be borne by the isolated individual. No friend or family member will accompany Everyman on his journey to the grave. It is something he must do unaided. In contrast to sacrificial ritual, where the public spectacle of death was shared by all, the Christian must cope with his or her own mortality alone. Yes, Christians also gather to mourn the death and celebrate the resurrection of Christ whose triumph over the grave gives them the hope of eternal life but what we have in *Everyman*, an individual facing the prospect of his own extinction, is almost unique at this moment in Western literature. For although the Bible explains the relation between life and death and indeed the entire history of humanity from the Creation and the Fall to the coming of Christ and the Last Judgement, none of this seems to offer any comfort to Everyman as he faces the remorseless and inescapable fact that he must die. In the universe of *Everyman* we glimpse the beginnings of the desolation we find in Beckett.

So is the play a tragedy or a comedy? Strictly speaking it is neither. It is an allegory, a play dealing in types and moral personifications. Nevertheless, *Everyman* is a tragedy to the extent that it has a sacrificial structure. It also contains tragic themes such as the nature of man and the relation between fate and free will but it presents them in a new way. We have not seen man as bestial before but that is now part of his make-up. In fact he has the potential to 'become much worse than beasts'.[50] Another new element is that man is now defined almost in opposition to the world he inhabits. His true nature lies in his relation with God. The novel element in the old debate between fate and free will is the burden put upon human responsibility. One's actions do not just have consequences in this world but in the world to come. The smallest decision bears the weight of eternity. It is a terrifying prospect and one, moreover, that has to be faced alone.

And here is another difference from classical tragedy. There is no sense of a relation between Everyman and a wider community as there is with, say, Oedipus and Thebes. He has no friends and belongs to no society. Everyman may be the first truly isolated figure in Western drama. And the fact that he stands for all humanity only means that each and every person must also stand alone. This is not only very different from Greek and Roman tragedy but also from folk drama, traces of which are present throughout *Everyman*. For example, the final speech is by a Doctor, and the Doctor, a comic figure, usually had the last word in the mumming plays mentioned earlier.

The comic aspect of *Everyman* lies in his ultimate salvation. He will be spared the pains of hell; he will reside in Abraham's bosom. But again the focus is on the individual, not the community, and it is the community which is the special concern of comedy. It aims to include everyone but the aim of Christianity, with its emphasis on sorting the saints from the sinners, the sheep from the goats, is to create divisions. Another fundamental difference between comedy and Christianity lies in their respective attitudes to the body. *Everyman* shows a contempt for the flesh whose pleasures are celebrated particularly in Old Comedy.

The hostility of Christianity to sex has its origins in Adam's and Eve's transgression. Eating the fruit of the Tree of Knowledge of Good and Evil opened their eyes to sexual difference and alienated them from God. This is in contrast to the ancient world where sex, as in the orgiastic rites of the various mystery sects,[51] appeared to bring people closer to divinity. Rejection not just of the body but also the things of this world means that *Everyman* cannot possibly be considered as a comedy. Salvation not fertility is the goal of the Christian religion. That's why death looms so large in the play. Its connection with life has been broken. The two are now opposites, a situation brought about by Christian enmity to man's embodiment in nature.

Perhaps the most important thing about sacrifice that we learn from *Everyman* is that is not tied to tragedy and comedy. Its strong presence in the play demonstrates that it can transcend these genres though they are its most natural form of expression. Sacrifice in *Everyman* is both an echo of Christ dying to redeem humans and a command that we sacrifice things of this world for the next. People in the ancient world could see if sacrifice worked or not and, if it didn't, they could change it. Sacrifice in the ancient world was designed to bring about tangible results but the outcome of the individual Christian sacrifice is uncertain. Will he or she go to heaven? There is no certain answer, and yet they must act as if there is.

6

Renaissance Drama

Going to the theatre in fifth-century Athens was mainly a civic duty; in sixteenth- and seventeenth-century London it was mostly a form of entertainment. The pleasures of the stage had to compete with those of the alehouse, acrobatic displays, brothels, bear-baiting, fencing, fireworks and the scaffold. The rituals performed at Great Dionysia were, in part, an expression of the city's identity. A similar function was fulfilled by the Cycle plays of the Medieval era. But, as a business, the main aim of theatre in Renaissance London was to appeal to the audience.

The rituals that preceded the main event at the Dionysia served to enhance the sacrificial element in the plays, particularly tragedy. The lack of such ceremonies at the Rose (f. 1587), the Globe (f. 1599) and the Swan (f. 1599) suggests that the drama's connection with sacrifice had been severed. Plays could still reflect the issues of the age – the dissolution of traditional hierarchies, scientific discoveries, religious conflicts and the new emphasis on the individual – but they no longer relied on sacrifice as a means of processing them. Theatre was the medium of experience. The pervasive metaphor of the age was life as a play. 'All the world's a stage,'[1] declares Jacques in *As You Like It* (1599).

The visibility of sacrifice also declined in Christianity. In the Medieval period the Mass was a piece of theatre and the Blessed Sacrament was paraded at the Feast of Corpus Christi. Since this was often the day when the Cycle plays were performed, the connection between drama and Christ's sacrifice was there for everyone to see. But all this changed on 31 October 1517 when the German monk and theologian Martin Luther (1483–1546) nailed his ninety-five theses to the door of All Saints Church in Wittenberg.[2] This bold action kick-started the Protestant Reformation whose central tenet was that humans could not be saved by good works, as Catholics claimed, but by faith alone. What was important in Protestantism was the individual's relation to God. The statues, sculptures, stained windows and carvings or pictures of Christ on the cross were all believed to be distractions from a person's encounter with divinity.

The Puritans took this belief to an extreme by smashing all windows and statues and whitewashing the painted walls of churches. Not only did the representation of Christ's sacrifice, his suffering on the cross, start to disappear from churches but Puritan theology also seemed to downplay his sacrifice. The doctrine of election, formulated by John Calvin (1509–1564), stated that at the beginning of time God had decided to save only a very few souls, the elect, and the rest, the majority, would be cast into hell. This ran contrary to the belief that salvation largely depended on accepting that Christ had died for our sins. The matter was greatly debated and though the theology is far more complex than I can indicate here, the basic point, that predestination creates problems for the notion of sacrifice, remains sound. Its arbitrary and ruthless determinism makes it the descendant of fate in Greek tragedy.

Was the eclipse of sacrifice in Christianity reflected in the tragedies and comedies of the period? A comprehensive answer is impossible, requiring, as it would, a detailed analysis of all the plays of the period. But, on the evidence of the four works discussed here *King Lear*, *The Revenger's Tragedy*, *A Midsummer Night's Dream* and *Every Man in His Humour*, the response is a tentative 'no'. A sacrificial structure is evident, in one form or another, in all of them.

Again, it is important to stress that the plays are not reducible to this structure which always exists in a complex relation to other elements. Christopher Marlowe's *Dr. Faustus* (1592), for example, reverses the sacrifice of *Everyman*: the eponymous hero gives up heavenly pleasures for earthly ones, an act that can only be understood in the context of the expansion of commerce, the voyages of exploration, the stirrings of science and the rise of humanist philosophy. It reinforces the idea, found in *Everyman*, that sacrifice is more of a personal rather than a social matter and that its exercise carries enormous consequences. It also registers the collision between a Medieval form of representation and more realistic portrayals of human psychology. There is even a reference to the Puritan anxiety about damnation in Faust's final descent into the stage prop known as the hell mouth.

Renaissance Tragedy

Before looking to see if sacrifice is operative in individual plays, it is worth making some general remarks about Renaissance tragedy. One innovation was the introduction of the sub-plot which was often quite comic until Thomas Kyd's *The Spanish Tragedy* (1587) where it added depth and complication to the main themes. Kyd's play, incidentally, anticipates some of the themes of *Hamlet* (1600) and contains the sort of spectacular violence associated with sacrifice. There were several sorts of tragedy in this period: those dealing with royalist politics or history, those dealing with revenge, those dealing with divine providence and those dealing with domestic traumas such as *Arden of Faversham* (1591).[3]

Based on the murder of Thomas Arden by his wife Alice and her lover this sort of domestic tragedy did not become popular until the eighteenth century. Critics tend to differentiate it from 'true' tragedy on the grounds that the characters are 'middle class', that the action is set in the present and often based on real events, and that the protagonist's downfall is a personal rather than a social matter; it does not have the potentially catastrophic consequences for the kingdom as the ambition of a Macbeth or the folly of a Lear. And yet, as Catherine Belsey has demonstrated, such plays did have wider ramifications. The scandal of Arden's crime, she claims, lay 'in the challenge to the institution of marriage, itself publicly in crisis in the period'.[4]

Robert N. Watson states that, apart from the domestic version, English Renaissance tragedy presents 'the struggle of a remarkable individual against implacable, impersonal forces, a struggle no less imperative for its ultimate failure'.[5] But he also notes that the tragedy of this period is 'essentially' a re-enactment of ritual sacrifice.[6] What, though, did contemporary writers have to say about the genre? The word 'renaissance' means rebirth and the period was partly characterized by the rediscovery of classical authors whose works could either be regarded as models to be followed or as suggestions to be developed.

Aristotle said that tragedy should imitate a single action and have a cathartic effect. But Shakespeare's Hamlet has a more ambitious view, being less interested in drama as a form of catharsis than as means of correction. Its aim, he declares, 'is to hold as 'twere the mirror up to Nature and to show Virtue her feature, Scorn her own image and the very age and body of the time his form and pressure'.[7] George Chapman (1559–1634), in the dedication of *The Revenge of Bussy D'Ambois* (1613), declares that the sole purpose of tragedy is to excite a love of virtue and hatred of vice. Sir Philip Sidney (1554–1586) has a slightly more expansive view observing that tragedy not only warns kings about the consequences of tyranny, it also 'teacheth the uncertainty of this world, and upon how weak foundations gilden roofs are builded'.[8]

Thomas Heywood (c. 1575–1641) promotes tragedy as a civic good: it polishes the language, teaches proper speech, imparts a knowledge of English history, inspires noble actions, is a guide to morality and can even bring murderers to justice. Heywood recounts the tale of a Norfolk woman who was prompted to confess to the murder of her husband after watching a play on the same subject. Shakespeare may have had the story in mind when he had Hamlet stage *The Mousetrap* in an attempt to make Claudius admit he'd murdered the prince's father. What is missing from Heywood's otherwise impressive list of the benefits of tragedy is any sense of death, suffering or fate.

A more practical objection to Heywood's ethical defence of tragedy is that it takes no account of the commercial context in which theatre operated.

People put on plays for money, not because they led to moral improvement. This is what lies behind the rejection of Aristotle's three unities and the principle that tragedy and comedy should not be mixed. We get a sense of the extent to which the unities were being flouted from George Whetstone's famous Dedication of *The Right Excellent and Famous History of Promus and Cassandra* (1575) where he fulminates against the English playwright because he 'grounds his work on impossibilities; then in three hours he runs through the world, marries, gets children, makes children men, men to conquer kingdoms, murder monsters, and bringeth gods from heaven, and fetcheth devils from hell'.[9] But plays had to be exciting if they were to attract an audience. A single action in one place in real time did not offer the same opportunity for breath-taking thrills as a number of episodes in different locations over many months or years.

The idea of the unities – which Aristotle said were specific to tragedy – might have made perfect sense in a small city state thirteen hundred years ago, but not in a bustling capital city in the sixteenth and seventeenth centuries. The unities symbolized a restricted outlook on the world which was fast disappearing due to scientific discoveries and cultures coming into more contact with each other through trade. Something similar was going on in the debate about whether tragedy and comedy were distinct or whether an author could mingle clowns and kings. Sidney was in no doubt. Mixing the two was like mixing 'hornpipes and funerals'.[10] The result was a ghastly hybrid, a mongrel form. The ancients kept tragedy and comedy separate, reasoned Sidney, and so should his contemporaries. But Ulpian Fulwell (c. 1545–c. 1584), in his Prologue to *Like Will to Like* (1568), claimed that it was an 'author's chief desire to please all men' and since 'divers men of divers mind be', it was necessary to mix 'mirth with care'.[11]

Such differences were symptomatic of wider issues, in particular the shift from feudalism to capitalism. Everyone had their place in feudal society and the sumptuary laws stipulated that they should dress according to their degree. But feudalism was crumbling; 'rank and status were giving way to wealth and property'[12] which helped fuel the new sense of individualism. Christopher Marlowe's Tamburlaine gives expression to this change when he says that he will be defined by his deeds, not his parentage. Exchanging his shepherd's clothes for armour he utters one of the most famous lines of the age: 'Lie here, ye weeds that I disdain to wear.'[13]

It doesn't take a great deal of ingenuity to see the parallel between the desire to maintain social distinctions and the desire to maintain the differences between literary genres. But both were beginning to dissolve in Renaissance England as the old order gave way to the new, one characterized by plurality rather than hierarchy. In drama, for example, the choice is no longer just between tragedy or comedy but, as Polonius notes, 'history, pastoral, pastoral comical, historical pastoral, scene individable or poem unlimited. Seneca cannot be too heavy nor Plautus too light for the law of writ and the liberty.'[14]

Shakespeare (1564–1616), *King Lear* (1605)

King Lear contains several themes that we have already encountered in our discussion of tragedy: the nature of man, the reality of the gods and the relation between fate and free will in human affairs. It also contains elements of comedy but of a dark kind: Lear's powerless posturing, Edmund's delight in villainy, the Fool's bitter wit, and the sexual intrigue between Edmund and Goneril and Regan. But are these sufficient to explain the towering stature of this play? Its battered canvas of waste, desolation and existential exhaustion make it one of the most deeply disturbing works of Western literature. We expect tragedy to generate a sense of loss and grief but not, if we are looking at it from the perspective of sacrifice, total devastation. For sacrifice is a form of cleansing that leads to new life. More profoundly, it is also a way of comprehending death – of making what is beyond imagination into a manageable image. Since *King Lear* holds out little hope of new life, especially as it ends with the death of all the female characters, and since the death of Cordelia seems wholly without meaning – 'Why should a dog, a horse, a rat have life/And thou no breath at all?'[15] – then it follows that sacrifice is absent in the play.

Or so it seems. In fact sacrificial elements are present even in the opening scene. First, Lear's demand that his daughters give a public declaration of their love for him has a ceremonial character. Second, it foregrounds the act of exchange which is central to sacrifice and third it deals with the passage of power from the old to the new. In ancient ritual, the old was often represented by a king who was killed because his advanced age meant that he was no longer able to guarantee the fertility of the land. We can see Lear in this way. First he is old and, second, he is closely associated with what is barren or sterile or a threat to fecundity. When he is sane he utters curses against reproduction. He calls upon the gods to 'dry up' in Goneril 'the organs of increase',[16] and when he is insane he is spotted 'crowned [with] all the idle weeds that grow/In our sustaining corn'.[17]

Sacrificial ritual depended on a certain conception of nature – that it was ruled by gods who needed to be appeased if it were to work properly – but it is precisely 'nature' which is in question in this play.[18] On the one hand it is conceived of as a moral order that governs human affairs. That is why Goneril's and Regan's treatment of their father is frequently referred to as either 'unnatural' or 'monstrous'. On the other hand it is seen as the ally of high ambition and sexual vigour. It is to this idea of nature that Edmund's 'services are bound'.[19] The storm in Act 3 scene 1 is a good example of nature's ability to generate different meanings. It signifies, simultaneously, the turbulence of Lear's mind, the chaos in the kingdom, nature's fury at the behaviour of Goneril and Regan, and the indifference of the elements to the plight of man. These various notions of nature complicate any account of the play that tries to link it too closely to fertility rituals.

It is not only nature that's a problem in *King Lear*, so too is culture and it manifests itself in the division between plain and rhetorical speech.[20] Kent and Cordelia represent plain speech and Goneril, Regan and Edmund rhetorical speech. The differences between the two are clearly marked in the opening scene. Goneril's and Regan's exaggerated expressions of love for their father – 'Dearer than eyesight, space and liberty'[21] – contrasts with Cordelia's moderate declaration that she loves him 'According to my bond, no more nor less'.[22] But Lear, who as king bears ultimate responsibility for this linguistic inflation, can no longer tell the difference between honesty and hyperbole.

The divorce between words and genuine feeling leads to divisions not just between Lear and his daughters but also in the kingdom itself. It's a similar story with Edmund. He lies to his father and brother in order to advance his own career. He has as little regard for social or familial obligation as do Goneril and Regan. In sacrificial terms their deaths purge the kingdom of artifice, deceit and verbal excess. As Edgar says at the end, we must 'Speak what we feel, not what we ought to say.'[23]

But society is not cleansed because the distinction between what we might term 'authenticity' and 'affectation' is not sustainable. Both that 'glib and oily art/To speak and purpose not'[24] and that 'tardiness in nature,/ Which often leaves the history unspoken that it intends to do'[25] are similar to the extent that neither conveys the speaker's true meaning.

The plainness of the good man or woman may be as artful as the well-practised eloquence of the villains. Cornwall says that Kent is one of those men 'Who, having been praised for bluntness, doth affect/A saucy roughness and constrains the garb/Quite from his nature.'[26] In other words Kent exaggerates the image others have of him as a straight-talking fellow. He plays at being himself rather than actually being himself. And he is an actor. He is disguised when he presents himself to Lear as 'a very honest-hearted fellow'.[27] He also tells Lear that he only fights when he 'cannot choose'[28] but this is clearly not the case since he attacks Goneril's servant Oswald. This confrontation, moreover, reveals Kent's talent for rhetorical inventiveness as he piles insults upon the hapless Oswald. For a plain, blunt man, Kent is also surprisingly adept at using similes as when he says the unkindness of Goneril and Regan has made Gloucester's castle 'harder than the stones whereof 'tis raised'.[29] The best we can say of him is that his dissembling is used for good rather than bad ends.

The failure to purge society of rhetoric and deception highlights the problem of identity. How do we know whether someone really is what they appear to be? Cordelia is a case in point. Cornwall's words to Kent 'plainness/Harbour[s] more craft and corrupter ends/Than twenty silly-ducking observant/That stretch their duty nicely'[30] apply more to her than to him. We know that Cordelia is her father's favourite but we rarely stop to ask why. How has she achieved this position? And did it involve creating a distance between him and Goneril and Regan? She knows Lear's temperament, his appetite for flattery, yet she refuses to match her sisters' outpourings of filial devotion. Perhaps she is thinking that she will win a third more opulent than them by using a different rhetorical tactic, 'less is more', but it backfires badly.

This is to attribute a degree of self-interest to Cordelia which is deeply at odds with the conventional view of her as a loving and dutiful daughter. After all doesn't she come back from France to help her father? 'O dear father/It is thy business I go about … No blown ambition doth our arms incite.'[31] She says this in front of various dignitaries and soldiers. Can this be the same Cordelia who shuns emotional exhibitionism? Clearly she wants to present herself as the selfless child who is only thinking about her poor father and who has no designs on the kingdom whatsoever. It would be easy to believe her but for the time scheme of the play which suggests that more selfish motives are at play.[32] Lear sends Kent with a message for Regan after Goneril has reduced the number of his knights. It takes Kent no more than two days to get there.[33] Either during that time or before, he has received a letter from Cordelia promising 'to give/ Losses their remedies'.[34]

But to which losses is she referring? It cannot be Lear's knights as that only happened two days ago and it would have taken more time than that for her to be informed of the matter and to have sent a reply. It therefore seems likely she means her own share of the land which was divided between her sisters. If so, then it is not simply her father's business that Cordelia goes about but her own, and swiftly too. Within a few hours of Kent reading Cordelia's letter, Goneril and Regan have shut Lear out of Gloucester's castle and a part of the French force has landed at Dover.[35] Given that Cordelia cannot realistically have been informed about the sufferings of her father her claim that she has been 'cast down'[36] for him seems rather hollow.

Assuming that this analysis of Cordelia is correct, then her death can no longer be regarded as evidence that we inhabit either a pitiless, indifferent or meaningless universe. On the contrary, it makes perfect sense within the sacrificial logic of the play. As a more artful representative of the evils of rhetoric she too, along with her father, his self-deceptions and the ills that flow from them, has to be removed if society is to flourish. What doesn't make sense, and what shows the ultimate failure of sacrifice is that the very person who demands that people should speak what they mean, not what they ought to say, is also the very person who is the most adept actor in the play. Edgar not only carries off the role of poor Tom with aplomb but also that of a mariner or fisherman and a West-country yokel. The fact that he is to be the new ruler shows that what was considered to be a danger to the kingdom, saying things you don't mean or pretending to be what you are not, has now been transposed to the very heart of it. The prodigious effort to rid the kingdom of all forms of pretence and chicanery has failed. Despite the use of numerous scapegoats from Edmund to Cordelia we are left with the disturbing suggestion that there is nothing but acting – that man is a creature quite without substance.

Here we again touch on one of the themes of tragedy, human nature. Lear thinks he has stumbled on its secret when he encounters Poor Tom.

> Is man no more than this? Consider him well. Thou ow'st the worm no silk, the beast no hide, the sheep no wool, the cat no perfume. Ha? Here's three on's us are sophisticated; thou art the thing itself. Unaccommodated man is no more but such a poor, bare, forked animal as thou art.[37]

But Lear is mistaken in his insight. Poor Tom is not 'the thing itself' he is Edgar playing the part of Poor Tom. In fact he is not even Edgar; he is an actor playing the part of Poor Tom who is playing the part of Edgar.

A similar idea is at work in *Hamlet* (1600). The sacrificial structure of that play consists in removing the taint of incest which is the something rotten in the state of Denmark. *Leviticus* 20:21 makes it plain that a man who marries his brother's wife, as Claudius does, becomes 'an unclean thing' and that the couple shall be childless. Hamlet's desire for his mother, meanwhile, comes across strongly in his hot imaginings of her in bed with Claudius.[38] Discussion of the play has tended to focus on why Hamlet doesn't take on revenge on Claudius for his father's murder. One explanation is that if Hamlet killed Claudius he would have to confront his own Oedipal guilt instead of being able to hide from it by projecting it onto his uncle. Another is that we should think of Hamlet not as a flawed man of action but as a consummate actor. Not only does he pretend to be mad for most of the play, but he also shows a superb knowledge of acting technique.[39] Hamlet is important because he embodies the Renaissance idea of life as a performance. This, though, implies that man is a creature without substance. As such he can never, as Edgar says, speak what he feels. Lacking any solid identity, he can only mimic emotion, not truly experience it.

Part of the reason for man's vacuity is that he is no longer in a clearly defined relationship with divinity, a relationship traditionally expressed through sacrifice. The conflict between Protestantism and Catholicism with their competing conceptions of God is one factor here, and the growth of science, which challenges biblical accounts of the world, is another. The confusion about the supernatural is reflected in the different attitudes to the gods in *King Lear*. Lear frequently invokes them when he is calling down curses on his daughters while other characters simply refer to the heavens. The belief that the gods are real prompts the question of their relation to humanity. Albany believes that the gods act in the name of justice[40] but Gloucester believes 'they kill us for their sport'.[41] We might also detect an allusion to the Christian acceptance of suffering in Edgar's admonition to his father 'Men must endure/Their going hence even as their coming hither./Ripeness is all.'[42] But then there are other characters such as Edmund who are either sceptical or downright dismissive of the supernatural. Edmund mocks Gloucester's belief in astrology as 'the excellent foppery of the world',[43] a belief that allows us to avoid taking responsibility for our actions. 'An admirable evasion of whoremaster man to lay his goatish disposition on the charge of a star,'[44] as he puts it. The uncertainty surrounding the existence of the gods has implications for understanding the operation of sacrifice in the play.[45] Sacrifice is based on a set of assumptions about human nature, the gods and the relation between the two. When these are thrown into disarray, as they are here, then humans lose their spiritual moorings and are faced with the task of redefining themselves and their relation to the cosmos.

How, then, can we sum up the problem of sacrifice in *King Lear*? By saying that the sacrificial structure of the play malfunctions. It aims to rid the kingdom of the rhetorical excess which leads to conflict and division. On the one hand this process appears to be successful because, by the end of the play, all those characters who delighted in verbal artifice are dead. On the other hand, it seems to have failed because the plain speaking that replaces ornate eloquence has been shown to have the same capacity for deceit and misrepresentation as its opposite. The failure of sacrifice may partly explain the recurrence of the word 'nothing' in the play. Sacrifice is about giving form and meaning to sex, society, suffering, death and the relation between humans and the gods, but it cannot fulfil this function if the concepts on which it depends, such as 'nature', are as unstable as they are in *King Lear*. But if the sacrificial mechanism fails in one sense, it succeeds in another for the deaths of the several scapegoats ensure that the qualities that die with them are reborn and refreshed in Edgar.

Thomas Middleton (1580–1627), *The Revenger's Tragedy* (1606)

Revenge tragedy is a distinct genre that flourished from approximately the 1580s to the 1620s. It is characterized chiefly by a protagonist bent on avenging the death of someone close to him or her. Other features are: that the protagonist may have been prompted to this action by the ghost of the deceased, that the protagonist will usually adopt a disguise, that the protagonist is usually melancholic and may suffer bouts of madness, that the protagonist may also have scruples about the action they are to take, and that the action itself comes to a bloody climax in a masque or play within a play.

Some of these features are present in *The Revenger's Tragedy*. The protagonist, Vindice, whose name means avenger, seeks retribution for the death of his mistress, whom the Duke poisoned when she would not respond to his advances. He disguises himself as 'a strange-composed fellow'[46] in pursuit of that end and he is also a man in whom 'much melancholy dwells'.[47] Far from having scruples about his undertaking, however, Vindice seems positively to revel in it. Not content with tricking the Duke into kissing the poisoned skull of his dead mistress, he strains to find more ways to 'afflict'[48] him as the venom slowly takes effect. There is more killing at the end as Vindice and his brother, Hippolito, stab Lussurioso and several nobles during a masque, the conventional finale of a revenge tragedy. The play also illustrates another meaning of revenge, namely that is a way of dramatizing the clash between the values of feudalism – honour and chastity – and those of capitalism – money and opportunism. 'Faiths are bought and sold./Oaths in these days are but the skin of gold.'[49]

A number of factors contributed to the growth of revenge tragedy. One is the various translations of the plays of Seneca, whose characteristic sensationalism was an important influence on the genre. So too was the prominence he gave to the theme of revenge which chimed more easily with Renaissance ideas of self-determination than the idea of fate or the notion that the gods controlled human destiny. A second factor in the development of revenge tragedy was the translation of French and Italian tales and histories which often had revenge as their main subject. There was a particular fascination with Italy because the vendetta was integral to its culture thanks to that symbol of villainy, Niccolò Machiavelli (1467–1527), whose book *The Prince* (1532) argued that effective government relied more on expediency than ethics. A third factor was the dissatisfaction felt with changes in the Tudor legal system which left those seeking justice frustrated and disappointed. This is very clearly illustrated in *The Revenger's Tragedy* where Antonio cannot get justice for his wife who was raped by Lussurioso, the Duke's son. 'My lord, what judgement follows the offender?' asks Piero, a nobleman. 'Faith, none my lord; it cools and is deferred,' replies Antonio.[50] Hippolito promises Antonio that if Lussurioso is not punished then he will 'let his soul out, which long since was found/Guilty in heaven', to which Antonio responds, 'I thank you in mine ire.'[51] That word 'ire' will prove crucial for understanding Antonio's action at the end of the play.

The most notorious feature of revenge tragedy is its spectacular violence. This is partly due to theatre's need to compete with such bloody forms of entertainment as bear-baiting and partly due to the new interest in anatomy.[52] But we can also understand it in terms of sacrifice. Girard argues that sacrifice is a way of channelling and controlling violence by projecting it onto a scapegoat. If this mechanism is absent then violence becomes endemic. But *The Revenger's Tragedy* presents a blow to his thesis for although it contains scapegoats, the blood flows freely. The most obvious scapegoat is the Duke himself who represents unrestrained sexuality. Vindice describes him as 'a royal lecher' and a 'grey haired adulter[er]'.[53] Lussurioso, as his name suggests,[54] is also a symbol of voracious sexuality. Having raped Antonio's wife, he then employs Vindice, who at this point is in disguise, to seduce Castiza, Vindice's sister, on Lussurioso's behalf.

Vindice uses the opportunity to test the virtue of his sister and her mother, Gratiana, because women, too, are seen as lascivious. Ambitioso, the Duchess' first son, airs the general view when he announces that 'Most women have small waist the world throughout,/But their desires are thousand miles about.'[55] Vindice's efforts are not successful with Castiza but, to his horror, Gratiana agrees to help him make sure that Lussurioso has his way. For that, he and Hippolito are prepared to kill her. But she is contrite and they spare her life. She can be forgiven, as long as she truly repents, for Christ's death redeemed the sins of all mankind.

The Christian concept of sacrifice exists uneasily, if not in flat contradiction, with the pagan concept of sacrifice. The former relates sacrifice to forgiveness; the latter relates it to revenge whose purpose is to rid the state of a rampant and incestuous sexuality represented by the Duke and Lussurioso. To insist on vengeance is to reject the Christian message that we should love our enemies, and it is also, if we take into account the Old Testament claim that vengeance belongs to the Lord,[56] to usurp the role of God. To that extent the Revenger, like Marlowe's Dr. Faustus (1592), aspires to the condition of divinity. Although the Christian and pagan notions of sacrifice are clearly differentiated at the level of ideas they do come together at the level of imagery. Gratiana's remorse is conveyed in terms that suggest a fertility festival as well as Christian repentance: 'The fruitful grounds and meadows of her soul/Has long been dry; pour down, thou blessed dew.'[57] But perhaps this is to be expected given the affinities we have noted between pagan and Christian sacrifice in previous chapters. Moreover what is fundamental to sacrifice, whether it is Christian or pagan, is an act of cleansing.

The Duke's prodigious appetite not only results in adultery which, in parts of Europe, was believed to blight the crops,[58] but it also overturns the natural order. If the sexual potency of the ruler is responsible for the land then the Duke, for all his prowess, is a threat to it because he is old. But then again his son, who has youth on his side, is no better for his energies are dissipated in sexual liaisons instead of in service to the state. For of course fertility and sterility are not to be understood literally but as metaphors for how the land is governed. It is the same with incest. Spurio, the Duke's bastard son, and the Duchess are involved in a sexual relationship which, while not technically incestuous, since she is not his mother, is nevertheless referred to as such. Lussurioso, for example, describes 'the incestuous sweets between them'.[59] Like adultery, incest was also considered a danger to the harvest. Here it is a metaphor for a preoccupation with private pleasures rather than public duties and so it too must be purged from the body politic.

There are two set-piece slayings in the play. The first is the killing of the Duke and the second is the killing of Lussurioso and several nobles. Both are sacrificial to the extent that the violence is highly theatrical and intended as an act of cleansing. Vindice dresses the skull of his mistress in a veil, a wig and a mask and Lussurioso is slain by Vindice, Hippolito and two Lords all wearing vizards. But there's a problem. The violence of both incidents is in excess of what we might expect for sacrifice. We noted earlier that Vindice wants to inflict as much pain and humiliation on the Duke as possible before the poison takes effect and, after Lussurioso and his entourage are stabbed to death, the Duchess' two sons, who had also plotted to kill Lussurioso, draw their swords on each other in a bid to become the new Duke. Spurio too enters the fray and is knifed by a nameless nobleman. How do we explain the extent of this carnage?

The answer is that one of the most important functions of sacrifice, the sanctioning, expressing and giving meaning to violence, has failed. There are many reasons for this, such as the low status of sacrifice in Protestantism compared to the one it had in Catholicism, but what is of interest here is the kind of violence that emerges when sacrifice breaks down. Part of it is Oedipal. Spurio and the Duchess, for example, want to kill the Duke. But Vindice, too, seems propelled by incestuous desire, something which he says afflicts the age: 'O hour of incest!/Any kin now .../Is man's meat these days'.[60] He derives a perverse pleasure out of trying to seduce his sister on behalf of Lussurioso and takes a strange delight in pressing his mother to help him in his suit. She, in her turn, responds with 'I blush to think what for your sakes I'll do.'[61] The fact that that she does not recognise him is no argument against the suggestively Oedipal nature of their encounter, for repressed wishes always appear in disguised form.

Vindice sounds like Hamlet when he remarks that, since his father's funeral, he feels that he ought not to be alive.[62] Hamlet's suicidal tendencies are, in part, the desire for punishment because he harboured hostile feelings against his father. His enmity towards him is disguised as admiration for his father's prowess as a warrior. But it is precisely because Hamlet, a scholar rather than a soldier, cannot live up to his father's image that he resents him. It is possible that Vindice, like Hamlet, feels guilty that he is alive when his father is dead and that his desire for death, though not as pronounced as Hamlet's, is also a desire for punishment. His aggression towards his father stems from his Oedipal feelings for his sister and mother. It comes out in his sadism towards the Duke, whose status makes him a symbolic father figure, and the savagery of his assault also serves to cover the guilt he feels for his own parricidal instincts. The Oedipal dimension of the play is also evident in the Duke's sons and stepsons each plotting to murder him. Their wish to kill their father is similar to that of brothers described by Freud in his mythical account of the origins of human society. The difference is that, in Freud's essay, the brothers unite to do the deadly deed. In *The Revenger's Tragedy*, they are riven by rivalry.

There is, then, an Oedipal dimension to the nature of the violence in the play, which surfaces again in the way Vindice and Hippolito are ready to stab their mother.[63] Freud, of course, argues that sacrifice is a symbolic version of Oedipal desire. It re-enacts and makes reparations for the murder of the primal father and is followed by rejoicing in which 'every instinct is unfettered and there is licence for every kind of gratification'.[64] One of the interesting things about The Revenger's Tragedy is the way that it reverses the order of these events. The play begins with disapproving references to the free play of desire and ends with the killing of several father figures. To the extent that the play gives limited expression to wayward desire by condemning it, it can be described as a comedy[65] but since that kind of anarchic desire leads to death – the Duke, Lussurioso, Vindice's mistress and Antonio's wife – then it can be described as a tragedy.

The terrible proximity of desire and death is at its most intense when the Duke kisses the painted skull. One of the functions of sacrifice is to distinguish between life and death even as it shows they are profoundly related. When, for whatever reason, sacrifice fails to function, the distinction between life and death collapses and the two become conflated. Freud noted that Eros and Thanatos, as he termed them, were very similar because they were both striving to reach a state characterized by the complete absence of tension, but the relationship between them is more complicated than this simple formulation suggests.

By searching for satisfaction, desire is seeking its end, for it expires when it fulfils itself. But as desire is only ever temporarily satiated, it is doomed to be renewed. Desire is therefore a source of anxiety and, in the worst-case scenario, can lead to thoughts of suicide in order to escape the angst, frustration and inevitable disappointment it brings. There are two other ways in which desire resembles death. First it can overwhelm us, undoing the unity of the self. Desire seems to invade, colonize and overturn our sense of who we are as it takes possession of us. Second, the fact that desire is necessary for reproduction is a reminder that we must die. The individual has to perish so that the species can continue. And no matter what symbolic systems we construct to try and transcend the inevitable decay of the flesh, we are bound to the body; its death is ours.

The failure of sacrifice in The Revenger's Tragedy, then, allows us to glimpse something of the nature of the violence it normally conceals. The excessive nature of this violence, evident in the pleasure Vindice takes in murdering the Duke, complements the excessive nature of sexuality in the play. The arrest and execution of Vindice and Hippolito at the end show that bloodshed will no more be tolerated than incest or adultery but, as suggested below, it is doubtful that these evils are truly eradicated. Hence the unsettling truth of The Revenger's Tragedy is that all our most worthy undertakings, in this case the pursuit of justice, may be little more than rationalizations for the indulgence of our worst instincts. By this logic sacrifice ceases to be a solemn ceremony, a communion with the god, and becomes, instead, a mere fiction that gratifies the base part of our nature – a nature that, as noted above, also has an impulse towards its own extinction.

Some of these ideas are apparent in Vindice's speeches about his mistress. In the first he describes how her beauty was such 'That the uprightest man (if such there be/That sin but seven times a day) broke custom,/And made up eight with looking after her.'[66] Vindice dwells on her power to disturb the opposite sex. She ignites such a fierce desire in them that they lose all sense of self. She is therefore a kind of death. This slightly undermines the revenge theme for, if Vindice's mistress arouses men against their will, if she makes them strangers to themselves, then the implication is that the Duke was compelled to try and seduce her. Vindice's mistress is associated with death in another of his speeches. Holding up her skull he says, 'Here might a scornful and ambitious woman/Look through and through herself; – see, ladies, with/false forms/ You deceive men but cannot deceive worms.'[67] In this context, the mistress functions not merely as a *memento mori*, a reminder that we must die, but as something altogether more profound, a symbol that death is truth and life is a lie. The skull and the mediations it provokes take us a long way from the idea, mentioned earlier, of man as god.

There is no sense of renewal in *The Revenger's Tragedy*. The corruption seems to have been banished but Antonio, who takes the Duke's place, is old and is therefore, in terms of sacrificial logic, incapable of infusing new life into his society. It is true that he revives the ideal of justice by having Vindice and Hippolito arrested for the murders they have committed but we cannot view this as an altogether positive step. First because Antonio himself sanctioned the killing of Lussurioso. And even though he did so in his 'ire', it does not excuse him from his part in the murder. The fact that he has benefitted from their actions means that revenge is not quite exorcized from the play. If civilization comes into being by replacing vengeance with law as in *The Oresteia*, then *The Revenger's Tragedy* shows that that is not a once-and-for-all process but a precarious and ongoing one.

The second reason we cannot afford to be sanguine about the apparent restoration of justice is because of the fascination with death in the play. The pervasive notion that it renders all human endeavour worthless means that it is pointless to aspire to anything higher than sensual gratification. But, of course, it is precisely sensual gratification which is the source of corruption in the play. The picture is further complicated when we consider the premium placed on chastity by Vindice and Antonio. Since Vindice's mistress and Antonio's wife die, chastity is associated with death but so too is sexual anarchy. Where then, in sacrificial terms, is the new life to come from? Not from Antonio nor, indeed, anyone else. And the fact that we don't know what happened to the Duchess suggests that elements of sexual pollution, like that of revenge, still have the potential to disturb the state. What's lacking is some mechanism for regulating the excesses of sex and violence as sacrifice regulates the relation between life and death. But since the sacrificial structure of *The Revenger's Tragedy* is, as we have seen, only partially successful, the world of the play can only offer a particular instance of Donne's general lament that society is indeed 'all in pieces, all coherence gone'.[68]

Renaissance Comedy

Renaissance comedy has its source in the works of Plautus (254–184 BCE) and Terence (185–159 BCE) whose works were studied in universities and grammar schools. They both adapted Greek New Comedy for their Roman audience and wrote about common life, mostly in verse, and their plots followed the same pattern of *protasis* (exposition), *epitasis* (complication) and *catastrophe* (resolution) often with an important recognition scene. Stock characters such as the slave, the bragging soldier, the young lovers and the old man were another common feature of their work. Each playwright contributed to the development of comedy in the Renaissance. Plautus bequeathed a fascination with wordplay while one of Terence's legacies was the overheard conversation. Although both writers were very similar, Terence is sometimes seen as the more subtle explorer of human behaviour. Medieval morality plays also influenced Renaissance comedy with the convention of naming a character after the moral quality they represented. The practice could be found in tragedy too, as we saw with Vindice and Lussurioso in *The Revenger's Tragedy*. This not only enhances the comic elements of that play, it also undermines the idea of character development which is crucial to tragedy. The hero, for example, is supposed to grow in self-knowledge. But a character who represents a single quality cannot progress; he or she can only repeat themselves.

Some Renaissance writers, such as George Puttenham (1529–1590), author of *The Arte of English Poesie* (1589), followed Aristotle in distinguishing between tragedy and comedy on the basis that the former portrayed the noble actions of noble men, while the latter concerned itself with 'common behaviours [among] the meaner sort of men'.[69] But this distinction, though it has some truth, quickly breaks down when we look at, say, Shakespeare's comedies whose protagonists are all from the nobility with the lower classes appearing in minor roles. William Webbe (1550–1591), in his *Discourse of English Poetry* (1586), argued that tragedy depicted persons of great state whose lives begin well but they then suffer 'miserable calamities' which continue to increase such that 'they come to the most woful (sic.) plight that might be devised'.[70] Comedy, by contrast, began in some 'trouble and turmoil' but 'always ended to the joy and appeasement of all parties'.[71] An obvious exception is *Twelfth Night* (1602) where the humiliated Malvolio will not be reconciled with his tormentors and storms off the stage at the end.

A further difference between tragedy and comedy is found in *Soliman and Perseda* (c. 1593), tentatively attributed to Thomas Kyd (1558–1594), when Death remarks that 'Love and Fortune play in comedies:/[But] powerful Death best fitteth tragedies.'[72] Again, this distinction is a useful rule of thumb but, as Aristotle pointed out, the best tragedies end happily. Moreover, if the hero of tragedy is a villain, then his or her death is a cause for celebration. Both comedy and tragedy were conceived in largely didactic terms, although this was not often realized in the plays themselves which were too complex to be reduced to a simple moral. Nevertheless Ben Jonson writes, in the Dedication of *Volpone* (1606), that the office of the comic poet is 'to imitate justice, and instruct to life, as well as purity of language, or stir up gentle affections'.[73] Comedy was also thought to have certain medicinal properties. It could relieve sadness and keep away the madness associated with melancholy. Laughter, it was believed, could also lengthen life.

Jill Levenson notes that Renaissance comedy was built out of diverse materials. From the late sixteenth to the early seventeenth century, comedy 'took in whole genres from romance and satire to sonnet and epigram; it borrowed subgenres or modes; it incorporated theatrical conventions like court masque; and it continued to admit the traditions of carnival and popular culture'.[74] That popular culture included various festivals, sports and games all designed, in one way or another, to promote fertility. The standard work on the connection between these pastimes and drama remains C. L. Barber's *Shakespeare's Festive Comedy: A Study of Dramatic Form and Its Relation to Social Custom* (1959 and 2012). It describes the diverse revels, festivals and holidays of Elizabethan England, how they were denounced by Puritans for being tainted with paganism, and how Shakespeare kept them alive by transforming ritual practice into artistic form.

Barber's main claim is that, at the heart of Shakespeare's comedies lies a saturnalian pattern involving 'inversion, statement and counterstatement, and a basic movement which can be summarised in the formula, through release to clarification'.[75] The word 'saturnalian' is derived from the Roman festival of Saturnalia held in honour of Saturn, an agricultural deity who was believed to have reigned over the world in the golden age when nature yielded her bounty freely and humans lived together in peace and harmony. The festival itself, held in December, involved a sacrifice, a banquet, gift-giving and a temporary overturning of social norms. The words 'inversion', 'statement' and 'counterstatement', are a reminder of the agon or contest that lies at the heart of comedy while the phrase 'release through clarification' means that, relieved of their customary responsibilities, characters achieve 'a heightened awareness of the relation between man and nature'.[76]

Barber sees a continuity between Elizabethan festivals and those of the ancient world. The phallic songs in worship of Dionysus, for example, contained two parts, an invocation to Phales intended to promote fertility, and abuse and invective intended to expel evil spirits. The May Games, which consisted of dancing, singing, sports and contests, comic speeches and mummers plays, were an invocation to nature, as was the 'bringing home of May', the gathering of hawthorn to decorate the houses and church. The Lord of Misrule represents the abuse and invective. He presided over eating and drinking in the winter season. The festivities were characterized by overturning the hierarchy of the household so that the servant would, for a short time, become the master and vice versa, the whole being accompanied by raillery and mockery.

The distinction between the May Games and the Lord of Misrule is one of emphasis rather than absolute division for the title Lord of Misrule could also apply to the leader of drinking and dancing in spring and summer. There was a clearer division between these sorts of revels and aristocratic entertainments, which took place in court and at selected country houses as the Queen and her entourage moved round the country in the summer months. The shows consisted of displays of allegorical dramas, enactments of myth, pastoral idylls and much solemn flattery of Elizabeth herself. But they also reflected the spirit of popular traditions and holidays. At Elvetham in 1591 Elizabeth was heralded as a May Queen, a harbinger of spring, and her departure marks the end of it, 'For how can summer stay, when Sun departs'?'[77] Having identified the various types of festival, Barber then examines how Shakespeare translates them into drama.

Shakespeare (1564–1616), *A Midsummer Night's Dream* (1595)

Barber makes two main claims about *A Midsummer Night's Dream*. The first is that the May Game provides the pattern for the 'whole action which moves "from the town to the grove" and back again, bringing in summer to the bridal',[78] and the second is that the mishaps of the night 'bring clarification about the tricks of strong imagination'.[79]

There is nothing contentious about his first point. The lovers departing for the woods and their being in the grip of strong desire roughly corresponds to the Puritan Philip Stubbes' (c. 1555–c. 1610) description of how, in May, 'all the young men and maids, old men and wives, run gadding over night to the woods, groves and hills … where they spend all the night in pleasant pastimes … And no marvel for there is a great Lord present among them … namely Satan, prince of hell'.[80] But Barber's second point is open to dispute. The overriding feeling among the lovers after experiencing the effects of the flower love-in-idleness[81] is one of confusion, not clarification. Demetrius, for example, cannot explain by 'what power' his love to Hermia has 'Melted as the snow'; Hermia sees the night's events 'with parted eye,/When everything seems double', and Helena's 'So methinks'[82] shows she shares her friend's perplexity. Bottom, too, cannot fathom what has happened to him, declaring that it is beyond the power of eye, ear, hand and tongue to report what his dream was or meant.[83]

It is true that the relation between the lovers has been either confirmed, as in the case of Lysander and Hermia, or corrected, as in the case of Demetrius and Helena. But even here there are questions. Is it right, for example, that Oberon tricks Demetrius into falling in love with Helena by coating his eyes with the juice of love-in-idleness? In terms of the plot, yes. For Demetrius was betrothed to Helena before meeting Hermia[84] and therefore it is only right that he should fulfil his obligation towards her – a theme that Shakespeare will revisit in the character of Angelo in *Measure for Measure* (1603). Even so, there is a sense of disquiet about the means used to bring about this end if only because Demetrius' love for Helena cannot be considered as either reasoned or genuine.

But then what is genuine love? How is it distinguished from desire? Lysander sees love in terms of obstacles that bring it to a quick end.[85] Helena makes contradictory claims about it. On the one hand she says that 'Love looks not with the eyes but with the mind' and on the other hand she says that 'Nor hath Love's mind of any judgement taste,'[86] a remark which is echoed in Bottom's observation that 'reason and love keep little company together nowadays'.[87] All these comments about love apply equally to desire. It too faces obstacles. When Lysander desires Hermia she rejects him. Desire can be brought to a quick end by the application of the antidote to love-in-idleness. And it certainly does not look with the mind. Love-in-idleness is dropped into the eye, not the brain. Helena says that 'Things base and vile, holding no quantity,/Love can transpose to form and dignity'[88] but it is the juice of the flower, not love, that makes Titania think that Bottom is an 'angel'.[89] Finally violence is much a part of love as it is of desire. Theseus wooed Hippolyta with his sword, Hermia is threatened with death or a nunnery if she doesn't accept her father's choice of suitor, Helena says the more that Demetrius beats her the more she will fawn on him[90] and Oberon uses love-in-idleness as a way of imposing his will on Titania.

The difficulty of distinguishing between love and desire is paralleled by the mechanicals confusing acting with 'real' life. Snout is worried that the ladies will be frightened by the sight of a lion in their performance of 'The most lamentable comedy and most cruel death of Pyramus and Thisbe' and Bottom agrees, suggesting that the prologue be expanded to explain that Snug the joiner, who plays the lion's part, is not really a lion and, just to make sure there is no confusion, he is to show half his face through the costume. The play-within-a play itself reflects some of the themes of the main action, for example, misunderstandings and the obstacles lovers have to face to be together.

The upper class audience pour scorn on the mechanicals' lack of ability and amateurish efforts. There is no inversion of hierarchy here. Quite the opposite. The actors are mocked precisely because of the gap between them and the classical figures they endeavour to impersonate. But we shouldn't forget that the lovers were themselves a source of amusement for 'higher' beings. Their antics under the influence of love-in-idleness prompt Puck to remark 'Shall we their fond pageant see?/Lord what fools these mortals be.'[91] What's more, the intellectually sophisticated lovers are more like the mechanicals than they imagine for they have the same difficulty in distinguishing between dream and waking as Bottom and his friends do in distinguishing the stage world from the workaday world. The latter mix up their words, often meaning the opposite of what they want to say 'If we offend, it is with our good will,'[92] while the former cannot sort out which of their perceptions are real and which fantasy. Like Hermia, they see 'double'.

There is at least a case, then, for querying Barber's view that *A Midsummer Night's Dream* clarifies the tricks that strong imagination can play. This is a play in which the solid world melts into something rich and strange, a blend of dream, magic and imagination. We saw in *Hamlet* and *King Lear* that man was a creature without substance, but here the great globe itself threatens to dissolve into thin air. And this has consequences for sacrifice since it depends on a clear demarcation between two distinct realms, the sacred and the secular. Without a division between humans and gods, sacrifice either becomes redundant or has to be redefined.

There appear to be two distinct realms in *A Midsummer Night's Dream* – that of the humans and the fairies though the dividing line between them is unclear since Oberon seems at one time to have been Hippolyta's lover and Titania Theseus'.[93] Oberon and Puck have, in addition, controlled the behaviour of the lovers and at the end the fairies bless the bridal beds. However, the humans seem to be unaware of the fairies' existence and certainly do not offer sacrifices to them. Nevertheless, sacrifice is present in the play and it centres on the little changeling boy. His mother was a 'votress',[94] that is a vowed woman member of Titania's order. The religious diction here elevates Titania from being a mere fairy to a near divinity thereby introducing an element of the sacred which is necessary to sacrifice.

The act of exchange is also necessary to sacrifice and the word 'changeling' usually refers to a child left by fairies in return for one they have stolen though that doesn't seem to be the case here. Titania looks after the boy because his mother, of whom she was fond, died. However, Puck tells a different story which is that the child was stolen from an Indian king. Either way, Oberon wants the boy as his henchman or page of honour. Because Titania refuses to surrender him the two have quarrelled and, as a result, the land has lost its fertility: 'the green corn/Hath rotted ere his youth attain'd a beard'.[95] The humans show no awareness of the terrible blight described by Titania, though from what she says it must affect them. In order to remove it, Titania must sacrifice the child – that is give up him to Oberon. But she doesn't. At least not when she is in her right mind. She delivers the boy to Oberon under the influence of love-in-idleness which has caused her to transfer her affections from the child to Bottom. And the result is that nature is presumably rebalanced. The seasons are in order, the fogs have lifted and the floods have retreated.

So what are we to make of all this? The changeling is an ambiguous figure. Was he abducted or did his mother really die? Certainly if he wasn't stolen before, he is now. Since sacrifice is meant to be an exchange, not a theft, then the changeling cannot be regarded as a sacrificial victim. On the other hand, his appropriation by Oberon brings fertility back to the land. Once more we find the sacrificial function in a play but, again, we find that it operates in a far from straightforward way. That's because, in this play, the changeling signifies on two levels. As a sacrificial victim he is an ahistorical figure but, as an Indian child, he is rooted in a specific historical context of trade and empire. Oberon's prising of the boy from Titania may also be an allusion to the upper-class custom of removing boys from their mothers to school or other households.

Another peculiarity of sacrifice in this play is that it is a relation between Oberon and Titania rather than between humans and gods. Sacrifice is not, in other words, a relation between two different kinds of being, one of whom is more powerful than the other, but between the same kind of beings. But this does not mean that the fairy king and queen are equal or that the relation between them is conflict free. Titania defies male authority just as Hermia defies her father's will that she marry Demetrius. Both are asked to sacrifice or give up something dear to them as a sign of their submission to male power.

Power is central to sacrifice. The gods were able to extract offerings from humans because they were believed to control the forces of nature and, in this play, males expect females to do as they say or, in the case of Hermia, face either death or a nunnery. And in this play, males usually get their way. Oberon tricks Titania out of the changeling boy. And Egeus only fails in his bid to have his daughter marry the person of his choice because he is overruled by Theseus, a male of higher status. Theseus makes this decision because Demetrius now loves Helena, but he does so only because he is under the influence of love-in-idleness. The play's happy ending relies on him being drugged. Does this mean that one of the functions of comedy is to substitute truth for delusion? No, because *A Midsummer Night's Dream* repeatedly shows that this distinction is not as straightforward as it seems. The key point here, however, is that the power dimension of sacrifice is also at work in gender relations. This should come as no surprise for, since the murder of Clytemnestra, the repression of women has been a factor in what we understand by sacrifice.

The sacrificial aspect of *A Midsummer Night's Dream* is most apparent in the frequent references to fertility. We have already mentioned that fertility is restored to the land by Titania giving up the Indian boy to Oberon and it is also closely associated with marriage. Theseus tells Hermia that it is better to bear children than to chant 'faint hymns to the cold fruitless moon'[96] and the fairies bless the bride-bed so that 'the issue there create/Ever shall be fortunate'.[97] Titania is an interesting case. She has no children. If she stole the boy then that implies a desire for a child. As does the imagery she uses in her conversation with her votress: 'we have laughed to see the sails conceive/And grow big-bellied with the wanton wind'.[98] Finally, she appears to treat Bottom very much as she treated the changeling, decorating both of them with flowers.[99] It is not impossible to see a reference to the unmarried Elizabeth in Titania's childlessness. The question of an heir to the throne was a source of anxiety in this period. A disputed succession could lead to war, a concern that is at the heart of Shakespeare's history plays.

In some ways the institution of monarchy is a formalization of the ancient transfer of power from the old to the new king in order to guarantee the success of the harvest. Vigorous sexual activity was also believed to bring about the same end. This, as we noted in chapter one, took the form of orgies. The impulse to promiscuity survives in comedy in the form of mistaken identities. They sanction the waywardness of desire before true identities are revealed and everyone is restored to their rightful partner. Lysander's and Demetrius' pursuit of Helena is a restrained version of the sexual congress that was part of the celebrations following a sacrifice. These desires are tamed and channelled into marriage. But, as we can see from the sexual adventures of Oberon and Titania, marriage is only partially successful in controlling them.

This is a reminder of the potency of desire – of how it disrupts monogamy, dominates actions and perceptions, and makes a person blind to all but the sought after object. Desire is a burden. That is why Theseus seeks a distraction from it. *A Midsummer Night's Dream* begins with him seeking release from the pain of non-fulfilment of desire and ends with him longing for a play 'To ease the anguish of a torturing hour.'[100] But desire should not just be seen in sexual terms; it is also an expression of a need to be part of something greater than oneself. This is one of Barber's main points about the May Games. Their 'wantonness has a reverence about [them] because [they are] a realisation of a power of life larger than the individual'.[101] But that desire to belong to the larger processes of life was under threat. The discipline demanded by the new economic order, Puritan attacks on traditional customs and pastimes, the new individualism and a more scientific understanding of nature all contributed to a weakening of man's connection with the world of flora and fauna. In time, this created the problem of trying to find a new symbol to express that connection. We are still struggling to locate it.

Ben Jonson (1572–1637), *Every Man in His Humour* (1598)

This play is quite different from *A Midsummer Night's Dream*. It has an urban setting and the characters are drawn from the merchant, trading and labouring classes. It is not so much about love as about London life and its aim is to moralize rather than enchant. *Every Man in His Humour* is one of the first examples of city comedy which flourished between 1598 and 1614, though there are also later instances of the genre such as R. Brome's *The City Wit* (1630). This type of comedy is partly an expression of the interests and ideas of that section of society known as the middle rank, a highly varied group, which existed in some tension with the monarchy and aristocracy. There was, for example, resentment towards Crown monopolies, that is the sale of exclusive rights of production of goods, as this was felt to damage competition and block the development of trade. But the city was able to retaliate by refusing loans to James I (1566–1625), who was also irritated by its being a haven for dissident religious views.

Very little of the simmering hostility between the city and the court is evident in *Every Man in His Humour*. The play, which helped to shape the genre of city comedy, is assembled from a number of different dramatic traditions. The father–son conflict can be traced back to the Old Comedy of Aristophanes; Brainworm, the clever servant, is a feature of the New Comedy of Plautus while the portrayal of a person in terms of a single quality has a long history dating from Theophrastus' *The Characters* (c. 286 BCE).[102] 'Humour' is the term mostly commonly used in the Renaissance for this convention. Up to the late middle ages it referred to the belief that there were four fluids in the human body: sanguine (sociable and pleasure loving), choleric (assertive and ambitious), melancholic (quiet and thoughtful) and phlegmatic (calm and relaxed). They corresponded, respectively, to the four elements: air, fire, earth and water. The ideal was for the humours to be in balance. If the strongest was not held in check it would dominate behaviour which then became a source of comedy.

Jonson explains what he means by humour in his next play, *Every Man Out of His Humour* (1599): 'Some one peculiar quality/Doth so possess a man, that it doth draw/All his affects, his spirits, and his powers,/In their confluctions, all to run one way/This may be truly said to be a humour.'[103] In *Every Man in His Humour* both Matthew and Stephen, the one a town the other a country 'gull' or fool, are both under, or imagine they are under, the sway of melancholy. But this is not reflected in their names whereas the opposite is the case for other characters such as Justice Clement and George Downright, a plain squire.

Jonson's use of the humours as the basis of comedy is not without wider problems. First it clashes with his belief, cited above, that comedy should correct behaviour. But how can it do this if it relies on a static conception of character? At the end of *Every Man in His Humour*, Justice Clement banishes Matthew and Bobadill, a boastful coward in the manner of Shakespeare's Falstaff, from his supper partly on the basis that they 'have so little of man in 'em.' Since they are clearly incapable of reform, 'they are no part of [his] care'.[104] The second problem with the humours is that they are close to caricature and this is at odds with Jonson's aim of portraying 'deeds, and language such as men do use'.[105] In other words Jonson aims at 'realism' but relies on an 'unrealistic' representation of persons as being motivated by a single passion.

This is not to say that *Every Man in His Humour* lacks lifelike features. A strong sense of place is conjured by the use of names: Old Jew'ry, Thames Street and Custom House quay. There are references to current events such as wars and threats to the state.[106] And the play is suffused with anxiety about the social structure manifested in Stephen's crass efforts to appear a gentleman and in the water-carrier Cob's parody of genealogies as he traces his ancestry from 'Herring', 'the king of Fish'.[107]

The general sense of dislocation is accompanied by the emergence of a new sensibility which appears in the character of the merchant Kitely. 'My brain (methinks) is like an hourglass,/Wherein my imagination run like sands,/Filling up time; but then are turned, and turned;/So that I know not what to stay upon,/And less to put in act.'[108] There is distinct echo of Hamlet in Kitely's dithering over how to act. He is worried about his wife's fidelity but these lines also speak of an experience of rootlessness, a loss of direction as the old order continues to disappear without a new one appearing to take its place. Knowell, the father of Edward Knowell, feels equally disorientated. He presents the upheaval in terms of the collapse of the father–son relationship. Age, for example, no longer provides the young with standards to live by, teaching them instead to embrace all the pleasures of the age. And we can read this surrender of authority as a crisis of patriarchy. This crisis is also evident in the behaviour of Brainworm, Knowell's servant. He flouts the feudal bond of loyalty by informing Edward that his father has read the letter the young gallant Wellbred intended for him.

By reading the letter, Knowell's worst fears about his son are confirmed – that he is spending time in dissolute company. He therefore proposes to spy on him. Although Knowell represents the mentality of the merchant class to the extent that he believes a person should be sober, save and work hard,[109] he is also conscious that the constant injunction to 'Get money …/No matter by what means'[110] corrodes the social fabric. This is apparent in the way most characters in the play view others in terms of the money they can make out of them. Knowell's servant, Brainworm, is typical in this respect, convincing Stephen to buy what appears to be a Toledo sword but is in fact just a rapier.[111]

The fact that Brainworm is, at this point, disguised as a soldier gives us a new perspective on the metaphor of acting in Renaissance drama. Previously it was a sign of the emptiness of man but in this context it underpins the success of trade. It is Brainworm's impersonation of a war veteran that gives credibility to his description of the sword, persuading Stephen to buy it. Not only does acting become a technique of commerce, it is also a means of social mobility. Brainworm's ability to perform different roles – a beggar and a Justice's clerk – means that he can move with ease through the different levels of society, a bit like Edgar in *King Lear*. Edward and Wellbred testify to his skill in this respect. 'Who would have thought thou hadst been such an artificer?' exclaims Wellbred. 'An artificer?' Edward responds. 'An architect!'[112]

Every Man in His Humour is then quite different from the other plays we have considered in this chapter. It depicts a world where commercial values are triumphant. A world where characters are defined almost as much by their function as by their 'humour'; Kitely's cashier, for example, is called Cash.[113] A world where even ordinary conversation can lapse into a form of advertising. 'This speech would ha' done decently in a tobacco trader's mouth.'[114] A world where the times are not merely changing but where time itself is being redefined. When Kitely asks Cash what time it is, Cash tells him that it is 'Exchange time'.[115] This is a world completely removed from the May games of *A Midsummer Night's Dream*. Here revelry does not mean a release of instinct or a realization of belonging to Nature rather it is a form of profanity and dissolution,[116] the enemy of sobriety and hard work. Here, surely, we will find no trace of sacrifice.

But we do. There is corruption and cleansing. The corruption manifests itself in bad poetry and possible adultery. Poetry appears to be despised at every level of society. Knowell dismisses it as 'a fruitless and unprofitable art' while Cob vents his spleen on what he calls 'vile, rascally verses'.[117] Matthew's execrable poetry, which he writes in a bid to woo Kitely's sister Bridget, is a summation of all that is wrong with the art. Not only doesn't it scan, it barely makes sense.[118] Although the suspicion of infidelity falls on several characters, it is Kitely who is obsessed by the possibility of becoming a cuckold. Will the young gallants who frequent his house succeed in seducing his wife?[119] Poetry and sexuality are connected in the play not merely because they symbolize, ideally, types of creativity but also because they are a threat to commerce. Knowell identifies poetry with idleness while Matthew is tempted to neglect his business so that he can keep an eye on his wife.[120]

There are two 'cleansings' in the play. The first involves the expulsion from Kitely's house of what Downright calls the 'lewd rakehells that ... come here to read ballads, and roguery and trash!'[121] It is a fairly chaotic affair involving mainly Downright, Matthew, Bobadill and Wellbred. Downright and Wellbred, who are half-brothers, draw their swords against each other, but before anything happens Kitely arrives and the would-be combatants are dispersed. Although there is nothing ceremonious about this episode, it clearly alludes to the sacrificial function of purging. The second act of cleansing takes place in a public setting and involves the burning of Matthew's poetry. 'Cleanse the air', cries Justice Clement, 'Here was enough [poetry] to have infected the whole City, if it had not been taken in time.'[122]

Clement's words make a connection between Matthew's verses and the plague which regularly afflicted London. Between about 1510 and the great visitation of 1665, there were only about a dozen years when the city was free from the plague. Outbreaks in 1563 and 1603 wiped out a quarter of London's population. The Puritans believed that the plague was a punishment for sin, and that sin was caused by plays.[123] To their mind, plays were not dramas of purgation but the very source of pollution. Matthew's verses are consigned to flames for the same reason as were the sheets that covered those who died from the plague, to prevent contamination, though in this case of an intellectual and spiritual sort rather than a physical one. There is nothing ceremonious or indeed ritualistic about this act of purification either. Justice Clement does it on the spur of the moment. But it is a more successful form of cleansing since the 'evil' is removed and, as with sacrifice, it is followed by a celebratory meal.

Part of that celebration is of the marriage of Edward to Kitely's sister Bridget. But this is not the sort of union normally associated with comedy. The two do not even speak to one another during the course of the play and Knowell and Kitely only learn of the wedding after it has taken place. The marriage cannot, therefore, symbolize the reconciliation, renewal or new life that the joining together of Shakespeare's couples does. It fails to fulfil the traditional comic function of drawing the community together. The divisions in this community are underlined by Clement's exclusion of Matthew and Bobadill from the festivities that close the play. And yet Clement does not rule out the possibility of accepting them back after they have shown due remorse. He orders them to 'penitently fast [and] pray ... that we may be so merry within as to forgive, or forget you when we come out'.[124] This, though, hardly shows any great commitment to reintegrating the pair. Not only is the choice between forgiving or forgetting them a huge one, it is also acknowledged to be dependent on drink. Drink is conventionally a symbol of inclusion in comedy but here it could just as easily serve as one of exclusion.

The hesitation between inclusion and exclusion highlights the ambiguity at the heart of sacrifice, namely that the victim is at once a part of the community and separate from it. He or she is a part of it because they symbolize its dark side but, for that very reason, they are also removed from it. Normally, this does not present a problem because the knowledge that the villain embodies an uncomfortable truth about the community is either not recognized or repressed. In *King Lear*, for example, there is no acknowledgement that Edmund and Edgar are similar to the extent that they both pretend to be what they are not. Only Edmund's deceit is emphasized thereby making him a scapegoat for what is, in fact, a general condition.

What is interesting in *Every Man in His Humour* is that Matthew and Bobadill are simultaneously scapegoats and non-scapegoats. They are scapegoats to the extent that they represent certain ills of the community and are therefore excluded from it. They are not scapegoats because they may be forgiven and brought back into civic life. If they are forgotten, well, that implies they were not important enough to be scapegoats in the first place. For it is a requirement of sacrificial victims that they have an aura which makes them both a worthy offering to the gods and a powerful enough symbol of the evil that has to be expelled from the community. To put this another way, *Every Man in His Humour* raises the possibility of dispensing with the figure of the scapegoat. And since the scapegoat is central to sacrifice, this also implies the potential disappearance of sacrifice itself. If that were to happen, then a particular conception of society would also vanish for, as we noted in the first chapter, sacrifice and the social are deeply entwined with one another.

The particular conception of society with which sacrifice is associated is monarchical, priestly and hierarchical. But the picture we have of society in this play is very different. It is fluid and fast moving, a search for identity rather than an expression of it. Sacrifice seems to have no place here especially as the representatives of this new order are Puritans whose religious beliefs, as we saw earlier, downplay its importance. But if there is no sacrifice, then how is society to be organized? How is it to be made into a cohesive whole? This is an urgent question for, as the conduct of Brainworm shows, commercial life is characterized by individuals preying on one another for financial gain. It is Thomas Hobbes' 'the war of all against all'.[125]

The answer seems to be the Law. It is Justice Clement who finally sorts out the tangled threads of the plot and sets everything in order. The Law stands opposed to patronage, patriarchy and the will of the monarch. The Law is consistent with the idea of a society based on the charter or contract rather than divine rule, though Clement's behaviour does suggest the arbitrariness that was always a danger of royal power.[126] But despite the Law's potential for binding citizen's together, sacrifice and its associated celebrations remain albeit in residual forms. Matthew and Bobadill are scapegoats and the marriage of Edward and Bridget negates the potential promiscuity that has worried Kitely and Knowell. But it is the uncertain status of the scapegoats which is most intriguing. For it reflects a dilemma faced by the leaders of this increasingly commercial society, namely whether to accept or reject what Matthew and Bobadill represent: self-promotion and the manipulation of appearance which Brainworm has shown are the prerequisites of success in the pursuit of money. And there may be one further reason for the stubborn persistence of sacrificial elements in *Every Man in His Humour*. They provide a symbolic structure that gives significance to life in a way that the Law does not.

7

Restoration and Eighteenth-Century Drama

When General George Monk (1608–1670) negotiated Charles II's return to England in 1660, the new king brought with him the culture of the continent chief of which, in terms of drama, was French neoclassicism – the belief that plays should conform to the rules laid down by Aristotle in the *Poetics*. The main forms of drama during Charles' reign were the heroic play, Restoration comedy and revivals of the work of Shakespeare, Jonson, Francis Beaumont (1584–1616) and John Fletcher (1579–1625). Revivals of Shakespeare continued throughout the period but the late seventeenth century sees the appearance of 'pathetic' tragedy which marks a significant departure in the history of the genre. It normally has a domestic setting and female protagonist, which is why it is also called 'she' tragedy. Tragedy declines during the reign of the three Georges (1714–1727, 1727–1760 and 1760–1820) while comedy diversifies. But the fact that there is a lot of discussion about the social role of both suggests that their purpose can no longer be taken for granted. This is largely due to the rise of more popular forms of entertainment to which both have to adapt. One of the questions we will look at when examining individual plays is whether the changes in tragedy and comedy spell the death of their sacrificial character.

Tragedy

The Enlightenment and the beginnings of Parliamentary democracy affected tragedy particularly. If we put sacrifice on one side for the moment, we can say that tragedy depends for its effect on hierarchy and religious belief. Hierarchy is necessary because, without it, the tragic hero or heroine cannot 'fall'. The drama resides in his or her descent down the social ladder, an event that, in Aristotelian terms, excites our pity and fear. But in the eighteenth century the old hierarchies of English society were beginning to crumble.[1]

The crown was becoming more subordinate to the Commons, the aristocracy was losing ground to the middle class in terms of wealth and cultural leadership and the labouring class were enjoying an unprecedented degree of social mobility or upheaval, depending on your point of view. These changes prompted the appearance of different classification systems in an attempt to understand the nature of this new society but the only thing they agreed upon was that it was in a state of flux. This was not conducive to the writing of tragedy which relies on a clearly defined social structure for its effect.

Gloucester's remark in *King Lear* that 'As flies are to wanton boys are we to the gods,/They kill us for their sport'[2] sums up the religious character of tragedy. The gods control human life. They do not explain the destiny they have chosen for the tragic hero nor justify the suffering it will bring. Since the hero or heroine has no power to resist their fate, the only sensible thing to do is to accept it, though that means foregoing the tragic greatness that comes from defying the inevitable. And if all else fails, there is at least a grim comfort in knowing that the gods take an interest in us, even if it is only as a source for their amusement.

This view of the relation between the human and the divine was tempered by the rise of Christianity. The tragic hero is now responsible for his or her actions but is saved from the consequences of them by Christ's sacrifice on the cross. If the hero shows remorse, he or she will be forgiven. Tragedy is not, as it was with the Greeks, an irreversible doom. Nor were humans helpless before the forces of nature. Scientific advances, new ideas about psychology and a recognition that a person's environment affects the way they behave all showed that people had some capacity to control their lives and perhaps even change them for the better.[3] Such developments were in direct contrast to the tragic philosophy of resignation in the face of disaster.

English Neoclassicism

Despite being doomed tragedy, rather fittingly, defied these developments and continued to be written. But how? Should English dramatists follow the example of French neoclassicism and produce tragedies that adhered to Aristotle's stipulations about plot, character and the unities of time, place and action? Historiographer royal Thomas Rymer (1641–1713) certainly thought so. All the faults of English playwrights were due to their 'ignorance or negligence of the fundamental rules and laws of Aristotle'.[4] He illustrated his point with an analysis of *Othello* (1693), a play 'fraught with impossibilities'.[5] Not only does it ignore the unities but the plot itself lacks all credibility. No one would take Iago's insinuations about Desdemona's behaviour as proof of infidelity nor would they fall down in a fit at the production of handkerchief. What's more, Othello doesn't behave like a general; Iago is not like any other soldier in tragedy while Desdemona resembles nothing so much as a 'country chamber-maid'.[6]

Rymer's position on how far the rules of the ancients should be applied to modern tragedy was considered extreme even by those sympathetic to his views. John Dennis (1657–1734), for example, responded almost immediately. In *The Impartial Critic* (1693) he takes issue with Rymer's demand that the chorus should be restored to English tragedy. This, he argued, would be an anachronism. The chorus in Greek tragedy was a product of a particular society and therefore could not be simply transplanted to the modern stage. In stating this Dennis was hoisted by his own petard for if, as he said, social conditions give rise to dramatic conventions, then he had no grounds for advocating the use of the unities, since the context in which they operated had long since vanished.

One of the greatest essayists of the early eighteenth century, Joseph Addison (1672–1719), objected to Rymer's requirement that poetic justice should be the primary aim of tragedy. The poet, wrote Rymer, 'must of necessity see justice exactly administered, if he intended to please'.[7] In other words, the good should be rewarded and the bad punished. Addison said that this defeated the 'principal Design of Tragedy, [which] is to raise Commiseration and Terror in the Minds of the Audience'.[8] That seems an unanswerable argument until we remember that Aristotle himself declared that the best tragedies end happily. His otherwise strange remark makes sense if we recall drama's origins in sacrificial ritual where death was used to create new life. Rymer's assertion that virtue should triumph over vice is the ethical equivalent of that process – the expulsion of moral evil from a community in order for moral good to thrive.

Reactions to Rymer demonstrate that the English response to French neoclassicism was one of dialogue rather than wholehearted acceptance. The merits or otherwise of neoclassical drama were summed up in John Dryden's *An Essay on Dramatic Poesy* (1668). It lists the faults of English plays as judged from the perspective of the ancients: subplots, a disregard for time and place, and the mixing of tragedy and comedy. Dryden (1631–1700) acknowledges the problems that arise from these, chiefly a strain on the audience's credibility, but he also defends them. The use of subplots is more intellectually satisfying because it makes the audience think about how the different actions are related and how they will be resolved, while the advantage of mixing tragedy and comedy is that 'Contraries set one another off.'[9]

Heroic Drama and Pathetic or She-tragedy

So much, then, for the context in which tragedies were written. What about the tragedies themselves? As we noted in the Introduction there were several kinds, of which heroic drama was, during the 1660s, the most interesting variety. It was partly a reaction to the demise of revenge tragedy and an attempt to restore English theatre to its former glory. Its basic template was an exotic or historical setting, a superhuman hero, the theme of personal honour versus public good, and the glorification of conquest and military might. Despite having a high-born hero torn between two conflicting impulses, heroic drama cannot really be considered as tragedy, and not merely because the good do not perish. With its lavish scenery and elaborate stage machinery, it is more properly described as a spectacle. In this capacity heroic drama can be viewed as a form of propaganda for the Stuart court, celebrating divine rule, providential history, the romance of the 'Martyred Monarch' and his 'Merry son'.

But its highly stylized nature also invites comparison with ritual. Dryden, whose own *Conquest of Granada* (1670 and 1671) is the apotheosis of the genre, claimed heroic drama was similar to magic and religion for it dealt not with real things but 'visionary objects' and its aim was 'absolute dominion over the minds of the spectators'.[10] Moreover, one of the main themes of heroic drama, the founding of a nation or a society, may very well have its roots in the creation myths enacted in ritual. It wasn't the parallels with ritual that struck contemporaries however. They focused more on the fanciful plots of heroic drama and the way characters spouted heroic couplets. Who, it was asked, spoke in neat rhymes in real life, especially when they were under duress? The genre was famously satirized by George Villiers, 2nd Duke of Buckingham (1628–1687) and others in *The Rehearsal* (1671).

One effect of Buckingham's satire was to stop dramatists from writing in heroic couplets, a practice that had been adopted from French drama. Another was to make them focus more on emotions and real life than on the impossible actions of even more impossible heroes. Of course it wasn't just Buckingham's play that was responsible for these changes. Others, too, poked fun at heroic drama. Thomas Duffet (fl. 1673–1676), for example, was well known for his parodies of Dryden's work among others. But these various burlesques were themselves not so much a cause as a symptom of wider changes that were happening in the culture, chief of which was the spread of middle-class values such as moderation, common sense and an appreciation of the practicalities of life.

These account for the focus on 'real life' but what about emotion? This appeared to be in short supply in some neoclassical tragedies. The eponymous hero in Addison's *Cato* (1713), for example, feels no grief at his son's death, only pride at his patriotism. From the point of view of a society still suffering from the trauma of the Civil War, the value of emotion was that it could act as a binding force, helping to heal wounds and divisions. People's religions may differ, but their feelings were the same. Whether or not we agree with the logic, it seemed an appealing argument at the time. Plays which foregrounded emotion were known either as 'she tragedies' or 'pathetic tragedies', so called because they portrayed the sufferings of an innocent and virtuous woman. Thomas Otway's *The Orphan*, discussed below, is generally regarded as the first of the genre and in Nicholas Rowe's *The Fair Penitent* (1703), it reaches its apotheosis. The play was an adaptation of *The Fatal Dowry* (1632) by Philip Massinger (1583–1640) and Nathan Field (1587–1620). It differs from the original by focusing on the infidelity of Calista instead of the legal and political affairs of her husband. The play is also, incidentally, the source of the word 'Lothario', used to refer to a man who seduces women.

Rowe's Prologue rejects the traditional subject matter of tragedy 'the fate of kings and empires',[11] and redefines the role of pity. Aristotle said that tragedy roused our pity in order to purge it but Rowe (1674–1718) argues that it excites our pity so that we may find common ground with one another. Ruined royalty may arouse our wonder but 'We can ne'er pity what we can ne'er share' hence 'a humbler theme our author chose,/A melancholy tale of private woes: here you will find sorrows like your own'.[12] Rowe's play, in short, signals a revolution in tragedy because it shifts attention from public action to private emotion which, because it is also deemed to be universal, helps to harmonize social relations. But it also marks the decline of tragedy's power because from now on its heroes are drawn from the middling classes rather than the nobility, and a merchant cannot fall as far as a king, nor does his fate have consequences for the nation.[13]

Thomas Otway (1652–1685), *The Orphan: Or, The Unhappy Marriage* (1680)

The Orphan initiates a new departure in the history of tragedy with its domestic setting and its focus on the feelings of the lead female character. It has a fairly simple plot. Acasto, a nobleman, is guardian to Monimia, whose parents are dead and whose estate was 'ruin'd in our late and civil discords',[14] a clear allusion to the Civil War even though the play is set in Bohemia. Acasto has twin sons, Castalio and Polydore, both of whom are in love with Monimia. Polydore tells Castalio of his feelings for Monimia but the confidence is not reciprocated. Castalio encourages his brother to woo Monimia despite knowing that his suit will be unsuccessful. Castalio and Monimia marry secretly and their plan to meet later is overheard by Polydore who tricks Monimia into thinking that it is Castalio who has come to her bed. Polydore did not know, however, that his brother was married. The fallout from these various deceptions is that Polydore provokes his brother into killing him, and Castalio and Monimia commit suicide.

Where, though, is sacrifice in all this? The simple answer is in the deaths of Castalio, Polydore and Monimia for these characters represent the two evils that afflict the world of *The Orphan*, incest and falsehood. At first these two evils seem quite separate, falsehood infects the court, incest the home but, in fact, they are closely related. Acasto has tried to escape from the fawning, feigning and flattery of court life by staying at home, keeping his two sons with him in case they become corrupted by such behaviour. But there is no escape. As we see from the machinations Polydore uses to sleep with Monimia, envy and deceit are as much a part of the private as the public world. The same is true for incest which is a useful way of describing the court's debased and inward-looking character. The incest in the home requires a little more investigation.

Polydore can be said to commit incest because he sleeps with his brother's wife. This may not be an act of incest as we understand the term but there were grounds for considering it be so in the seventeenth century when biblical injunctions were taken more seriously. Leviticus (18: 16) forbade intercourse between a man and his brother's wife because they were considered to be blood relations. It was not that long ago that Henry VIII (1491–1547) had argued for a divorce on the grounds that he should never have married Katherine of Aragon (1485–1536) because she had been his brother's wife.

Polydore doesn't just sleep with his brother's wife, he also sleeps with a woman who, if not his actual sister, is certainly his nominal one. Monimia has been brought up as if she were his and Castalio's sibling. Chamont is Monimia's brother but his behaviour towards her seems to be more that of a lover. It is not merely that he is jealous of her virginity but also that he has a disturbing dream about her in which she appears in 'garments flowing loose, and in each hand/A wanton lover'.[15] The symbolism of him drawing his sword and darting it at her is too obvious to require comment. But it is worth pointing out that this is one of several echoes of Shakespeare in the play. This particular scene recalls the behaviour of Hamlet in his mother's bedchamber (Act 3 scene 4). There is the same undercurrent of incestuous sexuality and the same lunge at an arras. The picture on the one pierced by Chamont is of Oedipus killing his father.

Incest is a recurring theme in tragedy. Its presence is partly explained by the fact that tragedy grew out of sacrificial ritual, one of whose functions was to either prevent or banish irregular forms of sexual activity such as incest which might otherwise blight the harvest. The hints of incest and the illicit sexuality in *The Orphan* are nothing to do with the failure of the crops, but with the corruption of the state manifest in envy, discontent, faction and the decline of religion and morality.[16] The character who is most associated with incest and unlicensed desire is Monimia. As a woman she is the scapegoat for all that's wrong with the world. 'What mighty ills have not been done by woman/Destructive, damnable, deceitful woman.'[17] If it hadn't been for Monimia, Castalio and Polydore would still be alive. She created the division between them, albeit unwittingly.

To appreciate the significance of Monimia we have to go back to the *Oresteia*. We argued that Clytemnestra had to be sacrificed[18] for civilization to come into existence. There were several reasons for her death and one was her association with female fertility goddesses whose excessive sexuality was deemed to be a threat to the new order. Monimia is no fertility goddess but, precisely because she is female, she retains the ancient power to disrupt a community. Her status as an orphan, an outsider, is indicative of women's dangerous otherness. And yet she is brought from the outside into the family, the heart of civilization, with predictable consequences. She arouses desire and divides Castalio and Polydore, both of whom resort to subterfuge in order to obtain her. In short Monimia brings sexual chaos and deception, the latter also affecting the wider society.

She does not do this intentionally but in virtue of the fact that she is a woman. Indeed her behaviour throughout is virtuous and we sympathize with her as she is tricked by Polydore and rejected by Castalio. That Monimia's being a woman dooms her rather than any action on her part is another instance of the theme of responsibility in tragedy. Do we determine our lives or the gods? Polydore thinks that we do; 'Twas my own fault,' he declares in his dying speech while Chamont thinks it is down to the gods. 'Tis thus that Heaven it's (sic) empire does maintain/It may afflict but man must not complain.'[19] But, this question aside, the fact remains that Monimia, as the source of contamination in the play, has to be removed, as do those whom she has infected. Since they all commit suicide, their deaths cannot be regarded as a sacrifice. Nor can they be seen as self-sacrifice since they lack any ritualistic element whatsoever. Nevertheless, they all fulfil the sacrificial function of the expulsion of evil.

The Orphan, then, is governed by the logic of sacrifice. We are shown a society in disorder and the cause of that disorder is identified and banished. But what is missing is any sense of ceremony which locates that 'sacrifice' in a wider system of meaning which comprehends the relation between life and death. In this play, death is a response to the destruction of a set of values, notably truth, honour and chastity, which give shape, significance and direction to existence. Without them, it ceases to have any meaning and so death becomes the preferred option. As in King Lear and The Revenger's Tragedy, death has become an escape from life rather than a prelude to it.

The Orphan also offers us something new. The usual pattern of sacrifice is death followed by the celebration of new life, which usually involves sexual activity. But in this play the order is reversed and death follows sex. The two are related to the extent that they both involve a loss of self, in sex temporarily and in death permanently. Monimia represents the extreme case of losing the self through sex. She has, in other words, lost her reputation, the immortal part of herself, and so her actual death is no more than a formality to what has already happened. Another example of how this play inverts the usual logic of sacrifice is that the young die for the old since Acasto is the only main character left alive at the end. And he is not going to be propagating any new life.

Neither is his one surviving child, Serina, who speaks the epilogue. She says that if her father dies she will become an orphan and asks if there is anyone in the audience who will take her in. If not she will withdraw from the world. Her position rather uncannily resembles Monimia's earlier. Serina may very well be an orphan, she is an outsider and she is a woman and therefore dangerous. There is not only a sense of something unresolved here, which underlines the absence of the sense-making properties of sacrifice in the play, but also something uncanny too. It is as if Monimia has come back in the form of Serina. Like in the horror film, there is a sense that the 'evil' will return.

Comedy

The conditions which proved near fatal to tragedy helped comedy to flourish. It was more attuned to the character of the age than tragedy. Its spirit of irreverence chimed with Enlightenment scepticism towards received wisdom while its celebration of improvisation was of a piece with the new faith in humans to determine their own destiny. There were several different types of comedy in this period. The Restoration saw the comedy of wit and the comedy of humours, while Georgian comedy was broadly divided into sentimental or laughing comedy.

Most of the contemporary discussion about comedy centred on its corrective function and how best that could be achieved. Should it delight or instruct? Both, ideally. The accepted wisdom was that comedy taught people to be good by ridiculing what was bad, namely the foolish, the affected and the downright villainous. The danger was that, because audiences laughed at such behaviour, they tacitly encouraged it which then prompted playwrights to produce ever more scandalous versions of it. To put this another way, delight ceased to be a means of instruction and became an end in itself.

This was certainly the opinion of the theatre critic and theologian Jeremy Collier (1650–1726) who, in his *Short View of the Immorality and Profaneness of the English Stage* (1698), argued that the devotion to pleasure in Restoration comedies had the brutalizing effect of reducing human beings to mere appetite. Nor was he the only one to think this way. The playwright William Congreve (1670–1729) wrote that he didn't care to see things 'that force me to entertain low thoughts of my Nature'.[20] There was a political dimension to both Collier's and Congreve's ideas about comedy. Collier objected to its ridicule of solid bourgeois values such as learning, industry and frugality while Congreve extolled the specifically English virtues of the comedy of humour. It reflects 'the greater Freedom, Privilege and Liberty which the Common People of England enjoy. Any man that has a humour is under no restraint or fear of giving it vent.'[21] This claim makes Congreve an early contributor to the project of defining English identity, which gets underway in earnest in the eighteenth century.

Sentimental and Laughing comedy

If comedy was not to improve people by making them laugh then how else was it to achieve its goal? Why, by holding up examples of goodness for them to imitate, of course. The change was largely initiated by Richard Steele's *The Conscious Lovers* (1722). It breaks with Restoration comedy by presenting scenes of emotional distress rather than contrived seductions and by portraying a hero who restrains his passions instead of indulging them. The key moment is in Act 4 when the hero, Bevil Junior, brings his anger under control and thus avoids a duel with his friend Myrtle. The hope was that the play would provide the middle-class audience with a different set of ethics to their aristocratic counterparts, one based on reason rather than rashness. The word 'conscious' in the title says it all. Think before acting.

Steele's other innovation was to depict marriage as a love match rather than an economic contract. Since Menander, comedy had, broadly speaking, ended in marriage. But Georgian comedy probes the state of marriage itself. Dryden's *Marriage à la Mode* (1673) could be said to begin the process. It contains the famous song 'Why Should a Foolish Marriage Vow' whose lyrics touch on the problems that come with the decay of passion. As might be expected, the constraints of marriage were a particular theme in the work of female playwrights like Susannah Centlivre (1667–1723) and Frances Sheridan (1724–1766), whose comedies celebrated women's manipulation of the conventions of courtship and marriage to their own advantage. But questions of power, control and the politics of gender were not always to the fore. Mary Pix (1666–1709) certainly portrays the pitfalls of marriage but more with the aim of sentimentalizing the heroine than protesting her plight.

The debate over whether comedy should portray images of goodness or provoke laughter at folly continued throughout the eighteenth century, culminating in Oliver Goldsmith's 'An Essay on the Theatre: Or A Comparison Between Sentimental and Laughing Comedy' (1773). Goldsmith (1730–1774) started by claiming that sentimental comedy, by focusing on distress, was closer to tragedy than comedy. Following tradition, he insists that the two genres should be kept separate. But his fundamental objection to sentimental comedy is not formal but ethical. It subtly encourages vanity, stupidity and ignorance. How so? Because we are encouraged to overlook the shortcomings of characters who are otherwise generous and good. In doing so, we become more indulgent towards people's faults in the real world with possibly serious consequences for the social order. It is therefore important, in Goldsmith's view, that we cultivate a type of comedy that renders folly ridiculous. This is 'laughing' comedy of which his own *She Stoops to Conquer* (1773) is an example. Indeed it is tempting to see Goldsmith's Essay as a piece of theatrical propaganda for the play which, incidentally, betrays its origins in ritual. Tony Lumpkin, for example, is the old lord of misrule; he pins Mr Hardcastle's wig to a chair, he tells Marlow and Hastings that his stepfather's house is an inn, and he pretends he is taking his mother and cousin to Miss Pedigree but just drives them round and round in a circle instead.

The argument about whether laughing comedy is better than sentimental comedy is actually just an argument about which technique best achieves the true goal of comedy, namely the celebration of virtue and the condemnation of vice. But this is also the goal of tragedy. The two genres are different means to the same end. The explanation of this lies in their common origin in sacrificial ritual. And they both function according to the logic of sacrifice; that is, in order to boost goodness, badness must be destroyed – in tragedy by death and in comedy by laughter. Of course there is far more to tragedy and comedy than their sacrificial character but we fail to appreciate them fully if we forget that fact.

William Wycherley (1640–1715), *The Country Wife* (1675)

The Country Wife belongs to the tradition of new comedy but differs from it in some significant respects. There is no young couple striving to overcome obstacles in order to be together and the play does not end in marriage but in a grotesque dance of cuckolds, the term used for men whose wives have been unfaithful. The play is an example of Restoration comedy which can be described as a comedy of wit, that is plays which exploit the different meanings of words, or a comedy of manners, that is plays which satirize the mores, manners and behaviour of social groups. Both terms are accurate but lack historical specificity because they could be equally applied to Alan Ayckbourn as they could to William Wycherley. One of the historically distinctive features of *The Country Wife* is that it still draws on the comedy of humours because half the characters are named after their defining trait. Horner, for example, is so named because of his sexual readiness and the cuckold's 'horns' he bestows on the heads of husbands he deceives.

But the main characteristic of Restoration comedy is its frank embrace of sexuality which, in part, is a reaction to the Puritan fear of it. The introduction of female actresses no doubt added a certain piquancy to the subject while the innovations of machinery and moveable scenery not only helped to create a sense of realism but also prompted more inventive uses of the stage. Dividing it, for example, so that the audience sees what the actors cannot, enhances the comic effect of one character trying to hide from another. But these developments, along with more opulent costumes, were dismissed, in some quarters, as distractions from the true purpose of drama. To paraphrase Addison, a huge plume of feathers does not hero a make. 'Our Minds', he wrote, 'should be opened to great Conceptions, and inflamed with glorious sentiments, by what the Actor speaks, more than by what he appears.'[22]

There are no 'great conceptions' or 'glorious sentiments' in *The Country Wife*. The main plot centres round Horner trying to seduce Pinchwife's bride, Margery, the country wife of the title. He has also caused a rumour to be spread about the town that he is impotent. Consequently, husbands consider their wives safe from his advances. Indeed, Sir Jaspar Fidget now considers Horner the perfect companion for his wife, Lady Fidget, as his presence will deter other rakes or gallants from approaching her. Even this brief summary should be sufficient to show that we are not dealing with the nobler side of human nature. This is a world of appetite, not of ideals – not even of common decency.

Love is derided, marriage is mocked and nothing is worthy of regard because all is acting or affectation. As Lady Fidget observes, 'We women make use of our reputation, as you men of yours, only to deceive the world ... Our virtue is like the statesman's religion, the Quaker's word, the gamester's oath, and the great man's honour-but to cheat those that trust us.'[23] Female duplicity may be a factor in the distinct hostility to women in *The Country Wife*. Horner is particularly virulent, castigating them as the source of disease and evil,[24] while Pinchwife is consumed with the thought that women have 'more desires, more soliciting, passions, more lust, and more of the devil'[25] than men. Such hatred is partly an expression of that fear of female power which we can trace right back to Clytemnestra and which must be 'sacrificed' for civilization to exist.

This hatred, though, does not inhibit the single-minded pursuit of sexual pleasure though it gives it a certain edge. Sex, indeed, seems to be an answer to the emptiness of existence. This has far deeper roots than the disorientation felt by a class who were exiled, who lost their lands and who now found themselves trying to reassert their authority in a changed political landscape. These simply intensified the crisis of identity that was already evident in the Renaissance and which found its most complete expression in *King Lear*. The idea that man, like the gods, has neither substance nor significance recurs here. Life is nothing more than performance. The character who best illustrates this is Sparkish. He is the archetypal Restoration fop, a follower of French fashion, a shrill peacock and a self-styled wit whose aphorisms always fail to impress. His sense of himself comes from appearing every day in the playhouse and public places. 'I love to be envied,'[26] he says.

The function of Sparkish in the play is to act as a contrast to the other male characters, his vanity and giddiness pointing up their self-assurance and purposefulness. Horner says that Sparkish is a 'false jewel amongst true ones', difficult to 'discern[] at a distance',[27] but easy close up. The contrast does not work, however, because it is one of degree rather than difference. Horner, Harcourt, Dorilant and Sparkish are all wits, dandies and libertines. The fact that Horner and his friends are better in the role than Sparkish does not alter the fact they are all playing the same part. And where each character is pretending, it makes little sense to say that one is real and one is fake. Sparkish's antics, his forays at wit and his courtship of Pinchwife's sister, Alithea, serve not so much as a contrast to the behaviour of the other characters as to deflect attention from the simple truth that they are as hollow as he is. They may despise Sparkish for his need to be seen, but it is difficult to imagine any of them alone.

It seems the only answer to this existential emptiness is sex. But while this gives a sense of reality to the body, it does nothing to satisfy the deeper craving of being for its own fulfilment. For this is a world drained of meaning. There are no symbolic systems to give shape, direction and purpose to life. Thomas Hobbes' philosophy reduced humans to machines whose actions can be explained in terms of simple cause and effect and the institutions of civil society, such as marriage and the family, have all been absorbed into a monetary idiom. 'Our sisters and daughters, like usurers' money, are safest when put out,' says Pinchwife while Lucy, Altihea's maid, observes that 'marrying to increase love is like gaming to become rich; alas, you only lose what little stock you had'.[28] Neither the mechanistic view of human nature nor the restricted language of commerce can aspire to that sense of transcendence offered by religion. It has the potential to connect humans to a larger sense of reality than mere profit and loss. And, in so doing, it nourishes that sense of 'being' which otherwise goes unsatisfied in this play.

Religion, though, is absent in *The Country Wife*. Indeed it is absent from most of the plays we have examined. But what has been present, in one form or another, is the sacrificial structure on which religion is based. This structure, as we have noted, fulfils a number of different functions, from giving meaning to death to authorizing sexual excess. But there appears to be no trace of it here. Theatre, in this play, has ceased to perform its symbolic sacrificial operations. For example, instead of being an exploration of communal values, it has become a place of self-display and sexual reconnaissance, an extension of social life itself. Sparkish goes to the theatre to prove he is more witty than the playwright[29] while Margery is typical of the women in having no interest in the play, only in the actors, 'the goodliest, properest men'.[30] Indeed Horner rejects the whole idea of ritual when he declares that 'ceremony in love and eating is ridiculous... Falling on briskly is all that should be done in those occasions'.[31] Horner also observes that while 'wine gives you joy', love is 'grief and tortures'.[32] In the ancient world drink and desire were part of the same celebrations but here they stand opposed – further testament to the fragmentation and failure of sacrifice.

Comedy, like sacrifice, controls sexuality. It gives limited expression to what Freud called its polymorphous perversity before channelling it into marriage where it reproduces the social order through the creation of new citizens. But sexuality in *The Country Wife* follows a different trajectory. Far from being absorbed into marriage it is a relentless assault on it. It is true that Pinchwife wants to preserve the integrity of marriage but we do not sympathize with him because he is constantly trying to confine or imprison his young wife Margery. Nor does the marriage of Harcourt and Alithea resolve the problem of anarchic sexuality, partly because they are secondary characters, partly because they seem bland and conventional compared to Horner and his mistresses, and partly because marriage itself is so thoroughly mocked.

The Country Wife, then, fails to regulate sexuality. Promiscuity has become routine rather than part of a licenced revel. One reason for this is that sexuality has lost its ancient connection with fertility as farming becomes more scientific and society more urban. It is now more about pleasure than reproduction. The contrast between town and country is an important theme in this play. Both have at least two meanings. The town is a place of refinement and sociability but also of immorality and needless expense; the country is a place of innocence and homeliness but also of boredom, confinement and even, Margery suggests, illicit assignations.[33] This opposition between town and country crops up in a number of plays such as *She Stoops to Conquer*, the conflict between them being part of a battle to define the nature of civilization.

A key aspect of civilization is the ordering of sexuality. In the ancient world, the taboo against incest served to ensure nature's bounty as did the sexual carousing after sacrifice. One symptom of the breakdown of civilization is a regression to Oedipal sexuality and that is largely what we have in *The Country Wife* in the form, for example, of Horner's pursuit of married women and Harcourt's prising Alithea away from Sparkish. The pleasure that comes from sleeping with another man's wife is the adult version of the child's desire to be at one with his mother and to be rid of his father. Horner appears to enjoy tormenting Pinchwife as much as he does his seduction of Margery. 'Did I not tell you I would raise his jealous gall?'[34] he boasts to Dorilant and Harcourt. The act of cuckolding is also a faint echo of the mythical murder of the primal father since it enables access to females who are the property of another male. And it is that 'murder', of course, which gives rise to sacrifice, the ritual that simultaneously repeats the deed and atones for it.

This collapse back into instinctual chaos seems a fitting symbol for a society that has itself lost direction after the upheaval of the civil war, the uncertainties of the interregnum and the difficulties of the Restoration. It is a society which seems to require a sacrifice that will make it whole and also sublimate the sexual desire which keeps it on the verge of dissolution.

But none is forthcoming. What we have instead is quite extraordinary – not the expulsion of evil, but the destruction of innocence. There is no purge of deviant sexuality and rampant affectation both referred to, on occasion, as 'monsters'. And it is the monster of affectation, coiled at the heart of the social, that particularly corrupts Margery.

Her candour forms a stark contrast to the deceit practised by other characters. She soon learns the art of simulation though. When Pinchwife demands she write a letter to Horner telling him that she detests him, she artfully substitutes it for one in which she says she loves him. Margery reverts to her natural openness at the end of the play when she informs the company that she loves Horner and that he is, to her 'certain knowledge',[35] not impotent. But the ladies instantly silence her. Such a revelation would mean they would no longer be allowed to keep company with Horner. Margery therefore reluctantly resigns herself to remaining Pinchwife's spouse and to lying about her encounter with Horner.

Her fate is the reverse of what normally happens in sacrifice; the evil is spread rather than being removed and, in the process, the distinction between the inside and the outside of society is blurred. This is important because the efficacy of sacrifice depends on clear spatial demarcations. There has to be a clear boundary between the inside and the outside. Putting it at its most basic, the inside represents the norm, the sphere of the social; the outside is the threat to the norm. When this threat erupts into the social, usually in the form of moral evil, it must be returned to the place from which it came. If there is no strong dividing line between the inside and the outside then sacrifice cannot function.

The confusion of inside and outside is already evident in the matter of Margery's sexuality. She hints in her letter that infidelity is not just something that happens in London. '"If you and I were in the country at cards together"-so-"I could not help treading on your toe under the table".'[36] She also appears dressed as her brother, a ruse of Pinchwife which he hopes will protect her from Horner's advances though it only serves to inflame his desires. Margery is thus a figure who not only conflates the distinction between inside and outside, that is between town and country, but also that between the sexes. She is part of the tradition, particularly marked in Shakespeare's comedies such as *Twelfth Night* (1602) and *As You Like It* (1603?), of cross-dressing which draws attention to the social construction of gender.

But Margery's male impersonation has a more specific meaning. It is a symbol of homoerotic desire. One of the reasons for the antipathy men feel to women in the play is because 'women serve but to keep a man from better company'.[37] The desires they arouse in men prevent them from enjoying the 'lasting, rational and manly pleasures' which are the qualities of 'good fellowship and friendship'.[38] Once again there is echo of the ancient anxiety that female sexuality is a threat to civilization, an anxiety which lies at the origin of sacrifice. The fact that the male characters do not take responsibility for their own desires is a reminder that sacrifice is also a form of projection of attributing to another the shortcomings of the self. Be that as it may, the key point here is that Margery's disguise is an imaginative solution to the problem of male–female relations in the play. It allows men to enjoy, in a symbolic fashion, the unity of mind and body whose perceived division in this play is part of the existential crisis mentioned above.

What conclusions can we draw about sacrifice from *The Country Wife*? The most obvious is that it has broken down. Evidence for this lies not just in the proliferation of deviant sexuality which is the job of sacrifice to control, but also in the absence of a scapegoat. Sparkish appears to fulfil that function because of his absurd affectations. However, since all the characters are playing some sort of role, Sparkish lacks the necessary 'otherness' required of a sacrificial victim. Hence, as Horner says, 'it is a very hard thing to be rid of him'.[39] It is not merely that sacrifice does not work in the play; it seems to go into reverse; that is, there is no cleansing, only further corruption. Margery, who occupies the traditional role of the outsider who brings the plague, is infected by those on the inside. The complications of sacrifice, which have their origins in the various intellectual crises of the Renaissance, help to explain the pervasive sense of meaninglessness in the play which is only alleviated by sexual activity. As yet, there appears to be no alternative to sacrifice as a means of ordering experience or endowing it with significance, by which I mean giving depth to the self, validating social relations and having a vision of humans as part of something greater than themselves. But in *The Country Wife* they can only frolic among the ruins.

New Developments

The degree of scrutiny that tragedy and comedy faced in the Restoration and Georgian period indicates that all was not well with either genre. One explanation for this is the appearance of other forms of entertainment. One was opera which arrived in England from Italy in the late seventeenth century. It was a spectacle of drama, music and dance whose highly stylized nature conferred great import on its subject matter, however slight it might appear in a different context. Neither tragedy nor comedy could offer the complete experience that opera provided. They lacked its sumptuous fusion of sense, emotion and intellect. Opera could therefore be more tragic than tragedy and more comic than comedy. The huge success of John Gay's *The Beggar's Opera* (1728), which ran for sixty-two consecutive performances, was something that comic dramatists could only dream about. A parody of Italian opera it offered, in place of noble characters, swelling music and portentous themes, a cast of crooks and prostitutes, popular tunes and a satire of England's first Prime Minister

Horace Walpole (1676–1745) who was castigated for corruption, presiding over rigged elections, bribery and the sale of votes.

Another Italian form that established itself in the eighteenth century was pantomime. Pantomimes initially took place after the main performance before becoming entertainments in their own right. Drawn from the *comedia dell arte*, the pantomime consisted of three characters, Harlequin, Colombine and Pantaloon. Harlequin's pursuit of Colombine is blocked by Pantaloon her father but Harlequin tricks him and wins Colombine. This comic plot, derived from new comedy, was interwoven with a more serious one drawn either from classical mythology, fairy tales or popular fiction. But pantomime's real appeal as John O' Brien has observed, 'lay in acrobatics, spectacle, song, dance, travelogue and special effects'.[40] In this, pantomime epitomized one of the main trends of eighteenth-century theatre, an increasing emphasis on the visual rather than the verbal character of drama evident from changes in scenery, lighting, costume and style of acting.

Against this development tragedy in particular had little defence and continued its decline. The comic spirit, by which I mean an impulse to laughter, appeared in new forms such as 'skits', 'revues', 'sketches' and burlettas, a type of musical farce poking fun at classical myth. On the one hand these developments can be seen as the dissolution of the comic genre; on the other they can be seen as a diversification of it. Richard W. Bevis sums up the general situation when he argues that 'the traditional genres, while still important, were crumbling, and their stones were being used to erect a variety of different buildings'.[41] One of those 'buildings' was melodrama into which, by the 1770s, tragedy had decayed. Along with the other sorts of performance mentioned here, it constitutes the beginnings of what will become, in the twentieth century, popular culture.

8

Victorian Drama

The standard view of nineteenth-century theatre is that it provided escapist entertainment in the form of melodrama and that nothing of any interest happened until the advent of Ibsen. Although recent studies have presented a more nuanced picture,[1] it nevertheless remains true that the intellectual upheavals and social dislocations of the age – the discoveries of geology, the theory of evolution, the move from the country to the city, the growth of factories and so on – were more likely to be negotiated in the novel than on the stage. To examine why this was the case would deflect us too much from our main theme, the role of sacrifice in drama.

At the same time we should remember that sacrifice is a way of negotiating turmoil and disturbance, as we shall see when we examine the sacrificial structure of Douglas Jerrold's *Black-Ey'd Susan*, Oscar Wilde's *A Woman of No Importance* and Ibsen's *Hedda Gabler*. These works may originate from different sources and address different problems but the element of sacrifice is common to them all. Indeed one reason for choosing a melodrama and a naturalistic play is to demonstrate that sacrifice is present in genres other than tragedy and comedy. We shall also discover that aspects of sacrifice are present in music hall, a major form of entertainment in this era. Its significance lies partly in its position between the comic forms of the late eighteenth century and the popular media of the twentieth and twenty-first centuries which will be considered in the final chapter, 'Conclusion: Tragedy, Comedy and Sacrifice in Popular Culture'.

The Triumph of Melodrama

Melodrama was the most popular form of drama in the nineteenth century. The English term derives from the French *mélodrame*, a dumb show accompanied by music. The word *melo* comes from the Greek word *melos*, which means music but the musical element gradually diminished.

Melodrama is characterized by boldly drawn characters, spectacular special effects and clear-cut moral schemes. Its basic plot is that a dastardly villain sets out to destroy the hero and the heroine. The hero can find himself disinherited, cast out, falsely accused of all kinds of heinous crimes, hunted by the police and assassins, exiled in strange lands, set adrift on the open sea, shot at, poisoned, hurled over cliffs, dropped down a well, tossed in a dungeon, or strapped to a railway track. The heroine is equally besieged, being forcibly married, half murdered, incarcerated in a tomb, removed, revived and stranded on a foreign shore or abandoned and left to die in the gutter. Although the villain comes close to realizing his evil schemes, he never quite succeeds. A dream-vision, the arrival of reinforcements, the discovery of a lost will, indeed a whole range of dramatic devices too numerous to mention conspire to frustrate his plans.

The subject of early English melodrama was influenced by German plays of Gothic horror and mystery but these gave way to plays concerned with rebellion, either abroad against oriental despots or at home against rampaging aristocrats or unprincipled factory owners as in John Walker's *The Factory Lad* (1832). The key figure of the 1850s and the 1860s was Dion Boucicault (1820–1890) who is most famous for his 'sensation scene'. These included an exploding steamboat, a burning house, a man climbing a prison tower and the last-minute rescue of a woman from under the wheels of an oncoming London Underground train. After Boucicault, we see the emergence of the conflicted hero whose chief struggle is with himself rather than with a moustache-twirling villain. Perhaps the most famous example of what David Mayer calls the 'divided hero-villain'[2] is Mathias in Leopold Lewis' *The Bells* (1871). It was the role in which Henry Irving (1838–1905), the first actor to be awarded a knighthood and the man believed to be the inspiration for Bram Stoker's Count Dracula, made his name. Set in Alsace, Mathias is an upstanding citizen, a magistrate and a good family man. But his outwardly respectable life hides a terrible secret, the murder of a Polish Jew. Mathias had committed the act to pay off his mortgage but is haunted by guilt and, waking from a dream in which he is condemned to death, has a heart attack and dies.

The action of melodrama resembles tragedy because it brings the good characters close to death without them actually dying. Historically, the tragic protagonist bears some responsibility for his or her suffering but this is not the case in melodrama where the hero is free of all flaws and faults. There is a faint premonition here of the meaningless universe that will appear in the work of Samuel Beckett. But such harbingers vanish with the eventual triumph of virtue, which proclaims the cosmos is ordered after all, and by melodrama's strong comic streak. Not only are the hero and heroine reunited but there is also at least one comic character whose job is to tell jokes and to comment on the action. He – for it is usually a 'he' – represents common sense in contrast to the idealism found in the main plot.

Melodrama and Sacrifice

It is customary to dismiss melodrama as an escapist form of entertainment. James Smith concedes that early nineteenth-century audiences 'wanted to forget the drudgery and drabness of everyday life and escape into a more colourful, less complex and plainly perfect world'.[3] But he also argues that melodrama was realistic because it accurately depicted the surface of Victorian life and portrayed the impact of new technology such as the railway and the telegraph. It also, he adds, 'takes the problems of real life and provides them with an ideal solution'.[4] This is something that is explored in a little more depth by David Mayer who argues that the hero's descent down the social ladder reflects anxieties about class and status in a rapidly changing society while the villain is a symbol for a whole cluster of social problems ranging from industrialization to revolution in Europe.[5] His main point, however, is that melodrama took on some of the functions that had previously been the province of religion. It 'provided an emotionally intelligible picture of the world to deracinated western cultures, severed by science and technology from former religious and "spiritual" truths'.[6] In particular, melodrama took on the responsibility for defining good and evil, a task which had become more difficult in an increasingly complex society with traditional morality under pressure and Christianity in apparent retreat.

Melodrama was able to satisfy some of the spiritual needs previously supplied by religion because its roots lay in ritual. First, it has a sacrificial structure. The villain represents the evil that must be expelled if society is to function properly. His disruption of the social order is symbolized by the suffering he causes the hero and heroine. Second, melodrama tends towards repetition which is an essential part of ritual. The key elements of the plot – the villain's ambition, the persecution of the hero and the heroine and the triumph of justice – change little, if at all, from 1800 to 1900.[7] The generic rules of melodrama have a similar effect as the repetitions of ritual: they quieten thought and breed an attitude of acceptance. They reassure audiences that there is order and harmony in the world by showing that good will prevail, evil will be destroyed and society replenished.

Third, melodrama, like ritual, depends for its effect on spectacle which is more likely to promote an emotional rather than a rational response. Ideally the spectacles of melodrama, from dioramas to exploding volcanoes, should reinforce the division between good and bad. The villain's end, for example, must reflect the extent of his wickedness and thus 'no ignominy is too terrible, no death too horrible'[8] for him. Being hurled from the Monument, entombed with a corpse or crushed under a descending lift are just some of the ways the villain perishes in melodrama. But, as we shall see, in our analysis of *Black-Ey'd Susan*, it is not always the villain who is at the centre of spectacle. Indeed spectacle can separate off from the moral scheme of melodrama. The appearance on stage of ships, trains and even an airship can be seen as celebrations of Victorian engineering and technology rather than as means of reinforcing the division between good and bad.

Douglas Jerrold (1803–1857), *Black-Ey'd Susan* (1829)

Black-Ey'd Susan is a nautical melodrama, aspects of which were parodied by W. S. Gilbert (1836–1911) and Arthur Sullivan (1842–1900) in their comic operetta *H.M.S. Pinafore* (1878). William is Susan's husband. He has been made to go into the navy by Susan's uncle, Doggrass, the villain of the piece. As well as driving the young couple apart, Doggrass connives in a plan to tell Susan that William is dead so that his partner, Hatchet, can marry her. To ensure the success of this scheme, Doggrass intends to make Susan homeless by demanding rent arrears from Dame Hatley, the woman with whom she is staying. But Gnatbrain, one of the good characters, prevents the eviction and Doggrass' scheme suffers a further blow when William returns from sea. The couple's troubles, however, are from over.

William's commanding officer, Captain Crosstree, drunkenly molests Susan and William gives him a near fatal injury in defending her. The penalty for a sailor striking an officer is death and William is duly sentenced. Just before he is executed, Crosstree arrives with a letter showing that he had discharged William from the navy as a reward for having saved him in battle. William was therefore not one of the king's sailors when he struck Crosstree and so, legally, cannot be charged with assaulting his superior. Doggrass had intercepted Crosstree's letter with the aim of ensuring that William would be hung. But, as he was waiting for the verdict, he fell out of his boat and drowned. The letter was discovered on his body.

It should be clear from even this brisk summary that *Black-Ey'd Susan* is a fairly typical melodrama. It shows its roots in tragicomedy by bringing the hero close to death but saving him at the last moment, and the comic resolution of the lovers' problems is enhanced by songs and humorous exchanges. In addition we see the villain who persecuted the hero and heroine duly punished for his actions. The play also raises a lot of other issues such as the treatment of the poor, conditions in the navy and the operation of the law. There are further considerations too, for example the impact of professional life on personal life. Both William and Susan are concerned about the time they spend apart and then there's the effect of all the nautical imagery in the play. 'There's my Susan...schooner rigged-I'd swear to her canvas from a whole fleet. Now she makes more sail!'[9] William's observation which, incidentally, echoes Mirabell's first sighting of Millament in William Congreve's *The Way of the World* (1700),[10] is typical of the way many of the characters speak. At one level it is a source of comedy, the humour arising from the mismatch between naval idioms and deep emotions. When Susan is attacked, William describes her as 'giving out signals of distress' and his running to her aid as coming up in his 'craft'.[11] At another level the ubiquity of seafaring terminology may prompt the reader to think about how looking at self and society purely through the lens of one's own profession limits understanding of both.

These and other aspects of the play reinforce the secondary argument of this book, namely that tragedy and comedy and, indeed, melodrama are not reducible to the sacrificial structure which underpins them. Nevertheless, our chief concern is with that structure and in *Black-Ey'd Susan* it can be divided into three parts; spectacle, the division of space and sexuality. In ritual the high point of spectacle is the slaying of the sacrificial victim. And in *Black-Ey'd Susan* that point occurs when William is led out to be hanged. A procession of naval personnel, a tolling bell, music and flags at half mast all create the air of a solemn ceremony. The difference from ritual, of course, lies in the fact that William is the hero and not the sacrificial victim. He symbolizes all the virtues of Britain illustrated by his embracing the Union Jack, while Doggrass symbolizes all its vices.

What we have, then, is a divorce between spectacle and sacrifice. Doggrass is the villain of the piece, and it should be his death which is dramatic. But though complying with the moral scheme of melodrama that the villain should be punished, his demise is almost incidental. Why is this the case? One possible answer is that the hero is given such high visibility because he is a moral exemplar. But then why not extend the same logic to the villain? Surely his fate should be seen as a warning to those tempted by a life of vice. What's more it was important, in sacrificial ritual, for victims to be on display because their deaths were proof that the evil they embodied was truly removed. If we do not see the villain die with our own eyes (Doggrass' death was reported), then we are not convinced that society has been truly purged of those ills which afflict it.

The ills which Doggrass symbolizes include exploitation, smuggling and, in his trying to separate William and Susan, an attack on the married state. As a landlord, Doggrass has no qualms about exploiting his tenants. When Susan protests that if he evicts Dame Hatley she will go to prison and probably die there his response is 'I have no time to hear sentiment,'[12] and though he slightly modifies his demands it is only because they make no difference to his plan of making Susan homeless. His role as 'chief encourager of the smugglers'[13] deserves more space than can be given here. In very general terms smuggling was a reaction to taxes not just on luxury goods but also on essential items like soap, leather and salt. Smuggling was obviously illegal but whole communities often connived in the trade. In addition, smugglers were endowed with a certain romantic glamour.[14]

Both these factors mean that smuggling blurs the distinction between law and criminality. It exists in some tension with the play's sacrificial structure because one of the functions of the latter is to make clear divisions between the sacred and the secular, right and wrong and the inside and the outside of society. The slaying of the scapegoat returns the evil that has invaded community back to the place from which it came. But the death of Doggrass fails to achieve that end because he doesn't symbolize a clear evil that exists outside society, rather a confusion of what is right and wrong within it. Smuggling may have been unlawful but it was also coextensive with the social and was, in some places, an economic necessity.[15] Doggrass may be the villain and the villain of melodrama has to die but the incidental nature of his death raises serious questions about whether it purges society of the ills he is supposed to symbolize or whether it hides them from view.

But what of William? Can we say that he really is a moral exemplar or is there something about him that qualifies him as a sacrificial victim? Is he, for example, a prototype for the conflicted hero who emerges later in the century? The short answer to that question is 'no'. He lacks the psychological depth necessary for such a figure. What does make William a possible candidate for sacrifice is the very thing that makes him a hero, his loyalty to the admiralty. He accepts without question the naval hierarchy that condemns him and doesn't even call witnesses in his defence when given the chance. William's cheerful resignation to his fate is in marked contrast to the temper of Britain in 1829.

The country was still feeling the effects of the French Revolution; there were protests against the Corn Laws and a mounting and sometimes bloody campaign for Parliamentary reform. William, in other words, symbolizes an attitude of deference and of putting up with one's lot that was elsewhere being challenged. Such attitudes had to be sacrificed if society was to change. But there was also a great deal of anxiety about change. The French Revolution had led to the terror and the Industrial Revolution was transforming not just the physical landscape of Britain but the social one too. The spectacle of William's near execution captures this ambiguity. It flirts with the possibility of ditching the principle of knowing your place but pulls back at the last moment.

Both Doggrass and William qualify as sacrificial victims but only partially because they also symbolize certain values of their society. Doggrass' various business activities ally him with Victorian entrepreneurs which means he is a force for social change. William, by contrast, stands for stability and continuity. But both men represent the extreme versions of these values. Doggrass' ambitions threaten to destroy the very foundation of society itself, as is evident in his attempt to wreck his niece's marriage, while William's deference to established hierarchies indicates the sclerotic nature of the old order – its failure to adapt neatly captured in William's habit of using naval terminology for each and every occasion. There is, then, no single or satisfactory scapegoat in the play nor do death and spectacle coincide. But that is not quite the end of the matter because there is a second death in the play – that of a black child. William describes it.

His fleet was lying off St Domingo in the West Indies. The crew wanted to go ashore to dance and drink but were forbidden to do so by the Admiral who also arranged for a shark to swim round the anchored ships as an added deterrent. One morning a native woman was on the deck of William's ship with her baby which suddenly 'jumped out of its mother's grappling'[16] and fell into the shark's jaws. One of the sailors leapt overboard and killed the shark. He came up 'all over blood with the corpse of the baby in his hand and the shark turned over dead upon its side'.[17] The sailors cut the shark open finding in it watches, tobacco boxes, an Admiral's hat and three telescopes. How does this story relate to the sacrificial structure of the play? It's important to note that the baby is not actually sacrificed. The toddler's death is an accident. Nevertheless, it has something of the character of sacrifice about it. First, it leads to the restoration of what was lost – the various items in the shark's stomach – and second, it enables access to what has been forbidden – drinking and dancing with the natives of St Domingo. The restoration of lost items such as watches, tobacco boxes and telescopes trivializes the notion of sacrifice as a religious phenomenon. It does carry faint echoes of the story of Jonah and the Whale which is about God's relationship to man and which also anticipates Christ's descent into hell before his resurrection of the third day. But there is no sense of deliverance or salvation here, just symbols of time, consumption, empire (telescope) and hierarchy – the paraphernalia of Victorian Britain.

In ancient ritual, sacrifice was followed by celebrations in which the usual rules governing behaviour were suspended. William's story clearly hints that what the Admiral had forbidden was carousing and sexual contact with native women. The social and spiritual uses of sacrificial ritual, the discharge of excess energy, the communion with the god and participation in the creative process of nature have here been perverted into a means of exploiting an already subjected people.[18] Freud argues that sacrifice is partly a re-enactment of the murder of the primal father. It is therefore, among other things, an act of rebellion and there is a faint trace of this in the killing of the shark since that enables the sailors to visit the island in defiance of their orders to the contrary.

There is more that could be said about this story. For example, it shows that William endorses rebellion even if he doesn't rebel himself. It also reveals the inhuman attitude of Europeans to the West Indians. William does not mention any feeling of sympathy for the woman who lost her baby, only delight at the death of the shark. But what is not so obvious is how this story connects with Susan who is, after all, the title character. She is called 'black-ey'd Susan' but no one seems to know why. It can't be because she has black eyes because humans do not have eyes of this colour. But their fabled blackness does mean she can be linked with the black women of St Domingo. They are viewed in largely sexual terms and so, it turns out, is Susan.

Doggrass insinuates that she may find it 'convenient' to have a husband at sea and she unwittingly provokes strong sexual reactions in both Hatchet and Crosstree, both of whom declare that they 'must' have her.[19] Of course she remains faithful to William, but her attractiveness and her association with the implied sexual freedoms of the women of St Domingo recall that fascination with, and fear of, female desire which has been a factor in sacrifice since the *Oresteia*. The *Eumenides*, the final play in that trilogy, showed that the sacrifice of female instinct to male rationality created a new type of society, one based on law rather than revenge.

Doggrass, in wanting to make Susan sexually available for other men, represents an urge to reverse that arrangement – to reintroduce female promiscuity. But this is no attempt to restore a more comprehensive sexuality. As in Plautus' *The Rope*, sexuality is reduced to a commercial exchange. Doggrass is effectively selling his niece to Hatchet. And the consequence of this action is to undermine all those bonds of care and affection on which society depends. Twenty years before Karl Marx (1818–1883) declares in *The Communist Manifesto* (1848) that money dissolves all social and family ties, Jerrold has dramatized it. One of the worries of the Victorian period was how the industrial revolution was not only producing a class of men wealthy enough to challenge the traditional aristocracy; it was also generating massive inequalities which were threatening to tear apart the social fabric. Since sexuality is also implicated in this process, it becomes associated with destruction rather than creation.

At one level, then, *Black-Ey'd Susan* has a clear sacrificial structure. The villain is expelled and the married couple will enjoy happiness and presumably children. But, at another level, this structure is more complicated. First, it lacks any religious dimension. There is no apprehension of a greater reality, only an attempt to expel evil. Second, it is difficult to identify this evil. Is it Doggrass' cupidity or William's conformity? The divorce between spectacle and sacrificial victim suggests that there is no clear answer to this question. William and Doggrass represent Victorian society poised between the old and the new order, between deference and self-assertion, between hallowed institutions and the rule of money. Finally, the riotous sexuality which is part of sacrificial celebration is projected onto the natives of St Domingo, but it is also present in Susan. It seems from all this that sacrificial structure is starting to disintegrate because society is becoming far too complex for its problems to be resolved simply by loading them onto a scapegoat. The psychological habit of sacrifice is still evident in *Black-Ey'd Susan* but it lags behind developments in the wider society.

Comedy

We said at the beginning of this chapter that tragedy had all but disappeared. By contrast, comedy seemed to have burgeoned. It generated different genres such as farce, pantomime, burlesque and extravaganza. But, in the process, the definition of comedy had become blurred. This lack of focus was aggravated by different elements from the tragic to the pathetic, from the satirical to the romantic, appearing in single works such as Edward Bulwer Lytton's popular *Money* (1840). Michael Booth notes that there was 'almost no such thing, in this veritable maelstrom of dramatic writing, as purity of form and singleness of genre'.[20] No doubt it was this lack of clarity which lay behind Ashley Thorndike's remark that it was 'not in comedies proper but in the operas of Gilbert and Sullivan that we find the chief Victorian tribute to the Comic Muse'.[21] It is a judgement still echoed today.[22]

There are many factors which account for this situation. One is the absorption of the single distinct form of comic play remaining at the end of the eighteenth century into melodrama. Sentimental comedy's appeal to the feelings found a natural home in the strong emotions of melodrama. Another is the influence of the Gothic, whose gloomy preoccupations with incest, murder and the nature of evil did not easily lend themselves to humorous treatment. Yet another factor, according to Rowell, was 'the complete subordination of comedy to spectacle, signs of which were apparent in the last years of the Georgian theatre'.[23]

Booth has suggested that one way of determining whether a work was more comic than, say, romantic or pathetic was to note which actors were in it. Charles Mathews (1803–1878) was renowned for his comic skills and talent for impersonation so his appearance in George Henry Lewes' *The Game of Speculation* (1852) highlights the comedy of the piece rather than the bleakness inherent in its themes of fraud, manipulation and bankruptcy and the sacrifice of a daughter for money.[24] Comic themes were present, if not always dominant, in a number of plays. They include the clash between old and new money, country virtue versus city vice and the importance of domestic bliss.

A key part of the ideology of home and hearth was the idealization of women either as sweethearts, wives or mothers. To view them in this way is to deny them their reality as complex human beings. As such it can be seen as a form of control which again takes us back to the founding moment of Western civilization, the suppression of the female nature. But of course it continues to defy all attempts to limit it and this can be seen in those mid-Victorian plays that deal with the problems of marriage, particularly where the woman tries to assume the dominant role in the relationship before being made to see the error of her ways as in J. S. Coyne's *My Wife's Daughter* (1850).

The residues of ritual can also be found in farce. Beginning as a one or two act afterpiece, the form changed under French influence into three-act plays which touched on adultery and sexual adventures. Here are hints of the promiscuity that characterized the celebrations following sacrifice. They were the seedbed out of which Old Comedy grew and its fantastical, slapstick action is echoed in the horseplay, improbabilities and sexual confusions of farce. Two other ingredients of farce may also be traced back to ritual. Booth has linked the high consumption of food in Victorian farces to the feasts of Dionysus,[25] while the sadistic element of farce, what George Bernard Shaw (1856–1950) called 'the deliberate indulgence of that horrible derisive joy in humiliation and suffering which is the beastliest element of human nature',[26] may have its beginnings in the slaying of the sacrificial victim. Ideally there is no guilt in witnessing such an event because it is an officially approved act with a necessary social purpose, namely the creation of new life. The pleasure in the spectacle of death is therefore a pleasure in that new life.

In the last twenty years of the century, the stage saw a return to more conventional comedy. French influence was a key factor in this development. It led to more skilfully plotted plays portraying more realistic situations with more credible characters. But both setting and *dramatis personae* were drawn from a narrow section of society. Comedy had moved upmarket. The playwright Arthur Wing Pinero (1855–1934) told the critic William Archer (1856–1924) that 'nothing of considerable merit but low comedy, has ever come from the study of low life'.[27] This exchange reflects a tension at the heart of the history of comedy. On the one hand it is a celebration of instinctual life; on the other it upholds standards of behaviour.

Oscar Wilde (1854–1900), *A Woman of No Importance* (1893)

The work of Oscar Wilde is typical of the upper-class comedies that were appearing in the 1890s but none could match his for wit or sophistication. Although he was born in Ireland, he lived and wrote in London. Wilde's comedies are very similar in terms of their wit and narrow social strata. The plot of *A Woman of No Importance* revolves around Lord Illingworth discovering the son he had by Mrs Arbuthnot, a woman he seduced many years ago. Gerald, the son, is now a young man and Lord Illingworth wants to employ him as his secretary but his mother is against the idea because she, not unreasonably, thinks he will be a corrupting influence on the boy. Gerald only learns that Lord Illingworth is his father when he is about to attack for him for having forcibly kissed Hester Worsley, the woman Gerald wants to marry. 'He is your own father,'[28] cries his mother as Gerald raises his hand. It is a moment worthy of the best melodrama.

But *A Woman of No Importance* isn't a melodrama; it's a comedy. In one way it is similar to Restoration comedy because its characters are mostly from the aristocracy and assert themselves through displays of wit. There is also the same dismissive attitude to the middle class and to nature which is considered quite inferior to artifice. One of the criticism of Hester, who is American, is that she is 'painfully natural'.[29] But the play differs from Restoration comedy in focusing on a social issue rather than the pursuit of sexual conquest and in having, nominally at least, a strong moral code. Tackling such problems as the fallen woman puts Wilde more in tune with the spirit of Ibsen (1828–1906) than with those who advocated that drama should focus on the good rather than the bad things in life, but he lacked Ibsen's naturalistic approach to the subject.

There are two sacrificial victims in *A Woman of No Importance*. The first is Mrs Arbuthnot and the second is Lord Illingworth, whom we will come to later. Mrs Arbuthnot fulfils the role of the scapegoat to the extent that she was cast out of society for being the mother of an illegitimate child. She bears the burden of wayward desire. Mrs Allonby is said to have run off with several men before she married and then there are hints of her affairs afterwards. Lady Caroline has been married four times and we also hear of a Lady Felpton who eloped with a Lord Fethersdale. This is another example of the disruptive nature of female desire which has haunted sacrifice in drama since the *Oresteia* but our concern here is with Mrs Arbuthnot's status as a scapegoat.

Normally, a play builds up to the dismissal of the scapegoat whose death or expulsion contains an element of spectacle. Both these testify to the deep-rooted importance of sacrifice as a means of binding a society together and dealing with its problems. But, as Mrs Arbuthnot has been exiled before the play began, her departure is neither climatic nor spectacular. Nor can *A Woman of No Importance* be said to end in a grand manner. The finale is less high drama than a quibble on the title. When Gerald asks who the visitor was – it was Lord Illingworth – his mother replies, 'Oh no-one. No-one in particular. A man of no importance.'[30] The element of spectacle has not disappeared but it has become separated from sacrifice. Once spectacle was an important event and so was set apart from the rest of social life but in this play it has become the principle of society itself or rather with one particular part of it, the upper class. It now consists of wealth, fashion, large houses, social gatherings and, above all, magnificent displays of wit rather than an existential counter with the deepest mysteries of human existence. Spectacle, it might be said, has lost its spiritual dimension and shrunk to a form of self-advertisement that is seen at its most attractive and most shallow in Lord Illingworth.

Mrs Arbuthnot's removal before the beginning of the action, and the almost causal way we learn of her fate, means that she is not an effective scapegoat. Even her status as a sacrificial victim is in doubt because she is not only admitted into society; there are those like Lady Hunstanton who actively seek her company. More surprisingly, it seems to be her choice whether or not she enters it.[31] All these factors mean that Mrs Arbuthnot's apparent status as an outcast does nothing to rid society of the sexual promiscuity, or at least the threat of it, which undermines the social order. Indeed, she represents a regression to instinctual confusion for there is a distinct Oedipal element in her relationship with her son.

Mrs Arbuthnot asks Gerald to come as close to her as when he was a little boy;[32] he tells her that she is both mother and father to him,[33] and announces to Lady Hunstanton that he doesn't wish to leave his mother.[34] These intense expressions of the bond between mother and son are precipitated by Gerald learning that Lord Illingworth is his father and by his mother's account of how he treated her. His attempted attack on his father needs to be seen in the context of these declarations of love and desire. It is true that, at the moment he tries to strike Lord Illingworth, Gerald does not know that he is his father but, given the forbidden nature of Oedipal desires, they are not going to be portrayed in a clear and unambiguous manner.

If Freud is to be believed, the return of Oedipal sexuality is another symptom of the breakdown of sacrifice. He argued that sacrifice was partly a response to the murder of the primal father. As an act of atonement, sacrifice was intended to prevent such an action happening ever again. It also marked the beginning of human society, the moment when the incest taboo was given frightening and compelling form. But if the sacrificial structure that we find in drama breaks down, then we see not only a regression to the Oedipal scenario but also a reversion to that state before the mythic murder. Mrs Allonby's comment, that there is no difference between the savage and the civilized,[35] may be significant in this connection.

A *Woman of No Importance* is perhaps unique among the plays we have examined because it operates with two notions of sacrifice both directed at the problem of unregulated sexuality. The first is the very basic one of identifying and expelling a scapegoat but this does not seem to work. The second is a Christian one. In this Christ is the sacrificial victim who takes on himself the sins of humanity and those who believe in him are redeemed. Hester reprises, in her change of attitude to the fallen woman, the shift from Old Testament condemnation to New Testament forgiveness. At first she takes a punitive attitude not just to the woman but also to the man: 'If a man and a woman have sinned, let them both go forth into the desert.'[36] But when she overhears Mrs Arbuthnot explain her feelings to Gerald she has a complete change of heart. 'I was wrong. God's law is only love.'[37]

The Christian idea of sacrifice also fails to cleanse social order. This is partly because Christianity is more about the relation of the individual soul to God than it is about the state of society. If a person does not repent, if they do not believe in the healing power of Christ, then they cannot be saved. Since Mrs Arbuthnot openly declares that she has never repented of her sin,[38] she is damned. But that is not the impression we get from the play. On the contrary Mrs Arbuthnot seems to form a new social unit with Gerald and Hester who want to marry. This unit stands for integrity, moral restraint and self-responsibility. What's more there are hints that this little family may move to America.[39] If that is the case then we have yet another variation on the scapegoat theme, namely that instead of bearing away everything that is bad about the society, they are bearing away everything that is good. This constitutes an admission that sacrifice, whether in its basic or Christian form, can no longer perform its ancient function of cleansing society.

But Mrs Arbuthnot, Gerald and Hester should not be seen simply as models of virtue. The whiff of incest between mother and son becomes decidedly more pungent when Hester asks if she can be Mrs Arbuthnot's daughter.[40] Now we have a slightly incestuous brother–sister relation to add to that between mother and son. This puts a different spin on their departure for now they can be seen as carrying away the ancient evil of incest of which all societies seek to rid themselves. In addition, they are also afflicted with what is most rotten in society, namely artifice. The alternatives, 'sincerity' and 'earnestness', according to Lord Illingworth, turn the human being into a 'bore'.[41]

It seems odd to claim that Mrs Arbuthnot, Gerald and Hester are infected with artifice. They do not indulge in clever, witty or outrageous remarks and, more importantly, they are associated with what is natural. Mrs Arbuthnot, for example, describes her life as 'a little vineyard'[42] while Gerald and Hester take pleasure in gardens[43] unlike their social superiors who see them only as shortcuts to somewhere else.[44] So wherein lies their artifice then? In the character of their speech. It is stagey, stilted and full of conventional pieties just like the language of melodrama. Mrs Arbuthnot's long speech about a mother's love[45] could be a classic of the genre.

The strain of artifice in the 'good' characters complicates our view of Lord Illingworth as a scapegoat. He qualifies for this role because he is the most brilliant symbol of artifice, of the triumph of style over substance, in the play. 'The future belongs to the dandy', he declares, 'It is the exquisites who are going to rule.'[46] Lord Illingworth also meets the criteria for being a scapegoat in the way that Mrs Arbuthnot does not. There is a build-up to his dismissal and it contains an element of spectacle in that he is struck across the face with a glove. In addition his departure serves to define the new community. It will be the opposite of what he represents.

But just as Mrs Arbuthnot's sacrifice fails to purge society, so too does Lord Illingworth's. If part of the scapegoat's role is to carry away the threat of incest, then he does not succeed. Indeed, his expulsion from Mrs Arbuthnot's *ménage à trois* only strengthens its incestuous character. It is precisely because Lord Illingworth represents the wider world that Mrs Arbuthnot expels him. She, Gerald and Hester want to withdraw into their own little enclave. Lord Illingworth's banishment from their little community is in fact a return to another, the upper class, the very milieu which is riddled with the artifice of which he is the prime example. Once again, there is a failure to remove the source of corruption. Indeed, it only seems to be more firmly entrenched. Finally, while Mrs Arbuthnot may imagine that in showing Lord Illingworth the door, she is getting rid of everything that is false, cynical, contrived and meretricious, the artifice in her own soul remains.

What we are left with in *A Woman of No Importance* is incest and artifice. They are both symbols for the masturbatory preoccupation with self and for the sterility of social life, its remoteness from nature and its division into separate classes. The quest of Mrs Arbuthnot, Gerald and Hester for 'green valleys' and 'fresh waters'[47] is less an attempt to reconnect with the creative forces of nature than a perfunctory nod to a Christianity under siege from the higher criticism, the fledgling science of geology and of course the theory of evolution. 'Green valleys' and 'fresh waters' recall Psalm 23 and the play refers several times to the Garden of Eden.[48] The desire to experience the power of Christianity is the desire to experience the healing power of Christ's sacrifice. But it is not one which is likely to be fulfilled. It would seem that late nineteenth-century Britain has become too complex for its various problems to be resolved by sacrifice, yet the yearning for it remains.

Henrik Ibsen (1828–1906), *Hedda Gabler* (1890)

We said above that Wilde shared with Ibsen an interest in social problems but that he had a different approach to them. Wilde treats them either as an exercise in style or else resorts to Christian pieties. Ibsen, by contrast, offers an uncompromising picture of the ills of modern life from syphilis to civic corruption. He is a 'naturalist', described by the French novelist Emile Zola (1840–1902) as the scientific observation of 'real' people, in 'real' settings, who speak and dress in a 'realistic' manner. The core assumption of naturalism was that people's environment determined their behaviour and, if it was desirable to change that behaviour, then it was necessary to change their environment.

This view of drama suggests that tragedy at least is no longer relevant to depictions of the modern world. But the tragic idea of people being in the grip of forces greater than themselves is still very much present in naturalism's notion that they are the product of their circumstances. And if tragedy is present in Ibsen's work then we may also expect to find traces of the sacrificial ritual that underpins it. Readers of this book may be more familiar with plays such as *A Doll's House* (1879) or *Ghosts* (1881) where the sacrificial element is fairly clear.[49] It is therefore more of a challenge to trace its workings in a play like *Hedda Gabler*. Like Wilde's *A Woman of No Importance* it focuses on the plight of women in contemporary society. Hedda, a general's daughter, is trapped in her marriage to the nondescript Tesman, a cultural historian from the class below her own. Hedda relieves her frustrations by manipulating those around her. In particular she persuades a former suitor, Eilert Loevborg, another cultural historian, to commit suicide, giving him one of her father's pistols to do so. On learning that his subsequent death may have been an accident, she shoots herself. But where, in all this, is sacrifice?

Well, if the need for sacrifice arises because there is something rotten in the state of society then there is no shortage of problems here – patriarchy, venality and financial irresponsibility to mention but a few. It is possible to see them all as symptoms of a much greater evil, namely the social conventions that suppress the human capacity to live life to the full. The remark 'people don't do such things'[50] is used to convey both shock and disapproval when they display genuine emotion which, because it has been repressed, erupts in an hostile fashion. Invalids, deaths and childlessness are all used to symbolize the moribund nature of this society.

The childless marriage of Hedda and Tesman reverses the ancient connection between weddings and fertility. Strengthening the impression that there will be no new birth is Hedda's destruction of Loevborg's tome on the future of civilization. Mrs Elvsted helped him to write it and as Hedda burns the book she cries, 'I am burning your child Thea...The child Eilert Loevborg gave you.'[51] We are approaching the world of Beckett where we are waiting for things to wind down and where there will be no new beginning. This is partly anticipated by Loevborg's fate. He wishes to 're-establish' himself, 'to begin again-from the beginning' and to be 'wash[ed] clean'[52] but he dies instead.

Society, then, is not only edging towards dissolution, it is also unredeemed. There is no scapegoat who can purge it of its various afflictions. If we view *Hedda Gabler* as a tragedy, then we might be tempted to say that the eponymous heroine's suicide makes her the scapegoat but she, like Loevborg, does not represent the ills of society so much as the very thing needed to revive it: the principle of vitality. 'Oh, Hedda! Hedda Gabler...It wasn't knowledge you wanted! It was life!'[53] We can only see Hedda, and indeed Loevborg, as scapegoats if we invert the entire logic of sacrificial ritual and argue that society's most profound desire is for death rather than life – that is for convention over conviction, propriety over passion, manners over morals, structure over spontaneity and habit over happiness.

The breakdown of the sacrificial structure impacts on how we understand drink, sexuality and even death in the play. In the model we have been using, sacrifice is followed by feasting and a suspension of the usual norms of sexual behaviour. The festivities signified, among other things, oneness with the god, the fecundity of nature and the celebration of community. None of these are present in *Hedda Gabler*. The men consume alcohol at one of Judge Brack's famous bachelor parties but there is no sense of fellowship. In fact Tesman's account of the evening focuses on Loevborg's drunken ramblings and the break-up of the group. A reformed drinker, Loevborg, was not going to attend the gathering but Hedda, to satisfy her vanity, manoeuvred him into doing so. It proved his undoing because he got drunk and lost his manuscript which Tesman finds and gives to Hedda at her insistence.

Just as drink has negative connotations in the play so too does sexuality. There seems to be no physical side to Hedda's and Tesman's marriage. The thought of marital relations seems to revolt her while he spent their honeymoon 'rooting around in libraries and copying old pieces of parchment'.[54] Judge Brack favours a triangular relationship, 'a delightful arrangement for all parties concerned'.[55] His preference is not a plea for a more liberated form of sexuality; it is a way of gaining power over women like Hedda.[56] It is therefore as much a perversion of sexual freedom as the commodification of sex in Mademoiselle Danielle's brothel. Brack's adulterous liaisons and Mademoiselle Danielle's business both disrupt the marital relation but the latter is positively anarchic with Loevborg's visit there ending in 'a general free-for-all'.[57]

The perception of death is also different from how it was seen in sacrificial ritual. In *Hedda Gabler*, it is no longer in a mutually dependent relation with life. The two are quite separate. Hedda makes a clear distinction between them when she states that life is a form of imprisonment and death is a release.[58] Hedda wants death to have a meaning because her life does not. Spectacle is an intrinsic part of the various meanings of death in sacrificial ritual and that's why Hedda urges Loevborg to make his death 'beautiful'.[59] Such a suicide will guarantee that, where life is stifled by petty convention, death can be a truly authentic act.

Of course, Loevborg's death is anything but. It is a sordid, botched affair. What Hedda learns from it is that we cannot ask anyone to act or, more precisely, to be a scapegoat for our own shortcomings. She had wanted Loevborg to kill himself in order to validate her own life – to reassure herself that the values of courage, freedom and sincerity had not disappeared from the modern world. But Loevborg's death was a ghastly accident and, what's more, his pistol had discharged itself into his groin, an image which suggests castration thereby underlining the fact that death is no longer related to the creation of new life, simply its destruction.

If Hedda wants to find in death the meaning that is missing in her life then she must commit suicide. By shooting herself she escapes the clutches of Judge Brack, but there is no spectacle in the affair since it takes place offstage, nor do the audience sense that Hedda has triumphed over circumstances. Her death merely seems a fitting symbol of her inability to live. But there is another dimension to it as well. In many ways Hedda is reminiscent of the powerful female who always haunts the margins of sacrifice. She can be traced back to Clytemnestra whose unavenged death functions as the sacrifice which precipitates Western civilization into existence. Hedda, like Clytemnestra, has masculine qualities – she is associated with her father's pistols – and, despite her distaste for her husband, she has a powerful sexual presence. But it is hard to accommodate such women within the framework of civilization and so they are repeatedly pushed out. Hedda's suicide can therefore be seen as another version of the sacrifice of Clytemnestra. It removes a challenge to the patriarchal order and no one will be held to account for it.

Music Hall

Music hall was one of many forms of entertainment available to the Victorians. Others included, for the upper classes, opera and operetta and, for the lower classes, sport, fairs and circuses. But it was music hall which proved to have the most appeal. The first purpose-built halls appeared in the 1840s but the heyday of music hall was from the 1890s to the 1910s.[60] Its risqué pleasures formed a contrast with the age's famed prudery. But compared to the religious festivals of ancient Greece, or to the Roman Games, or to Medieval folk plays or to the revels of the Renaissance, the music hall was a very restrained affair. The typical music hall bill, in no particular order, consisted of comic singing, a two- or three-handed domestic farce and speciality acts. The comic songs can broadly be divided into two main types: the swells and the costers, an abbreviation of costermonger, the term for street sellers of fruit and vegetables. The swells aped their social betters, 'swaggering round the stage in spats, sporting monocles and outrageous suits of garish cloth'.[61] One of the most popular was George Leybourne (1842–1884) best known today for the song 'Champagne Charlie' (1866). The costers, meanwhile, sang humorously of the hard lives endured by their audiences. Kate Carney (1869–1950), known as the 'Coster Comedienne', specialized in songs about working-class girls and their lives.

The domestic farce presented a more humorous and rough-edged version of the problems of marriage than could be seen in the plays of Pinero, Haddon Chambers (1860–1921) or Henry Arthur Jones (1851–1929) though it too endorsed the view that wives should submit to their husbands. The speciality act ranged from tightrope walking to performing crows. There was Zazel, real name Rossa Matilda Richter (1860–?), the first human cannonball; Jules Léotard (1838–1870), the original 'daring young man on the flying trapeze'; John Bottle (1875–1956) the memory man; William Ellsworth Robinson (1861–1918) known as Chung Ling Soo who caught bullets fired at him from a gun until one fatal night when the trick went wrong, and perhaps the most memorable performer of them all, the great escapologist Harry Houdini, real name Eric Weisz (1874–1926). In addition there were ventriloquists, jugglers, knife throwers, fire heaters and 'human curiosities' or 'freaks' such as Hermann Unthan (1848–1929) who, despite being born without arms, could use his feet 'to sharpen pens, shoot accurately, play the violin and cornet, shuffle cards and offer a glass of wine'.[62]

There does not seem to be too much here to invite the condemnation of social reformers. Nevertheless, music hall was regarded as the seedbed of drunkenness and sexual immorality. A case in point was the 'can-can', a dance that had originated in the working-class district of Montparnasse in Paris. The *Pall Mall Gazette* opined that its characteristic immodesty meant that it was a dance 'no woman should witness and no man should applaud'.[63] The high kicks and display of petticoats caused such outrage at the Alhambra that the theatre lost its licence and was closed. The perception of music hall as a somewhat base form of entertainment points to the existence of a divide between high and low culture. It was enshrined, to some extent, in the 1843 Theatre Licensing Act which forbade music halls from staging plays as they were considered the preserve of the theatre proper. The aim of the act was to protect dramatic performance from 'mindless, lascivious and degrading spectacle' but it was not particularly successful as music halls continued to stage plays or extracts from plays.[64]

The division between 'respectable' and 'non respectable' kinds of performance stands in sharp contrast to the unified experience of ritual from which all performance ultimately descends. Sex and drink were integral to the whole ceremony of sacrifice. They were manifestations of divinity and the new life created by the imposing spectacle of death. Spectacle, indeed, is the only other equally faint echo of sacrifice to be found in music hall. But it was not used as a form of comprehending religious or existential issues and it was entirely secular. Houdini was one of a number of artists who were at great pains to show that their acts were based on skill and not on supernatural aid. In Houdini's case this led to a row with his close friend Sir Arthur Conan Doyle (1859–1930), the creator of Sherlock Holmes.

It is probably easier to appreciate music hall's kinship with sacrifice by highlighting its relationship with comedy. In both the body is accepted and celebrated. It is at once a source of pleasure and amusement. One of the most popular music hall acts was the *'fartiste'*, a person who could use their anus to play tunes, blow out candles and spout water.[65] Cross-dressing is a feature of comedy from Aristophanes to Shakespeare and beyond. The most famous male impersonator in music hall was Matilda Alice Powles (1864–1952), otherwise known as Vesta Tilley, who mocked the upper class with her characters Burlington Bertie and Piccadilly Johnny. Such satire of those in power has always been one of the characteristics of comedy. Another is its pronounced air of community. The music hall audience tended to know each other and the performers. They engaged in banter and joined in with the songs. Jacky Bratton describes how one of the biggest stars of music hall, G. H. Macdermott (1845–1901), 'had a song whose chorus ended "I'll stand glasses all round; how much can you drink?" to which the mendacious audience response was "Not much!"'[66]

How, then, does music hall fit in with the argument of this book, namely that sacrifice, in one form or another, acts as template for tragedy and comedy? After all, there is no 'sacrifice' in music hall. No one dies and nor is there a scapegoat. Nevertheless, we can see that music hall is related to sacrificial ritual through its relationship to comedy. It is the Victorian incarnation of the festive side of sacrifice. As such it fulfils a number of functions associated with sacrifice, for example, a temporary suspension of social norms and the strengthening of communal identity.

But music hall also looks forward to the format of modern entertainment, in particular the fragmentation of spectacle into a series of smaller spectacles with little link between them except that they appear on the same bill. In that respect music hall anticipates the format of television. Television, in fact, is not just the product of technological innovation it is also the culmination of the standardization of entertainment that had been going on throughout the nineteenth century in a movement often summed up as 'from pot house to palace'.[67] A major consequence of this development is the commodification of qualities like sexuality and subversion as they are pressed into the service of profit instead of being used to explore what it means to be human. And yet, as we shall see in the last chapter, what we witness in television and, indeed, in cinema is a return of the scapegoat.

9

Twentieth and Twenty-First-Century Drama

The conditions which gave rise to classical tragedy and comedy have long gone and the forms themselves have changed in response to various historical developments including Christianity, the rise of science and the spread of democracy. To these can be added, in the twentieth and early twenty-first centuries, the growth of secularism and the emergence of new technologies such as cinema, television and the internet.

Despite these changes the comedy of today is not altogether different from the slapstick of Aristophanes, the mistaken identities of Shakespeare or the complications of love in Wycherely, though it is definitely more diverse – a trend which was apparent at the end of the eighteenth century. The case of tragedy is more difficult because it has traditionally been associated with the downfall of a high-born hero partly due to some fatal flaw in his or her character and partly to the actions of the gods. But as we are no longer ruled by monarchs nor consider ourselves the playthings of fate, the idea of tragedy is more problematic.

It all depends on how we define it.[1] We have taken the line that tragedy, like comedy, originates in sacrificial ritual which, at its simplest, is based on the idea that death is necessary for the renewal of life. The advantage of this approach is that it allows us to see continuities as well as changes between tragedies from different periods. Shakespearean tragedy may look very different from Greek tragedy and both bear little resemblance to a later manifestation, such as Tennessee Williams' *A Streetcar Named Desire* (1947) which is itself quite remote from Samuel Beckett's *Waiting for Godot* (1956); and yet all contain elements of sacrifice. In doing so they raise the question which, sadly, space does not permit us to even begin to answer – of whether the sacrificial mindset is hard-wired into the human brain.[2]

It is not easy trying to assess the place of tragedy and comedy in contemporary society. Not only do they have to compete with many other types of drama from kitchen-sink[3] to the Broadway musical but these forms themselves often contain elements of tragedy and comedy. As we shall see in the final chapter, 'Conclusion: Tragedy, Comedy and Sacrifice in Popular Culture', the same is true for other types of entertainment such as cinema and television. Tragedy to a greater extent, and comedy to a lesser, may no longer enjoy the generic purity they once had, but neither have they completely disappeared as their influence is apparent in new kinds of media and drama. Whether the diluted form of tragedy and comedy and the greater diversity of comedy mean that they are unable to confer the sort of meaning and significance on the great questions of existence that they did formerly remains to be seen. Their sacrificial character not only provided powerful narratives on the relation of life and death, identity and community they also offered ways of dealing with these issues that some of the new forms have yet to develop. Take YouTube, for instance. It is a fabulous resource for all kinds of dramatic and filmic material but often as extracts, clips viewed in isolation from their original context. Ultimately, this may have implications for how we tell stories: narrative may give way to a succession of unconnected incidents, high on sensation and low on meaning. In terms of sacrifice this would mean the triumph of spectacle over story, the relation between life and death dissolved into series of intense but separate images as is perhaps already evident in internet pornography and videos of executions.[4]

Fascinating as such speculation may be, our focus is on staged dramatizations of tragedy and comedy in the twentieth and twenty-first centuries. This chapter will look at a handful of plays mostly from Britain and America that have achieved notable success in the period and will seek to answer the question of whether tragedy and comedy appear differently in each. The tentative conclusion is that they do not for, as the discussion below shows, sacrifice remains a significant, if problematic, element in all of them.

Samuel Beckett (1906–1989), *Waiting for Godot* (1956)

The work of the Irish playwright Samuel Beckett has often been identified with the theatre of the absurd. The term was coined by the critic and translator Martin Esslin (1918–2002) to describe a type of play that had neither a realistic setting nor recognizable characters. It also lacked a plot and 'a fully explained theme'.[5] This certainly applies to *Waiting for Godot*. Even after seeing or reading the play we have learnt little about the two main characters, Vladimir and Estragon. We don't know where they came from, or how they know one another, or most importantly, why they are waiting for Godot. The lack of a plot prompted one reviewer to write that it is a play in which 'nothing happens, twice'.[6] Nor does there seem to be a clear theme. When Beckett was asked what Godot meant, he replied, 'If I knew, I would have said so in the play.'[7]

Esslin sought to explain this type of theatre in the context of the decline of religious faith and the horrors of the Second World War.[8] Scepticism about the existence of God leads to doubt about the purpose of life. If we are simply the result of blind evolution, then what possible meaning can our existence have? The existentialist may answer that we have to create our own meanings, but that is exactly what the Nazis had done. Their atrocities raised profound questions about human nature. Were we fundamentally incapable of being 'good'? The death camps had made a mockery of all our vain narratives about progress and civilization. We might have made great strides in science but we remain ethically stunted. Man is still wolf to man. The problem faced by artists was how to convey this shattered post-war landscape.

Dramatists could not rely on the old conventions for representing character and action because they rested on the very assumptions about self and society which had perished in the light of Hitler's final solution and the mushroom cloud of the atom bomb. The bizarre figures and peculiar scenarios of the theatre of the absurd were an attempt to reflect this disturbing new world. In Esslin's words, 'The Theatre of the Absurd strives to express its sense of the senselessness of the human condition and the inadequacy of the rational approach by the open abandonment of the rational devices and discursive thought.'[9]

It is important to recognize that the theatre of the absurd is a response to a specific set of circumstances, but we should remember that its roots also go back to the modernist rejection of realism in the early twentieth century. Well before Beckett there were those, like Wyndham Lewis (1882–1957) and Gordon Craig (1872–1966), who discarded conventional notions of plot and character in pursuit of a completely different theatrical experience. Even the basic premise of the theatre of the absurd – the pointlessness of human existence – is not particularly new. Laments about the emptiness of life can be found in Sophocles and Shakespeare. The difference is that they, unlike Beckett, did not make such nihilism the basis of their art.

With Beckett, then, we come to the end of tragedy as we have known it. There are no high-born figures; there is no plot – which for Aristotle was the soul of tragedy – and no death or renewal. But, of course, it is not as simple as that. For example, Beckett describes *Waiting for Godot* as 'A tragicomedy in two Acts'. Clearly he believed the play had a tragic aspect. What's more he understood that tragedy and comedy belong together. Only by putting them in relation to each other can we appreciate the true value of both.

But there is a suggestion in the play that tragedy and comedy cancel each other out. 'The tears of the world are a constant quantity. For each one who begins to weep, another stops. The same is true of the laugh.'[10] This presents a picture of a static world, a world in which everything seems to stand still, a world in which nothing happens. The very first line of the play is 'Nothing to be done'.[11] In short, the relationship between tragedy and comedy does not appear to be very fruitful. There is even a question about how far we can use the word 'comedy' to describe the play since, as Vladimir says, laughter is 'prohibited'.[12] It seems as if Beckett is draining the word 'tragicomedy' of meaning thereby dramatizing, at the level of language, one of the main themes of the play, namely the lack of purport in life. Not even words, it seems, can help us imagine how things may change for they too partake of the senselessness of existence.

But to fully understand how *Waiting for Godot* is a tragicomedy we have to isolate its tragic and comic elements and see them in relation to their respective traditions. The comic element is swiftly dealt with. Vladimir and Estragon, as their quick fire patter shows, are descended from music hall comedians rather than from the tradition of Old or New comedy. One of the staples of comedy is the love interest which also functions as a symbol of fertility. The absence not only of love but also of women indicates how the comic, in this play, is quite separate from any notion of regeneration. The kinship of *Waiting for Godot* to tragedy is much stronger than it is to comedy. One of the constants of tragedy is a despairing outlook on the world. Pozzo comments on the brevity of life: 'they give birth astride of a grave, the light gleams for an instant and then it's night once more';[13] Estragon complains of its tedium: 'Nothing happens, nobody comes, nobody goes, it's awful';[14] while Vladimir gives a picture of life as a largely grief-stricken journey to death: 'We have time to grow old. The air is full of our cries. But habit is a great deadener.'[15]

There is a very strong sense in Greek tragedy of humans being subject to the will of the gods. Vladimir and Estragon may not be manipulated by Godot but they are nevertheless in thrall to him. When Estragon asks why they can't drop Godot, Vladimir replies that 'He'd punish us.'[16] One of the refrains running through the play is that the pair want to go but cannot because they have to wait for Godot. Even when they agree to leave at the end the stage direction reads: *They do not move*. This suggests that they cannot adapt to a world where there is no supernatural agency – if that is what Godot symbolizes – to guide their actions. They still rely on a deity to shape their lives and fill them with meaning.

Waiting for Godot is also related to Renaissance tragedy. For example the set, a country road with a single tree, evokes the heath on which Lear has his insight into man as nothing more than a 'poor, bare forked animal'.[17] There is also something of Hamlet in Vladimir and Estragon to the extent that they are incapable of action but they differ from him in avoiding thought. They converse so they do not have to think.[18] Hamlet's conception of man as 'this quintessence of dust'[19] comes to mind when Vladimir, Estragon and Pozzo all fall down and remain on the ground, especially when Vladimir then says, 'We've arrived.'[20] The play breaks from the tradition of Renaissance tragedy not just by having clowns as the protagonists but also by deconstructing the soliloquy. This is evident in Lucky's long speech which continues for two and a quarter pages without any punctuation. In Renaissance tragedy such a speech was the expression of the coherent and unified self but, in *Waiting for Godot*, it is an expression of the breakdown of that self and it also represents a loss of faith in the Enlightenment project. For example, Lucky uses the phrase 'for reasons unknown'[21] at least ten times during his speech which suggests that, despite our efforts to know the world and our place in it, we remain in ignorance. He also repeats the expressions 'waste and pine' and 'shrink and dwindle'.[22] These introduce what will be the main theme in Beckett's next play, *Endgame* (1957), namely the desire for life to finish which it stubbornly refuses to do. This state of limbo, where there is neither life nor death, once again points to the absence of sacrifice which regulates the relation between them.

As well as giving a speech Lucky is made to dance. Dance was a mainstay of sacrificial celebration. It is therefore apt that Estragon guesses the dance is called 'The Scapegoat's Agony', but its real name is 'The Net.'[23] This suggests a very different conception of dance to what can be found in ritual where it served to act as a communion with the gods and to cement social bonds. But there is nothing social or divine about Lucky's writhings which signify a solitary self unable to escape the confines of its own miserable being. Just as Lucky's speech shows all the learning of the past smashed to smithereens so does his dance demonstrate the ruin of ritual. And if there is no ritual, there is no new life. The grape harvest that Vladimir and Estragon used to gather is now 'all dead and buried' and they have rejected 'Nature.'[24]

Yet there does seem to be some new life because the tree, which had no leaves in Act 1, has several by Act 2. 'Seem', however, is the operative word because the leaves, far from being symbolic of new life, are associated only with tears and the voices of the dead.[25] They also represent the fact that, while there may be small differences between Act 1 and Act 2, they are more or less the same. The second act is merely a variation of the first. For example in Act 1 Vladimir gives Estragon a carrot; in Act 2 he gives him a radish.[26] As Vladimir says: 'The essential doesn't change.'[27] Each act begins with the two friends being reunited; there is a middle section with Pozzo and Lucky and a final one with a boy coming to tell Vladimir and Estragon that Godot won't come today but will tomorrow. There are also repeated exchanges about, among other things, dreams, boots, passing the time, the desirability of doing nothing and suicide.

In short what we have in *Waiting for Godot* is not ritual but repetition. This includes Beckett's reprisal of aspects of *Oedipus Rex*. Oedipus goes blind and so too does Pozzo. Oedipus means 'swollen foot' and Estragon not only has difficulty taking off his boots he is also kicked by Lucky so that he finds it difficult to walk.[28] Furthermore, Oedipus learns that he is guilty of a terrible crime, one which has led to a blight on Thebes. The crops do not grow, the animals are dying and women do not give birth. There are hints that Vladimir and Estragon are also guilty of a crime. Vladimir suggests they repent but of what we don't know. Later he finds it difficult to believe that Estragon should be beaten for no reason but, again, the subject is quickly closed.[29] These intimations do not really point to actual crimes so much as to existential defects for which, if God does not exist, we must take responsibility. There is no space to explore what these defects may be but they are implicated in the barren setting of the play. And, unlike in *Oedipus Rex*, this desolation looks set to continue. Oedipus at least learns what he has done and acts accordingly. But there is no salvation through self-knowledge in *Waiting for Godot*.

Although ritual and repetition are distinct they are also closely related. Repetition is integral to ritual. The same words and actions must be repeated if they are to have the desired effect. If a priest changed the marriage ceremony each time there was a wedding none of the couples would feel that they were properly joined. But if repetition is a necessary part of ritual, it is not the case that ritual is a necessary part of repetition. Repetition, in fact, may be regarded as a degraded form of ritual. An important difference between them lies in their relationship to time. Ritual is an acknowledgement that time is differentiated – that some moments, such as the change of seasons, are more significant than others.

Ritual is also a way of linking past, present and future. Sacrifice looks forward and back as it removes old life to bring in the new. By contrast repetition seems stuck in an eternal present. Vladimir says that 'Time has stopped.'[30] This explains Estragon's poor memory: 'He's forgotten everything,' his companion declares, Vladimir's own tendency to forget, 'can't think of the name of the man', and Pozzo not remembering whom he met yesterday or what he has just said: 'I don't remember exactly what it was [I just said] but you may be sure there wasn't a word of truth in it.'[31] The past, as Lucky's shattered monologue demonstrates, can only be recalled in broken and obscure fashion and the future, as the broken appointment with Godot shows, is one of perpetual unfulfilment. All Vladimir and Estragon can do is find ways to pass the time by, for example, exercising or putting on boots[32] which they experience, more or less, as an extended single moment. As the philosopher George Santayana (1863–1952) remarked, 'those who cannot remember the past are condemned to repeat it'.[33] And so Vladimir and Estragon will continue to meet at the same place and wait for Godot again and again.

Another difference between ritual and repetition is that ritual requires a belief in a deity whereas repetition does not. But this difference is not clear-cut in the play because of the residual presence of Christianity. Beckett said that Godot was not God but he has a 'white beard'[34] which is how Lucky describes God at the beginning of his speech.[35] What's more Vladimir and Estragon offer him 'a kind of prayer'.[36] If Godot is God then that would make the boy a Christ-like figure. His speech certainly echoes Christ's when he talks about tending the sheep and the goats:[37]

Vladimir	What do you do?
Boy	I mind the goats sir ...
Vladimir	Ah you have a brother.
Boy	Yes sir.
Vladimir	What does he do?
Boy	He minds the sheep sir.[38]

In addition the tree is replete with Christian symbolism. There is the tree of knowledge of good and evil, the tree of life, and finally Judas hung himself from a tree which is exactly what Vladimir and Estragon propose to do. All these references to Christianity suggest that there is a possibility of salvation which of course depends on accepting the sacrifice of Christ. But, at the same time, these references are not presented in an unambiguous way. Moreover, a note of scepticism is struck early on when Vladimir wonders why only one of the four Evangelists tells the story of the two thieves crucified alongside Christ when all of them were present.[39]

Waiting for Godot, then, has a complicated relation to tragedy but less so to comedy. Its laughter comes from the music hall rather than the trials of lovers. But while this means there can be no regeneration, humour at least helps in coping with the grimness of existence. When Vladimir asks how he looks in Lucky's hat Estragon replies, 'Hideous.' To which Vladimir responds, 'Yes. But no more so than usual?'[40] The play alludes to Greek and Renaissance tragedy and also to Christian theology. But what distinguishes it from previous tragedies is the absence of a sacrificial structure. There is no scapegoat and there is no renewal. The absence of a sacrificial structure actually highlights its importance. Sacrifice provides a narrative, a relationship to time, and confers meaning on notions of self and society. Without it there is no time, no real sense of self and only a wilderness where society should be. Beckett shows us the exhaustion of the traditions he evokes but, at the same time, he cannot quite relinquish them. Like Vladimir and Estragon, he still hopes. Sarah Kane, to whom we turn next, seems to pick up where Beckett left off. Among other things she looks back to the rawness of Greek tragedy as a way of redeeming the present.

Sarah Kane (1971–1999), *Blasted* (1995)

Sarah Kane's *Blasted* premiered at the Royal Court Theatre Upstairs in January 1995. It caused outrage. The *Daily Mail* called it a 'disgusting feast of filth'. The reviewer had a point. The play contains scenes of rape, masturbation, blinding and eating a baby. Was Kane just out to shock her audience? Was this nothing more than a young writer's attempt to attract attention? If so, she was part of a zeitgeist. Kane was an exemplar of what Aleks Sierz calls 'In-Yer-Face' Theatre whose chief characteristics are sensation, challenge and a fascination with the forbidden.[41] By these means, it is able to tell us 'more about who we really are'.[42]

A similar approach was evident in the visual arts. The work of Damien Hirst (b. 1965) and Tracey Emin (b. 1963), for example, compel the viewer to confront ideas about, among other things, death and female sexuality. Advertising, too, was noted for its shock tactics. The Benetton group caused controversy in the 1990s with its adverts for clothing, one of which portrayed the deathbed scene of aids activist David Kirby. But the group defended its campaign by claiming that they were making people aware of social issues.

And the same argument can be used for Kane. *Blasted* does not have a plot so much as two parallel situations. Ian, a journalist, and Cate arrive at a hotel in Leeds. He is 45 and dying; she is 21 and suffers from epilepsy. He bullies her, demands sex and rapes her when she falls into one of her fits. Kane wanted to show 'the connection between a common rape in a Leeds hotel room and what was happening in Bosnia'[43] and so she creates a third character, the soldier who bullies and rapes Ian. The 'seeds of full-scale war', said Kane, 'can always be found in peacetime civilisation'.[44] One of the characteristics of this civilization is the way the media turns violence into a form of entertainment. Ian reports on 'shootings and rapes and kids getting fiddled by queer priests and schoolteachers'[45] and it is clearly implied that what matters in such stories is not tragedy but titillation. This desensitizes us to violence and its consequences one of which, as the case of Ian demonstrates when he rapes Cate, is to make us more likely to use it ourselves. Kane therefore wants to make us recognize the true horror of aggression and brutality and, if we recoil from her images, she has been successful.

Where, though, does sacrifice fit into this argument? Does *Blasted* have a sacrificial structure? The short answer is 'no'. One of the functions of sacrifice is to prevent the spread of violence in society by focusing it on a scapegoat. But there is no scapegoat in the play. The violence is all-pervasive. Another function of sacrifice is to narrate and regulate the relation between sex and death. But in *Blasted* they are fused together. Ian, for example, has a sexual climax on the word 'killer' while the soldier recounts, in sickening detail, his part in rape and killing. In one instance he knifes a woman between the legs and 'on the fifth stab snapped her spine'.[46] However, the absence of a scapegoat and the collapse of the distinction between sex and death do not necessarily mean that sacrifice is absent from *Blasted*. First, there are different ways of understanding sacrificial violence and, second, there are a number of sacrificial elements in the play.

Georges Bataille (1897–1963), whose various writings covered anthropology, economics, literature, philosophy and sociology, argued that the violence of sacrifice 'restores to the sacred world that which servile use has degraded, rendered profane'.[47] Simplifying greatly Bataille claims that, as society has developed, we have become alienated from nature and each other. The process of alienation involves two steps. The first is to separate all living creation into 'individuals' and the second is to turn these 'individuals' into objects that can be used. According to Bataille sacrifice redeems us, temporarily, from this condition. It returns us to what he calls the 'intimate' world, a world characterized by the absence of individuality, a world where everything is in direct communion with everything else. Bataille does not expand on what he means by 'intimacy', saying that it 'cannot be expressed discursively'.[48] He therefore resorts to a poetic idiom to give some sense of it. It is 'plenitude', the 'prodigious effervescence of life', and 'the profound immanence of all that is'.[49]

Seen in this light, sacrifice is essentially a protest against society where that term is understood as the realm of use – value. It is because society can only see things in terms of their use – value that it cannot tolerate waste. But sacrifice creates waste to the extent that it does not use a human or an animal for its intended purpose and it celebrates this waste as an example of nature's excess or bounty. Bataille suggests that madness is the best way to describe this process. 'I submit that madness itself gives a rarefied idea of the free subject, unsubordinated to the real order and occupied only with the present.'[50] Bataille is using 'madness' as an analogy for that state of ecstasy which can be found in the followers of Dionysus. It is a feeling of liberation, an immersion in the present moment and a sense of oneness with nature.

This admittedly very abbreviated account of Bataille's account of sacrifice throws some light on the violence in *Blasted*. We have argued that its excess has a moral purpose, namely to reawaken us to a knowledge of its true nature. But if we take Bataille as our guide then the torture, rape and mutilation in the play are a means of rejecting the values of a civilization that denies the exuberant, 'wonder-struck cry of life'.[51] Sacrifice is the negation of individuality and the affirmation of ecstatic communion. To put this another way, all the deaths in the play are really a sign of life because they signal a refusal of the death-in-life that society offers. By Bataille's reasoning, the excessive nature of violence in the play would be a celebration of the endless bounty of nature; the number of deaths moments of what he calls 'glorious consumption';[52] a demonstration of how much nature can afford to lose without ever being diminished. Bataille's theory may also account for the fusion of sex and death in *Blasted*. In negating individuality, sacrifice is abolishing the principle that one thing is different from another. It also regresses us to that intimate life in whose 'intense heat' all distinctions 'melt'.[53] The conflation of sex and death in *Blasted*, which seems so shocking may, in fact, be a symbol of some deep and indestructible life force, at least in Bataille's scheme.

The value of his ideas is that they give us a new perspective on sacrifice. It is not an exchange with the god and it is not a matter of scapegoating; rather it is a way of protesting against the limitations of civilization and it is also a symbol of the sublime creative power that resists rational description. Bataille's ideas parallel some of Freud's, though not on the subject of sacrifice. Bataille's claim that religion is 'the search for lost intimacy'[54] is a version of the Oedipus complex or the desire to recover the sense of oneness with the mother's body. His distinction between the instrumental and the intimate world is clearly based on Freud's distinction between the conscious and the unconscious mind and, finally, his notion that death is a form of liberation has close parallels with Freud's discussion of the death instinct. Bataille differs from Freud, however, in giving a profoundly existential sense of what is at stake in sacrifice. Whether he is right or wrong there is no denying that he is a highly provocative writer.

We said above that although *Blasted* does not have an obvious sacrificial structure, it does contain sacrificial elements some of which exist in a highly distorted form. For example the ritual murder that Ian reports and the atrocities that the soldier describes, such as cutting a woman's throat, hacking off her nose and ears before 'nail[ing] them to the front door'[55] are perversions of the spectacular nature of sacrificial violence since they lack the spiritual beliefs which justify – or at least rationalize – it. Similarly Ian's demand that gays, immigrants and sections of the working class should be killed[56] is a corruption of the sacrificial desire for cleansing. But there are other elements which evoke the culture of sacrifice directly. Cate's fits, for example, have parallels with Dionysian ecstasy because she temporarily loses herself just as she does when she masturbates. 'Feels like I am away for minutes or months sometimes, then I come back just where I was.'[57]

It is rain, however, which most directly conjures up the life-giving properties associated with sacrifice. Scene one ends with the sound of 'spring rain', scene two with the sound of 'summer rain', scene three with the sound of 'autumn rain', and scene four with the sound of 'heavy winter rain'. This may appear to reverse the usual chronology of sacrifice since it moves from life to death. But in the final scene, scene five, we have another shower of rain which falls on Ian just as he 'dies with relief'.[58] The rain revives him; it returns him to life. This miracle is quite at odds with the otherwise largely realistic nature of the play. It is also faintly reminiscent of the story of Dionysus. Ian can be seen, in part, as a secularized and badly degraded form of the god because of his excessive drinking, because he is mutilated – the soldier sucks out his eyeballs – and because he is resurrected.

Another aspect of sacrifice is the sharing of food which serves to strengthen the social bond. We see this at the end of *Blasted* when Cate returns with bread and sausage which she appears to have acquired in exchange for sex. After eating her fill she feeds the rest to Ian who responds with the last words of the play 'Thank you.' Prior to this moment food has acted as a source of division between Ian and Cate; he is a meat eater and she is a vegetarian, but here it brings them together. However, they are not completely united as Cate sits apart from Ian sucking her thumb, something she has done at various moments in the play. So although we have a sense of reconciliation, it is not an entirely satisfactory one. Moreover, questions remain not just about their relationship but also about the war raging outside – its causes and who the combatants are. Nevertheless, *Blasted* ends on a note of hope, albeit a fragile one.

The play also has strong links to the tradition of tragedy. It revisits the issue at the heart of the *Oresteia*, namely the destructiveness of revenge and how it must be replaced by the operation of the law. The soldier who has taken part in atrocities because of what happened to his girlfriend learns that nothing is to be gained by an eye for an eye: 'doing to them what they do to us, what good is that?'[59] When he blinds Ian, he is not doing anything that hasn't been done on stage before. Cornwell gouges out Gloucester's eyes in *King Lear*. There's another echo of *Lear* when Cate allows Ian to think he has committed suicide in order to bring home the point that 'It's wrong to kill yourself.'[60] This is very like the episode where Edgar makes Gloucester think he has jumped off a very tall cliff. What's more, we find the same questions about the nature of humans in *Blasted* as we do in Greek and Renaissance tragedy. Ian, blind, masturbating, defecating, and clutching the dead body of the soldier for comfort presents a stark image of humanity. Man was supposed to have been made in God's image but if, as Ian says, there is 'No God. No Father Christmas. No Fairies. No Narnia. No fucking nothing'[61] then what is he? Just appetite? Kane pulls back from that conclusion when she shows Cate reaching out to Ian. Even in the most brutal circumstances it is possible to act kindly.

Perhaps the most shocking moment in *Blasted* occurs when the starving Ian digs up a baby that Cate has buried under the floor and starts to eat it. A woman gave it to her, presumably so that it could be saved, but the child was too weak and died. This incident serves to illustrate what people will do when they are at their limit but it is also associated with sacrifice. In Greek mythology Cronus ate his own children to prevent them from overthrowing him. His action prevents new life from replacing the old. The death of the baby in *Blasted* has a similar function. It suggests that society is becoming incapable of renewing itself. The acceptance of violence as a form of entertainment, which leads to a greater tolerance of it, and the inability to see the connection between individual abuse and the atrocities committed by armies are important factors here. But again, in Greek mythology, the death of a child can also be a prelude to his or her resurrection. That is certainly the case with Dionysus. However, it is not the baby who returns to life in *Blasted*; it is Ian. His devouring infant flesh ensures that the old order will rot instead of being renewed.

Kane's allusions to the myth of Cronus and to the *Oresteia* suggest that she is reaching back to the very beginning of civilization and even beyond. As we argued in the chapter on Greek tragedy, Aeschylus' play can be regarded as one of the founding moments of Western civilization because it substitutes the blood feud for the law, an act which depends on the sacrifice of Clytemnestra. The myth of Cronus, plus others such as Atreus serving

Thyestes his own offspring which provides the backdrop to the *Oresteia*, may be based on the practice of child sacrifice. This was not common in the ancient world, but nor was it unusual. One possible reason for such an horrific act was that the gods, being offered brand new life, would offer the same in return. The story of Iphigenia, whom the goddess Artemis substitutes for a deer as she is about to be sacrificed by her father Agamemnon, may be a reference to the moment when the Greeks abandoned human for animal sacrifice.

Be that as it may, the point to emphasize is that Kane seems to be going back to the very roots of sacrifice in an attempt to revive what appears in Beckett to be an exhausted tradition. Beckett's *Endgame* (1957) seems to have been one of the influences on *Blasted*. Cate and Ian are like Hamm and Clov in *Endgame* to the extent that they are more or less confined to one room, they each have something wrong with them, their relationship is a struggle for power and there is an acknowledgement of the non-existence of God. Moreover, just as we are unclear in *Endgame* as to why the characters are there and what has happened outside their room so, in *Blasted*, we don't know what the war outside the hotel room is about. Finally, both plays have a pronounced apocalyptic tone, a sense that things are coming to an end. But *Blasted* differs from *Endgame* in having an actual as opposed to a symbolic setting and in raising political rather than metaphysical issues. Perhaps the biggest difference between the two playwrights is that Beckett is caught in the ruins of sacrifice and can neither move forward nor back whereas Kane revisits the spectacular nature of sacrificial violence though to what end is debatable. One thing is certain and that is that sacrifice, in one form or another, shapes the thinking of both. A return to Greek myth is also a feature of *A Streetcar Named Desire*, the play to which we turn now.

Tennessee Williams (1911–1983), *A Streetcar Named Desire* (1947)

Blanche Dubois comes to New Orleans to stay with her sister Stella who is married to Stanley. There is a great deal of tension between the husband and sister-in-law which culminates in him raping her on the night Stella is in hospital giving birth to their child. The play ends with Blanche, whose nervous disposition has been emphasized throughout, being removed to a mental hospital. This bald summary hardly does justice to *A Streetcar Named Desire*, one of the greatest plays of the twentieth century. It fuses together the two main trends of the thirties and the forties in American drama, the social problem play and the psychological play. *Streetcar* is related to the first because it raises such issues as domestic violence and it is related to the second because we see in detail why Blanche behaves the way she does. The play also contains expressionist flourishes as when lurid reflections appear on the wall shortly before Blanche is raped. Its themes include the nature of post-war America, the changing face of the South, the power of sex, prejudice and mental breakdown.

But our interest is in how the play relates to tragedy and whether or not it has a sacrificial structure. Blanche is a tragic heroine to the extent that she is high born – she hails from Southern aristocracy – and has a flaw that contributes to her downfall. This flaw is her desire for 'magic'[62] rather than realism, an attitude which is symbolized by her putting paper lanterns over light bulbs.[63] Whether this weakness is the result of her guilt at her husband's suicide or whether it is part of her temperament – Stella says Blanche was 'always flighty'[64] – is a moot point. But Williams certainly conjures up an air of tragic inevitability by using images which anticipate Stanley raping Blanche such as his rifling through her suitcase.[65] Blanche differs from the protagonists of classical and Renaissance tragedy by not arriving at self-knowledge through her suffering. She may claim that the value of suffering is that it 'makes for sincerity',[66] but this is hard to reconcile with the fact that she lies about her age and her past.

Looking at *Streetcar* in terms of sacrifice – which underpins tragedy – then other matters come into focus. Blanche Dubois, for example, means 'white woods' like 'an orchard in spring'.[67] Her very name, therefore, connects the play with the issue of fertility. And yet Blanche is also the 'evil' that must be expelled. Stanley sees her as a threat to his marriage to Stella. He tells her that 'it's going to be all right after [Blanche] goes' and that everything is going to go back to 'the way it was'.[68] If Blanche poses a danger to marriage then she also poses a danger to society, since marriage is its foundation. Certainly the good citizens of Laurel see her as threat to the social order. She is forced to leave their community for working as a prostitute in various hotels and for abusing her position as a teacher by seducing a seventeen-year-old boy,[69] a story that is given credence by Blanche's advances to The Young Man at the end of scene five.

The tale also carries a faint Oedipal suggestion given that Blanche is the older woman and incest was the original evil that had to be avoided or removed if the land was to thrive. However, Blanche's desire for young men has much more immediate explanation: namely that she is trying to recreate, through her relationship with them, her marriage to her husband and for him to find her sexually attractive which, being gay, he didn't. Despite this obvious psychological explanation it is also the case that Blanche belongs to that tradition which makes women the scapegoat for society's anxieties about sexuality. It goes right back to the *Oresteia* and the murder of Clytemnestra. As we saw in the chapter on Greek theatre, her death precipitated civilization into existence. But Blanche is not so much the enemy of civilization as the advocate of some of its best qualities. Art, she tells Stella, has nurtured tender feelings 'that we have got to make grow! And *cling* to and hold as our flag! In this dark march towards whatever it is we are approaching'.[70]

If anyone is the enemy of civilization – defined as progress, enlightenment and perhaps kindness to strangers – it is the brutish Stanley. Nevertheless, it is Blanche who is cast out. This introduces a new view of sacrifice. Here the removal of the scapegoat does not lead to the safety or renewal of society but to its surrender to instinct or to the 'ape', the 'animal'.[71] With Blanche go those aspects of civilization for which we use the word culture – art, literature, music, philosophy – and without which it would be the poorer. The purpose of culture – or what we might call symbolic thought – is, in a very general sense, to give meaning and significance to human experience. Sacrifice is an example of symbolic thought in that it gives shape, depth, purpose and value to the instincts of life and death. But Blanche's mental breakdown, and her expulsion from the ironically named Elysian Fields, indicate that the principle of symbolic thought is in crisis. And not just the principle of symbolic thought but, arguably, the very basis of the social itself: namely the process of mutual recognition on which human interaction depends. Without the ability to acknowledge others, to accept that they have needs or to enter in a relationship with them, society simply cannot exist. Blanche is the only character in the play to understand that, to realize that without others we have no sense of ourselves, 'you've got to have your existence admitted by someone', she tells Stella.[72] When she goes, so too, in a way, does the very possibility of sociability.

The curtailment of symbolic thought affects the portrayal of desire. Sacrifice makes desire an integral part of society celebrating it as a means of regeneration, a connection with others, a communion with nature and contact with the gods. But the rejection of symbolic thought, or culture, causes desire to regress to mere instinct. Stanley is the most obvious example here. Blanche describes him as a 'survivor of the stone age'.[73] His sexuality is simply another manifestation of his habit of 'always smash[ing] things'.[74] He pulled Stella off the columns of Belle Reve[75] and raped Blanche. His sexual demands trump all other considerations. Stella, for example, excuses Stanley's ill-treatment of her by saying that what happens between a man and a woman in the dark 'sort of make[s] everything else unimportant'.[76]

The destructive nature of Stanley's desire is the very opposite of the creative nature of desire in sacrifice. Ritual slaughter distinguishes very carefully between life and death and seeks a balanced relationship between them. But, in *Streetcar*, they are conflated. Stanley may appear to be a powerful symbol of vitality but he lives in the land of the dead. Elysian Fields is the name of a real street in New Orleans. In Greek mythology, however, it denotes the abode of souls. At first it was reserved for relatives of the gods but later heroes and the righteous were admitted. Stanley is none of these. So not only does Elysian Fields reinforce the convergence of desire and death, it also serves to critique Stanley's much-emphasized manliness by implicitly contrasting it with the courage and nobility of the ancients.

Stanley is driven by desire and so too is Blanche. For Stanley desire is a form of self-assertion but, for Blanche, it is more complicated. At one level she needs to prove her appeal because her husband did not desire her; at another she is trying to recreate what she should have had in her marriage and, at still another, she is compelled to use sex to gain the protection of men because they 'don't even admit your existence unless they are making love to you'.[77] But Blanche's desire, like Stanley's, has a death-like quality. We have already noted its faintly incestuous nature but it is also associated with 'that rattle-trap street-car that bangs through the Quarter, up one street and down another'.[78] In other words desire is in danger of becoming mechanistic, repetitive and completely divorced from ideas of growth and renewal.

This may reflect the change, partly charted by *Streetcar*, from an agricultural way of life identified with Belle Reve and the Old South to the more industrial way of life found in New Orleans.[79] Desire in agricultural society is based on the rhythms of nature and its characteristic form of expression is ritual. Desire in industrial society is based on the rhythms of the machine and its characteristic form of expression is repetition. We noted a similar shift from ritual to repetition in *Waiting for Godot*. In both cases there is a breakdown in the symbolic system that orders the relations of life and death with the result that the two become confused with one another.

There are no references to sacrifice in *Streetcar*, but its characteristic concerns erupt in the horrific rape scene, which has strong parallels with the myth of Philomena. She too went to visit her sister and she too was raped by her sister's husband, Tereus. He made sure Philomela could never tell of the crime by cutting out her tongue. Stanley does not go that far but he has so traumatized Blanche that she can barely communicate with others. Like Blanche's, Philomela's name, 'lover of fruit', instantly conjures up images of fertility. The myth also has connections with Dionysus. Philomela, for example, is rescued by her sister, Procne, from the prison in which Tereus has incarcerated her during the triennial celebrations of Dionysus. What's more the two women escape dressed as followers of the god. Stella is not like Procne. She refuses to believe that her husband has raped her sister and, far from rescuing her, is actually responsible for her confinement, though she is greatly upset when she realizes what she has done. 'What have I done to my sister? Oh God what have I done to my sister?'[80] But this difference does not in any way diminish the significance of the myth for *Streetcar* which is to highlight the negative effect of rape on fertility.

Rape, in fact, is a form of perverse sacrifice. Stanley does not kill Blanche but he annihilates her subjectivity. He can therefore be said to kill her metaphorically. The rape also contains elements of spectacle, which suggest rather than portray the act. These include Stanley's brilliant silk pyjamas, Blanche's tiara, the menacing shapes on the wall, the inhuman voices and the sound of the 'blue piano' which gets louder and louder eventually turning into 'the roar of an approaching locomotive'.[81] The fundamental use of violence in sacrifice is to create life but the rape of

Philomela results in death. Procne kills Itys, the son she had by Tereus, in revenge for what he had done to her sister.

Stella does not commit infanticide but neither does she seem consumed by motherly love. She is not even with her newborn baby who is upstairs with a neighbour, Eunice. While her remark 'How is my baby?'[82] may be construed as an indication of maternal anxiety, it also hints at how the child has to be kept out of the way – that he or she is not part of life in the Kowalski household. Stella barely seems to notice when Eunice later places the child in her arms. And Stanley is positively oblivious of his offspring. He doesn't acknowledge the child when he goes to comfort the sobbing Stella after Blanche's departure. And his method of dealing with her grief is to 'find the opening of her blouse'[83] reaching for the breast that is the baby's source of comfort and nourishment.

But perhaps the most important point about Stella's baby is that he or she is born on the night of the rape. It is a brutal and unsettling juxtaposition. One which, at some level, invites us to make a connection between the two events. Which would mean the child sprang directly from the rape without the proper period of gestation. This makes the child seem unnatural as does the fact that it has no gender. We do not know if it is a boy or girl. As such the child can never be part of the process of regeneration; it can only stand as a symbol for the death of sexuality. While this may be overstating the case there can be no doubt that the child is hardly a convincing or reassuring harbinger of new life. In appropriating the elements of sacrifice, such as spectacle, violence and new birth, rape has put life where death should be and death where life should be.

Although there are similarities between *Streetcar* and the myth of Philomena, there are also differences. The major one is that while the play offers no consolations the myth, as befits its roots in sacrifice, ends on an upbeat note. Philomena's suffering replicates that of the god because she too suffers a ritualistic dismemberment. And just as the death of the god leads to new life so do Philomena's torments result in her transfiguration. She becomes a nightingale, a symbol of beauty and poetic creativity. But there is no such comfort at the end of *Streetcar*. Blanche who, like Philomena, represents the arts and culture, is shepherded away to an asylum. Her removal leaves Elysian Fields a darker place – Blanche only covers light bulbs, Stanley smashes them. Instinctual brutishness triumphs over empathy and imagination. The very thing that should, perhaps, be removed, is the very thing that is strengthened.

Does this mean that the mechanism of the scapegoat has also ceased to function properly? We have seen that the symbolic system of sacrifice, the means by which life and death are ordered, has failed but the role of the scapegoat appears to be intact because Blanche is expelled from the community. One reason for her removal was her wayward sexuality but this also applies to Stanley. He is not faithful to Stella when he rapes her sister. Blanche is also cast out because she is a liar and a fantasist yet her departure makes no difference to the fact that other characters connive in untruths. Stella, for example, refuses to believe that Stanley raped Blanche for to do so would mean she couldn't go on living with him.[84] This seems to suggest that the function of the scapegoat is not to expel evil from society only to give the appearance of doing so. In other words evil, or even simple wrongdoing, are not really threats to society, they are rather an essential part of it. But that is a truth which must never be acknowledged. The value of the scapegoat may be that it sustains the illusion that we know the difference between right and wrong and act accordingly when the reality could not be more different. Sacrifice protects us from knowing ourselves too well. Its various problems are also evident in *Top Dog/Under Dog* which won the Pulitzer Prize for Drama in 2002, a half century after Williams won it with *Streetcar*.

Suzan-Lori Parks (b. 1963), *Top Dog/Under Dog* (2001)

Top Dog/Under Dog is about the relationship between two black brothers, Booth and Lincoln. They are named after John Wilkes Booth (1838–1865) and Abraham Lincoln (1809–1865). Booth assassinated Lincoln on the 14th of April 1865 at Ford's Theatre during a performance of *Our American Cousin* (1858). Their father gave the brothers their names as 'a joke'[85] but it is more of an invitation for history to repeat itself, which it does – but this time as farce rather than tragedy. Booth shoots Lincoln, not because he believed in a cause – John Wilkes Booth believed in the independence of the Southern States – but because he lost to him in a game of 3-Card Monte in which a person has to guess which is the red card among two black ones or vice versa.

Top Dog/Under Dog's historical references are obviously important. The shooting of Lincoln is a key moment in black history. The play invites the audience to make links between this history and the poverty endured by blacks in contemporary America. Lincoln lives with Booth in a single room with no toilet and no sink. They survive on Lincoln's wages but his job – pretending to be assassinated as Abraham Lincoln – is under threat 'They're talking about cutbacks at the arcade'[86] and he also has to accept lower wages than a white person.[87] After covering all their outgoings each week – rent, food and so on – the brothers have forty-four dollars and thirty cents left for spending.[88]

Although their straitened circumstances are an important factor in how they live, the focus is not so much on the brothers' privations as on their identity. The concern with identity was one of the staple themes of tragedy. Who are we? Where do humans stand in relation to the cosmos? Booth and Lincoln do not put the question of their identity in such grandiose terms. For them, it is bound up with 3-Card Monte. Their sense of self depends on the recognition they receive for their manual dexterity with the cards. Booth wants to change his name to '3-Card'.[89] He also wants to be as good if not better than his brother at the game. Lincoln is only himself when he plays it. 'I was the be all and end all. I was throwing cards like throwing cards was made for me. Made for me and me alone.'[90] He stopped playing when his friend Lonny was shot[91] but when he loses his job he returns to the game and his identity is restored. 'Link', he says to himself, 'you got it back you got yr shit back in thuh saddle, man...Walking in Lucky's you seen how they was looking at you.'[92]

The 3-Card Monte is a form of theatre. It requires a cast of players, the dealer who must 'act like he don't wanna play',[93] the 'stickman', who pretends to be a customer, the sidemen who keep an eye out for the police, and a paying audience. There is a rough script which always begins with an invitation to watch the cards closely and props consisting of cards and a table. Finally the game poses questions about what is and isn't real since it involves illusion. When Lincoln tells Booth he is 'doing it for real', Booth can only respond that it 'didn't feel real'.[94] The 3-Card Monte suggests that identity is neither certain nor substantial, a notion which is familiar from the history of tragedy and indeed comedy where it most often arises in situations involving disguise. The laughter of comedy makes palatable a truth of tragedy – that there is no authentic self, only a performing one.

The question of identity in the play is also bound up with another persistent motif of tragedy, the Oedipus complex. The same feelings of ambiguity that characterize a son's relation to his father are present in the relation between the two brothers. On the one hand Booth loves Lincoln and models himself on him; on the other hand he feels not just competitive but also quite hostile towards him. This is partly because he believes that Lincoln has not been a father to him in the sense of taking care of him. 'I told her that I was the little brother and the big brother should look out after the little brother.'[95] Another aspect of the Oedipus complex, according to Freud, is the child's desire to occupy the father's place with the mother. This is reflected in Booth sleeping with Lincoln's wife. 'I had her. Yr damn wife. Right in that bed.'[96]

Top Dog/Under Dog also touches on another topic in tragedy: the question of whether or not we have free will. Here again the symbol of cards is important. Parks picks up on a discussion in *Streetcar* about whether winning at cards is a matter of luck or judgement. For Stanley 'luck is believing you are lucky'.[97] In other words if you have confidence in yourself, you will be a winner. Lincoln's view is slightly different since he emphasizes application and expertise rather than just belief. 'Ain't nothing lucky about cards. Cards ain't luck. Cards is work. Cards is skill.'[98] Nevertheless, both he and Stanley take one of the great symbols of chance, the deck of cards, to show that modern humans, thanks in part to the scientific revolution, have more control over their lives than had their predecessors. There's now no need to look at the heavens to see what will happen in human affairs.

Set against this, however, is the strong sense of inevitability in the play. Booth's killing of Lincoln seems unavoidable partly because of the historical precedent of the assassination of President Lincoln and partly because of the recurrent references to guns.[99] But this tension between the designs of the gods and self-determination has always been central to tragedy.

Top Dog/Under Dog doesn't just engage with the key themes of tragedy in a general way. It also echoes specific plays in that tradition. Park's play is set in one room as are *Endgame* and *Blasted*. It focuses on the power struggle between two flawed males as does *Waiting for Godot* and *Endgame* and there is also a power struggle between Ian and Cate in *Blasted*. Booth waits for his girlfriend Grace whose name, like that of Godot, suggests the possibility of salvation. She, like Godot, promises to appear but never does. The language of Top Dog/Under Dog has the same demotic quality as that of *Blasted* – 'one motherfucker shit'[100] – and in both plays there is a sense of history impinging itself on the characters.

Of course there are huge differences between these plays but they are all, in one way or another, groping for a new idiom in the wake of tragedy's decline, one that will have sufficient magnitude to encompass suffering and death. But the demise of tragedy, either as a genre or indeed as a philosophy, need not entail the disappearance of the sacrificial structure of plays. Elements of it, such as death, spectacle, cleansing and sexual licence, are evident in Top Dog/Under Dog, but they exist in isolation from one another. Once again we are picking our way through the ruins.

There are two deaths in the play: those of Lincoln and Grace. Neither fulfils the sacrificial function of cleansing or the creation of new life. In the first place it is difficult to know what it is that requires 'cleansing'. The focus of the play is more on the relationship between the two brothers than on their relationship with the wider society and so, if the term 'cleansing' is applicable at all, it is to their psychological condition rather than the social order. And the spotlight falls mostly on Booth's mental state. We have already noted that he has a somewhat Oedipal relation to Lincoln whom he regards as a failed father figure. This relation is evident again just before Booth kills Lincoln. His mother gave him five hundred dollars wrapped up in a stocking before abandoning him. He bets this on his being able to detect the right card in 3-Card Monte but Lincoln is too quick for him and he loses.

Booth is particularly agitated when Lincoln tries to untie the stocking to check the money. 'Oh don't, open it, man ... You won it man, you dont gotta go opening it.'[101] His anxiety is out of all proportion to Lincoln's proposed action. It appears to spring from his intense feelings for his mother. Booth regards the money as proof of his mother's love for him. To verify whether she actually did give him that amount is to admit the possibility that she may not have loved him. If Lincoln unpicks the knot in the stocking Booth may have to face the fact that his mother deceived him and that is not something he can cope with. Nor can he handle Lincoln using a knife when the knot proves too difficult to undo. It is as if Lincoln has wrenched their mother away from Booth and is now about to penetrate her.

That proves the tipping point and Booth shoots him though not before telling him that he had killed Grace who appears to function as a substitute mother. She is absent like the mother, Booth idealizes her like his mother, he excuses her like his mother and she abandons him like his mother.[102] In killing her, he vents the aggression he feels towards his mother which makes it all the more important that the one symbol he has of her, the knotted stocking, remains inviolable. The complexity of Booth's feelings towards his mother strengthens rather than weaken the claim that he has an Oedipal relation with her or at least the image he has of her. When Lincoln tries to take the symbol of the mother away from him and insert the phallic symbol of the knife into it Booth guns him down.

We said that Kane particularly reaches back to the roots of sacrifice. Parks does something even more radical. She returns us to the ghostly scene of the murder of the primal father. It was this, said Freud, which led to the institution of sacrifice both as a re-enactment and a restitution for the deed. Freud also claimed that entry into society depended on the successful resolution of the Oedipus complex. Booth is certainly trying to enter society in the sense that he wants to change his name and be accepted as an expert at 3-Card Monte. But, as the last scene shows, he will never be as good as his brother. He therefore remains at the Oedipal stage, killing Lincoln his father figure and reclaiming his mother in the form of the money and the stocking. Booth, in short, cannot escape his psychological past any more than he can his historical past. He is doubly conditioned to shoot Lincoln first because of his Oedipal desires and second because of his name.

Spectacle has several functions in sacrifice: it gives meaning to death, it dramatizes the relations between humans and the gods and it is a display of priestly power. But what happens over the centuries is that spectacle and sacrifice begin to separate. This is evident as early as the Roman Games but the process gathers pace with the arrival of the secular society. One of the consequences of this development is that while spectacle remains key to the representation of death in popular culture it lacks the symbolism to give it meaning, at least a religious one. In *Top Dog/Under Dog*, however, there is a divorce between spectacle and death.

The spectacle of Lincoln's death occurs in scene 3 where Booth encourages Lincoln to die in what he believes is a more convincing fashion for the benefit of visitors to the arcade. He suggests that he screams and thrashes about on the floor but Lincoln worries that if his acting looks too realistic he will get the sack. Lincoln's 'actual' death is entirely free of spectacle. Booth puts a bullet in his neck and Lincoln slumps to the floor. The contrast between the two is similar to the one Kane establishes in *Blasted* between the media depiction of violence and its reality.

The degradation of spectacle, its ability to deprive death of meaning while still making it visually imposing, is illustrated in Lincoln's job which is to sit in an arcade while everyone from children to businessmen pretends to shoot him. This is, as we have said, a re-enactment of the assassination of President Lincoln. Now it's time to add that Lincoln's assassination was seen as a sacrifice, especially as it took place on Good Friday, the day of Christ's crucifixion.[103] In the words of one commentator, 'He had died for the American sin of slavery, a sacrifice for national resurrection; as in Leviticus, he had proclaimed liberty throughout the land, leading "all the inhabitants thereof" from bondage into the promised land of freedom.'[104] President's Lincoln's sacrifice, in other words, has become a game in an amusement park. His death, which ushered in a new America, has dwindled into a moment's entertainment, a passing diversion.

It's not only sacrifice that has degenerated in *Top Dog/Under Dog*, so too has sexuality. One of the functions of sacrifice is to regulate the relation between sexuality and death. The two are intimately connected. According to Freud the instincts of sex and death are similar to the extent that each, in its own way, aims to reduce the amount of a tension in an organism by returning it to an earlier state of things. The sex instinct does this by seeking restoration of oneness with the mother, the death instinct by seeking a return to inanimate nature. But the two instincts are also different. The sex instinct aims to prolong life, the death instinct to shorten it and the two do battle within the individual.[105] In this play, however, they are simply regarded as being each other's equivalent. Booth says that if he doesn't have 'sexual release' he will be 'shooting people and shit'.[106]

In addition to being conflated with death, sex is also seen as masturbatory and voyeuristic. Booth has a stack of girlie magazines which he tries to hide under his bed. His sex life, despite what he says about Grace,[107] seems to be more fantasy than fact. Both brothers watched their parents having sex but not with each other. Booth saw his mother having sex with her lover and the two are in collusion about keeping the adultery a secret. The five hundred dollars, indeed, appears to have been payment for his silence.[108] Lincoln watched his father have sex with a variety of women. 'He made it seem like it was this big deal this great thing he was letting me witness but it wasn't like nothing.'[109] He also, in another manifestation of Oedipal desire in the play, had sex with one of his father's 'ladies' while his father lay beside them, 'sleeping and snoring'.[110] The promiscuous nature of the parent's sexuality is repeated in their sons. Each brother flouted the principle of fidelity, Booth with Grace and Lincoln with Cookie.[111]

The ritual of sacrifice created a space where the traditional norms governing sexual behaviour were temporarily suspended. This served, among other things, to siphon off excess energies that might otherwise prove disruptive to the social order. But in this play these energies are simply the symptom of a warped upbringing whose adulterous consequences undermine marriage which, in the tradition of tragedy and particularly comedy, is portrayed as the very foundation of society. The antisocial and death-like nature of sexuality in *Top Dog/Under Dog* is further underlined by the absence of women, a feature it shares with *Waiting for Godot*. Parks does not highlight infertility in the way that Beckett does with the symbol of the tree but she certainly hints at it with the reference to Lincoln 'shooting blanks' and with the mention of Grace's apparent plan to have a baby coming to nothing.[112]

The play, then, contains some of the typical elements of sacrifice: death, spectacle and sexuality but they are in disarray. Moreover this is the first play in which we do not have a scapegoat, someone whose removal rejuvenates society. Instead we have the story of one brother killing another. But even this is related to sacrifice if we take into account ancient stories of fratricide such as Cain and Abel. Cain kills his brother because God accepted Abel's sacrifice of 'the firstlings of his flock' but not Cain's of 'the fruit of the ground'.[113] Then there is the ancient Egyptian tale of 'Two Brothers', Anpu and Bata, a fertility myth that has parallels with the story of Dionysus. One of the brothers, for example, slices off his genitals and cuts out his heart but he is restored to life – several times in fact – before eventually becoming Pharaoh. The key point for our purpose, though, is that while sacrificial elements are clearly present in *Top Dog/Under Dog*, none of them seem to work.

This is evident partly from the problematic presentation of death and the parlous state of sexuality but mostly from the idea that history repeats itself: Booth must always shoot Lincoln. One of the functions of sacrifice, as we noted in the discussion of *Waiting for Godot*, is to regulate the relation between past, present and future. If there is no scapegoat to cleanse society of its problems then they will only recur. Grace is the one character who seems able to offer redemption: 'she wiped her hand over the past'.[114] She is often referred to as 'Amazing Grace',[115] a clear reference to the famous hymn of the same name written by the English clergyman John Newton (1725–1807). Its message is that anyone can be saved providing they believe, but Booth symbolically rejects that offer of salvation when he kills Grace. There is, in other words, a working model of sacrifice in the play – Christ's death on the cross – but the characters, particularly Booth, choose to discard it.

But 'Amazing Grace' isn't just signifier of Christianity. The hymn also figures in African-American identity. Its author was, even for a time after his conversion, captain of a slave ship. Despite that the hymn became a classic of African-American spirituals which developed in response to slavery. It should be remembered, though, that slaves were forced to convert to Christianity so 'Amazing Grace' is also a sign of their oppression. This provides an additional context for understanding Booth's attitude to Grace. It can now also be seen as an opening into the traumas of black history and the strategies they developed to cope with it. Religious services were, perhaps, the only places that slaves could gather and express themselves but, at the same time, their feelings and grievances had to be filtered through an essentially alien religion which, moreover, promoted only one of a number of the responses to suffering found in tragedy, namely resignation.

Quite how all this impacts on Booth's relationship with Grace is too big a topic to be entered into here. But it is a reminder that *Top Dog/Under Dog*, like the other plays we have discussed, has many layers. The question, as always, is how to reconcile the workings of sacrifice with the portrayal of social and historical issues. One way is to emphasize that sacrifice is a mode of thinking about these very matters since they are often depicted in terms of spectacle and sexuality whose malfunctions we have charted in Parks' play. But sacrifice is not just a means of representing problems; it's also a technique for dealing with them. The scapegoat, for example, is a simple way in which a society can rid itself of its various ills. But what happens when there is no scapegoat, as is the case here? What we seem to be left with is an impasse. It's as if drama cannot think beyond its sacrificial mindset, even though that mindset is cracked.

We have seen from our account of the above 'tragedies' that sacrifice remains a key element even if it only functions in a spasmodic fashion. The same is true of comedy though its generic status remains more intact than that of tragedy. But this does not means it is without problems as we shall see in the discussion of Charlotte Jones' *Humble Boy*.

Charlotte Jones (b. 1968), *Humble Boy* (2001)

Humble Boy is largely based on *Hamlet*. Felix Humble arrives home for his father's funeral from Cambridge, where he is a research fellow in theoretical astrophysics. He is upset because his mother, Flora, is about to be married to a widower, George Pye. He is shocked to learn not only that their affair has been going on for years but also that his father, Jim, knew about it.[116] Felix had a not very satisfactory relationship with George's daughter, Rosie, and discovers that he is the father of her daughter, Felicity. There is also a character called Mercy Lott, a spinster, who tries to keep the peace whenever conflict breaks out. She is teased by George, on whom she has a crush, and despised by Flora.[117] The first half of the play builds up to the meal to announce Flora and George's engagement. It goes horribly wrong, and the second half of the play portrays the aftermath.

Felix is very like Hamlet. He is a scholar, he dotes on his mother, he cannot sustain a relationship with a woman his age, he has thoughts of suicide and he is in his thirties and overweight. He even sounds like Hamlet at times. His observation that 'just because you can't see something doesn't mean that it isn't there'[118] echoes Hamlet's 'There are more things in heaven and earth, Horatio, than are dreamt of in your philosophy.'[119] More importantly, Felix, like the prince, encounters the ghost of his father. Jim kept bees as a hobby and there is a constant riff on the various meanings of 'be' throughout the play. All allude, in one form or another, to Hamlet's famous speech that begins 'To be or not to be'.[120] Felix is not as eloquent as the prince, he stutters on words beginning with 'b' but, like him, he needs 'to make a decision about what I should do next'.[121] Rosie offers him one option: getting to know his daughter. 'Don't you realise... I am offering you a chance to be. Just to be.'[122] This is in contrast to Felix's usual state of fretting about astrophysics and his relation to his parents.

George as Claudius and Flora as Gertrude depart more from their originals more than Felix does. George is a buffoon not a villain, and Flora is certainly more vain than Gertrude. Also it is hard to imagine Felix berating his mother for her lovemaking as Hamlet does his[123] since Flora seems strangely passionless. 'Please don't get ardent, George,' she tells her enthusiastic suitor, 'It's only half past twelve.'[124] Rosie loves Felix as Ophelia loves Hamlet but she is not as obliging as her Shakespearean counterpart. 'What did you expect me to do after you left me?' she asks in a clear allusion to Hamlet's famous dismissal of Ophelia, 'Hie myself to a nunnery?'[125] Far from being the vengeful ghost of Hamlet's father, Jim is a gentle spirit who tends the garden, has conversations with his son about bees and flowers and restores Flora to herself by reminding her of the first time they met. Finally there's Mercy. Although nothing like as pompous or verbose as Polonius she is equally officious and ineffectual. She is impatiently dismissed by Flora when she is trying to keep the peace between mother and son. 'Oh please go in Mercy... Wreak havoc with some potted shrimp for Christ's sake.'[126]

What is the purpose of these borrowings? Partly it is to show that stories from the past continue to be relevant in the present. This is a small illustration of one of the arguments of this book: that it is possible for a particular mindset, namely sacrifice, to persist over a long period of time. But chiefly the presence of *Hamlet* in *Humble Boy* serves to make us think about the relation between tragedy and comedy, especially in an age where tragedy, as a genre, has more or less vanished. The distinction between the two crops up when Felix and Flora are discussing Jim's death. Felix is determined to see it as a tragedy because he thinks his father, who was working alone in the garden, could have been saved if his mother had not been in the house convalescing from a nose job, the latest manifestation in his view, of her vanity, and part of her increasingly absurd efforts to recapture her lost youth.[127] But Flora is having none of it. She takes an almost vicious delight in telling Felix that his father did not die from a heart attack but from being stung by one of his beloved bees. Mercy echoes Felix in saying that it was a tragedy but she is sharply reproved by Flora. 'No. It was not a tragedy. Sad and pathetic and shockingly stupid, ironic, funny even, yes, comical, hilarious but not a tragedy.'[128]

This little exchange is important because it shows that the labels 'tragedy' and 'comedy' have become somewhat indeterminate. Nevertheless, they are still used in framing a response to death: a reminder, perhaps, of the origins of tragedy and comedy in sacrifice and of the need to make sense of our mortality. The description of Jim's death as a tragedy changes when we learn that he did not die from a heart attack but from a bee sting. Oscar Wilde, in 'The Ballad of Reading Gaol' (1898) wrote that 'each man kills the thing he loves'.[129] In Jim's case it seems that the thing he loved killed him. Either way it is a small reminder of the connection between love and death.

But what needs to be emphasized here are the different ways in which his death is viewed as this illustrates how, in our secular society, we are no longer certain about how to approach the subject of mortality. In all the major faiths, death is held to be a doorway from one order existence to another. But such beliefs are likely to be greeted with scepticism in our postmodern culture where death, like everything else, has become relative. Tragedy in particular, with its roots in ritual, helped to bolster the existential gravitas death had in religion but, as it moves ever further away from its origins in sacrifice, the most it can do is lend death an aesthetic identity.

We said that tragedy – as a genre – has almost disappeared from contemporary society but Flora's remark suggests that comedy too is beginning to disintegrate. How best to describe it when there are so many types of humour: 'ironic, funny…comical, hilarious'? Certainly *Humble Boy* does not conform to the conventions of New Comedy. If anything it reverses them. It's not the young couple trying to overcome obstacles in order to be together, but the old ones. Flora particularly must win her son round to the idea that she would like to marry again. But, thanks to Felix's objections and to the fact that Jim discovered a new species of bumblebee and named it after her, she decides there can be no wedding after all. At this moment Flora resembles a tragic heroine, one who has arrived at self-knowledge – 'To want things has always been my gravest error'[130] – and who now accepts her fate of growing old and being on her own with graceful resignation.

A much darker interpretation of Flora's rejection of George is that it marks the triumph of incest in the play, which arises largely from its debt to *Hamlet*. Felix, no less than the prince, is fixated on his mother whom he believes has never loved him. 'You don't love me mother.'[131] He has a recurrent dream about her placing him on the lawn where he feels 'complete'.[132] A difference from *Hamlet* is that Felix tells Rosie that it was his mother he was close to, not his father. He describes his relationship to them in terms of the laws of physics. 'It's like my mother was the big force – gently wrapping everything around her. And my father was the little force, fizzing away on the microscopic level.'[133] Here, the language of science is used to connect human beings to the operations of cosmos in the way that religion used to do.

Hamlet's idealization of his father[134] masks his fear that he can never be like him: the prince is a scholar not a warrior. Felix does not seem to be intimidated by his father but Jim does represent, albeit faintly, the threat of castration. He tells his son about the queen bee who flies away with the 'torn-off genitals [of the drones] still inside her',[135] an image that also resonates with those anxieties about female sexuality which hover around sacrifice. The ghost of Jim revives the mixed feelings Felix had for his father in relation to his feelings for his mother. Felix's defence of his father against his mother's criticism, wearing his father's suit at the party and his outrage on his father's behalf when he learns of his mother's adultery,[136] can all be read as atonements for his fear and possible hostility towards him when he was alive.[137] Finally, just as Hamlet is angry with Claudius so is Felix with George, as when he mocks him for confusing astrology with astronomy.[138]

The Oedipal streak in the play becomes even more evident when we consider that the thrust of the drama is to remove from the stage everyone who is not a member of the Humble family. Mercy runs away when she realizes that she has used Jim's ashes to season the soup, Rosie has to get back to Felicity and George is chased off by a bee. These various disappearances serve to eliminate all the obstacles to Felix being alone with his mother. It is true that Felix says he will return to Cambridge but our last sight of him is standing uncertainly in the garden. Will he accept Flora's invitation to leave in the morning or will he go now, or even at all? One reason for drawing attention to the Oedipal subtext is to emphasize how *Humble Boy* subverts the comic tradition. It does not end in marriage, it promotes an acceptance of death rather than life and it gives expression to the theme of incest which, since at least Sophocles' *Oedipus Rex*, has been a curse on fertility.

Hamlet is not the only Shakespeare play haunting *Humble Boy*. The humour of Felix's line 'Exit pursued by a bee'[139] is partly dependent on the audience knowing the most famous stage direction in *The Winter's Tale* (1623): 'Exit pursued by a bear'.[140] That play's themes of forgiveness and reconciliation are central to *Humble Boy* as are its explorations of the relation between art and life. The two come together in the final scene of Shakespeare's play when the 'statue' of Hermione 'miraculously' comes to life and forgives her husband, Leontes, for having wrongly accused her of adultery sixteen years earlier. Similarly, in the final scene of *Humble Boy* Flora, like Leontes, comes to realize the value of the love she weighed so lightly when Jim was alive. Seeing his spirit before her she is reminded of the moment they first met and becomes herself again, a transformation symbolized by the recovery of her sense of smell which she lost when she had plastic surgery.

As Jim guides her round the garden, and they recall the names of flowers, he their Latin ones, she their English designations, they seem to conjure up Perdita and her bouquet from *The Winter's Tale*. She is the daughter of Leontes and Hermione but he had ordered her to be abandoned because he thought he was not the father and she was brought up by a shepherd. At the beginning of the sheep shearing scene in Act 4 scene 4, arguably the most pastoral moment in all Shakespeare, Perdita invokes the goddess of spring, Prosperina, and welcomes the guests with flowers, telling them the various properties of each. Sheep shearing took place in June and it culminated in general feasting, merriment and dancing. The trace of this scene from *The Winter's Tale* in *Humble Boy* connects the play to an ancient tradition. In doing so it implies a need to be part of the rhythms of nature, the cycles of the seasons, which has always been one of the lessons of comedy, perhaps because it has always been more rooted in the body than tragedy.

But this faith in the return of new life as opposed to the repetition of the old one which we found in Beckett and, to a lesser extent in Williams, is somewhat darkened by the emphasis on death. This is not just a matter of Flora accepting that she must grow old; it is also that the play, like *Blasted*, moves from summer to winter, a season which Flora can't do on her own.[141] The urge to self-destruction also resurfaces in the most life affirming moment of the play, namely when Jim shows Flora the flowers. For it evokes not just the memory of Perdita but also Ophelia. She too hands out flowers and explains their meaning but she does so when her wits have turned and she is about to commit suicide.[142] Once again death stalks Arcadia.

There's even an impulse to remove the very means of life. Mercy and George, for example, are associated with food and drink.[143] Add to this that George is also closely identified with music, particularly Glen Miller, and it seems that the aim of *Humble Boy* is to cast out the festive spirit altogether. Indeed it barely seems to get going. For centuries the shared meal has acted as an enduring symbol of social solidarity and communal harmony but the meal in this play is anything but. It is meant to celebrate George and Flora's engagement but tensions are simmering even before Felix appears wearing his father's suit. Soon politeness can barely conceal hostilities and the party quickly disintegrates into squabbles and even downright viciousness. 'Piss off,' George tells Felix at one point.[144] It is possible to see in this general breakdown an image of Britain at the turn of the millennium, particularly since the characters divide along class lines. 'Perhaps Rosie was right,' opines George. 'We're not good enough for the Humbles.'[145]

But this should not blind us to the sacrificial aspects of the scene. It is reminiscent of ritual in its close connection with nature. The set is a country garden in summer and one scene even takes place at the summer solstice. Prior to the meal there are worries about the lack of rain[146] which, put into the context of all the allusions to nature's bounty, links them to ancient anxieties about poor harvests. The fact that the meal takes place in the garden is itself highly suggestive. In Christian symbolism the garden is a place of innocence,[147] Rosie's first appearance is as Eve offering Felix an apple. 'Do you want a b-b-bite?' she asks teasingly.[148] This, together with her sexual appetite, associates her with the figure of the unruly woman who is often the unacknowledged victim of sacrifice. But the garden is also a place where innocence is lost. If Eve hadn't fallen for the serpent's charm, humanity would never have developed nor needed Christ's sacrifice on the cross.

Freud's theory that civilization began with the murder of the primal father is another faintly reverberating myth in the party scene. The unwitting consumption of several spoonfuls of Jim's ashes can be seen as a comic take on Freud's claim that sacrifice involves the killing and eating of the animal who represents the slain patriarch. Mercy, in one of the funniest scenes of the play, calls into question the very foundation of sacrifice, when she says that she is on 'a sabbatical from God'.[149] But disbelief in a deity does not necessarily mean that sacrifice, whose origins lie partly in an acknowledgement of human dependence on divine power, disappears. For sacrifice isn't simply a set of beliefs, rather it is a mode of apprehending the relation between life and death that finds only partial expression in those beliefs.

Another way of putting this is to say that sacrifice provides an integrated understanding of the key questions of existence. And that is exactly what Felix is seeking in *Humble Boy* by trying to discover an equation that unites quantum mechanics and general relativity. 'The superstrings will give us a quantum theory of gravity-that's what I want, what we all want.'[150] Not only would it unite all the physical forces, it would also harmonize art and science. The cosmologist Stephen Hawking's equations (b. 1942), Felix's observes, showered through him 'like Shakespearean sonnets.'[151] Most important of all, in terms of the argument of this book, is that such a theory acts as a metaphor for redemption and resurrection. As already noted, Felix describes his parents in terms of 'the big force' and 'the little' force and by bringing them together he redeems their marriage and his relationship with them. It is the 'Eureka moment',[152] for which he has been longing. Finally a theory of quantum gravity, like sacrifice, shows the interdependence of life and death – that they are part of one continuous process. Yes, a person would be killed if they passed through the event horizon of a black hole, says Felix, but their essence would survive. 'It's a kind of immortality.'[153]

Felix's search for what physicists call 'a unified field theory' shows the need for a holistic understanding of human experience. In the past this had been provided, to a greater or lesser extent, by sacrifice. And there is some evidence that sacrifice is at work in *Humble Boy*. The bees, banished at the beginning, return at the end. And Jim and Flora are reconciled. But a closer examination reveals a different picture. For a start, despite Felix declaring that 'The bees are back'[154] only one is and, in chasing off George, the creature is instrumental in establishing the Oedipal atmosphere at the end of the play. Ironically, this is strengthened by Felix bringing Jim and Flora together. Why? Because Jim disappears immediately afterwards leaving Felix alone with his mother.

The strong suggestion of incest is one reason for saying that sacrifice has failed. It is meant to ensure fertility, not sterility. And in this connection it is worth noting that Jim is the only one who tends the garden. Neither Felix nor Flora appear to have any aptitude with plants. Another reason for saying that sacrifice has failed lies in the ambiguity surrounding Jim's death. One of the functions of sacrifice is to give death a meaning but the question of whether Jim's demise is a tragedy or a comedy or, if the latter, what kind of comedy, remains unanswered. And if sacrifice no longer works, then something else must take its place. That's where Felix's search for a quantum theory of gravity comes in.

The fact that he doesn't find one takes us back to *Hamlet*. T. S. Eliot, in a famous essay on the play, said that the hero's feelings about his mother were out of all proportion to anything she had actually done. What the play lacked was an objective correlative, 'a set of objects, a situation, a chain of events which will be the formula of that particular emotion.'[155] In other words it lacks a principle of organization in much the same way that *Humble Boy* does. The same problem that afflicted Shakespeare's play afflicts Jones' but where Denmark is purged of incest by the death of Hamlet, his mother and Claudius, the 'pretty country garden'[156] is still haunted by Oedipal longing. Like other playwrights we have examined in this chapter, Jones ultimately goes back to Greek tragedy but she can get no further than the incest with which Sophocles starts.

The discussion of Sarah Ruhl's *The Clean House* is longer than that of the other plays because it brings together nearly all the issues we have discussed in new and fascinating ways.

Sarah Ruhl (b. 1974), *The Clean House* (2004)

Matilde is from Brazil. She cleans Lane's house but it makes her sad. She really wants to tell jokes and spends much of her time trying to devise the perfect one, even though she fears it may kill her.[157] Lane is married to Charles. They are both doctors. Lane has a sister called Virginia who feels her life has lost direction but cleaning makes her feel better. Charles falls in love with Ana on whom he has performed a mastectomy. Matilde divides her time between Lane's house and Ana's house and increasingly seems less of a maid and more of a friend. Ana's cancer returns but she refuses treatment. Charles goes to Alaska to chop down a yew tree whose properties, he believes, may cure her. Ana complains that Charles wants to be an explorer rather than a nurse. She moves in with Lane. Finally she asks Matilde to kill her with a joke which she does. We do not hear what the joke is.

The play is both realistic and non-realistic. The non-realistic elements include the play being set in a 'metaphysical Connecticut',[158] Charles' adventures in Alaska and the appearance of Matilde's deceased parents who are played by the same actors as play Charles and Ana. There are also several flashbacks. The scenes are very short and a number consist of addresses to the audience. In many ways this is the most self-consciously theatrical play of all those discussed in this chapter. Does it, like them, still show a connection with sacrifice? Yes. But, again like the others, it does so in its own manner. The very title touches on one of the key functions of sacrifice, to purge society of its afflictions.

What is not clear, though, is what these afflictions are. Or, to be more accurate, they are mentioned but not emphasized which seems to diminish their importance. The chief affliction is the state of the world. Virginia thinks it is 'sick and ugly'[159] which is why she didn't want children but this may be a rationalization of the fact that her husband is barren.[160] Ana also did not want children[161] and, in this context, her mastectomy may signify more than cancer – the loss of the maternal function perhaps. The fact that Lane and Charles are also childless suggests that the world is physically as well as morally degenerate; in other words it is incapable of bring forth new life. Certainly it seems inimical to the formation of loving relationships from which new life might spring. Lane and Charles are both too busy as doctors to have any time for each other.[162] And the essentially barren nature of their relationship is symbolized by the fact that they met over a corpse.[163]

There seem to be three ways of dealing with the problem of infertility, if it can be so termed: love, cleaning and humour. Charles's relationship with Ana is quite different from his relationship with Lane. They loved each other in a balanced and rational manner but his love for Ana, like hers for him, is completely overwhelming and transformative. It is almost offered as a proof of God's existence partly because it signifies the power of invisible forces before which a person has to give way and partly because both Charles and Ana speak of each other as soulmates.[164] What's more Lane imagines Charles kissing Ana in a form of 'sacred ritual'.[165] Charles looked at Lane with admiration but he looks at Ana with adoration.[166]

But changing the nature of love solves nothing. First Charles and Ana grow apart as he travels in search of a cure instead of nursing her and so she turns to Lane and Matilde for support. Second Charles' adventures, such as trying to get a tree on a plane, show love as more of an absurd fantasy than a solution to a barren relationship. Third, there is something Oedipal about Charles' attraction to Ana. She is a much older woman. The overpowering desire they feel for each other may thus arise from forbidden desire rather a transcendent force. Moreover there is something childlike in the way that Charles tries to impress Ana in his efforts to save her. The Oedipal taint in Charles' and Ana's relationship means that it is another expression of infertility rather than a cure for it.

Marriage has traditionally been comedy's solution to social problems such as the tensions between the classes or the generations. It has also been a way of controlling sexuality by giving it socially approved and time-honoured expression. But *The Clean House* is typical of modern comedies in breaking with that tradition. There are many reasons for this departure such as secularism, feminism, increased social mobility and a more liberal attitude to sexual behaviour. Since marriage is shown to be sterile in this play – Virginia makes eggs for her husband but throws them away – [167] sex is more likely to occur outside it. Virginia is attracted to her brother-in-law, commenting on his charisma and his physical appearance, and Lane owns black underwear which, since she never sees Charles, implies either that she has a lover or aspires to one.[168] In general, there is an air of reserve, hesitation or even fear surrounding sexuality in the play which reinforces the sense that the world is a corrupt and dangerous place.

Cleansing has a clear meaning in sacrificial ritual. It purges society of its problems by projecting them onto a scapegoat. But the term 'cleaning' in this play has more of psychological than a social inflection. Matilde says that cleaning makes her sad but Lane says it makes Matilde depressed.[169] Lane's use of this term demonstrates the assumption that the white middle-class professional has the power to label the experience of the immigrant, but it is a power which is contested. It is also an instance of the tension between a medical and an existential approach to disease in the play.

The tension is at its strongest and most profound in Ana's relationship with cancer. She rejects treatment because she does not want a relationship with a disease but with death.[170] She is seeking, in other words, the very thing that sacrifice offers: a meaningful conception of mortality. Part of that meaning lies in the connection between her love for Charles and the cancer that is eating away at her. Love obliterated her sense of self[171] just as death will. But if love can give her a new sense of self in exchange, then who is to say that death won't do the same?

If cleaning makes Matilde sad, it gives Virginia a sense of achievement. To dust is to make a small difference to the dirt of the world. Virginia also sees cleaning as an expression of love and female solidarity.[172] She claims that people who are truly in love like to clean up after each other.[173] But this should be set against her remark that a wife can tell by her husband's 'dirty underwear'[174] if he is sleeping with a prostitute. This implies that Virginia is speaking from experience[175] in which case cleaning is also a way of checking for infidelity and removing the trace of the 'other woman'. And while cleaning may be a means of drawing women together on some occasions,[176] it also divides them, for the subject provokes arguments between Lane, Matilde and Virginia.[177]

In fact cleaning is an expression of Virginia's neurosis about her own sexuality. She hints unwittingly that she washes her own underwear in a somewhat compulsive fashion.[178] She also laughingly admits that cleaning prevents her from slitting her wrists.[179] Cleaning does not make Virginia sad like it does Matilde, but it certainly signifies her deep-seated misery. Both want to do something else. Matilde wants to be a comedian, and Virginia wanted to be a scholar specializing in Greek ruins.[180] To that extent cleaning may stand as a symbol of women's oppression. It is something that they are expected to do, not men. But Virginia's desire to understand ancient Greece is also another instance of a play reaching back to the past in order to revitalize drama's ability to make sense of the present.

At one point, cleaning is seen as a religious practice.[181] In anthropology there are many different types of purifying ritual, all designed to remove dirt and filth. To the extent that Ruhl's play highlights the opposition between cleaning and dirt it harks back to these ancient rituals. Mary Douglas (1921–2007) famously defined dirt as 'matter out of place.'[182] In other words dirt and cleanliness were not simply matters of hygiene. Rather they are part of a symbolic system whose purpose is to uphold and reinforce social hierarchies. Hence those who step out of their allotted role in society are treated as possible sources of infection or pollution for the whole of it. The novelist Edward Bulwer Lytton (1803–1873), for example, coined the phrase 'the great unwashed' to describe the threat of the industrial masses in the nineteenth century and it is still occasionally used today.

The difference between cleaning and dirt is a marker of social boundaries in the play. Lane's professional status means that she does not use a broom or a duster and Virginia is apologetic that as 'an educated woman' she enjoys making her home spotless.[183] Although Virginia is happy to clean Lane's house, Lane objects to the arrangement. She is annoyed at her sister's blurring of social boundaries. She wants 'a stranger'[184] to clean her home. As is clear from her first conversation with Matilde, Lane does not want to know anything about her.[185] The stories people tell about their lives are what makes them human. In denying Matilde the opportunity to tell her story Lane is denying her her humanity. She maintains the border or, as she calls it, 'context'[186] between those who work with dirt and those who don't. And that border is also a border between the human and the non-human.

But it is not an absolute. Where it is drawn differs according to point of view. Lane may think that her profession is an index of cleanliness but, for Virginia, it is hospitals that 'are places of human waste'.[187] Waste here does not just refer to debilitating or terminal illnesses but also, as Ana points out, to the way doctors dismiss or cast aside patient's descriptions of their diseases. 'As long as I live', she says, 'I want to retain my own language.'[188] The shifting border between what is clean and what is dirty, what is useful and what is useless suggests that these apparent opposites may be closely related. They certainly weren't clearly differentiated in the early stages of religious thought. Frazer wrote that they were both 'blent in a sort of vaporous solution to which we give the name taboo'.[189]

Freud argued that, in mental life too, opposites were more apparent than real.[190] The neurotic is dominated by guilt because he or she is still tempted by their repressed desires. Their symptoms are a compromise formation of unconscious desire and conscious censorship. The symptom both expresses and represses the desire. It takes the form of some trivial but obsessive act such as compulsive handwashing or habitually straightening a tablecloth. This disguises the true meaning of the action from the person who performs it thereby allowing them to get some measure of satisfaction from the repressed instinct. The compromise formation, however, is unsteady and leads to ever greater adjustments as the unconscious finds more new ways of breaking through the conscious defences. Freud's theory of neurosis is partly analogous to the logic of sacrifice in that the conscious mind constantly has to find ways of repelling unconscious invasions that disturb its equilibrium. Virginia's constant cleaning, for example, is comparable to the purifying rituals found in religion.[191]

Lane loses interest in having a clean house when Charles leaves her. She wants to experience dirt, chaos and abandonment. These are the very things she wanted to keep out of her home but they have entered it in the form of adultery. However, she has no wish to rid her house of the mess it has caused. Quite the opposite. 'I WANT THERE TO BE DIRT AND PIGS IN THE CORNER AND LOTS OF DIRTY FUCKING SOCKS – AND NONE OF THEM MATCH-BECAUSE THAT'S HOW I FEEL.'[192] At one level this is analogous to the breakdown of the conscious defence system against unconscious desire. At another, it is the willed destruction of a ordered life in order to exploit the expressive possibilities of disorder. Virginia, meanwhile, discovers the pleasure of states of disarray when she makes 'a gigantic operatic mess in the living room'.[193]

Both sisters have lost one version of themselves but that gives them the opportunity to find another. Clutter is a form of psychological carnival in that it jumbles up ideas about self and the world, forcing us to re-examine what we hold most dear. This has implications for how we think of sacrifice. At its most basic it is an act of purification, removing whatever threatens to pollute the social order. But, in *The Clean House*, it is purification which proves to be the danger to society. It thins and dilutes life, boils it down to a series of sterile 'oughts'. That's why Lane finds it so hard to understand why Charles should fall for Ana, when she, Lane, is so smart, athletic, poised and the best doctor in the hospital.[194] The new found delight in dirt, however, and the stirring of long repressed instincts, has a potentially energizing and life-enhancing effect. The play is not so much about cleaning as clearing out.

So far, then, untidiness is the one thing that holds out the possibility of renewal in the play. It is a symbol of freedom and awakening instinct. It is also reminiscent of the spirit of Old Comedy but lacks something of its anarchic vigour. Nevertheless, *The Clean House* is not just concerned with renewal. Its real goal, like that of *Humble Boy*, is to find a way of unifying experience, of capturing its contradictory qualities in a single formula. Such a task had traditionally fallen to sacrifice; here it falls to what Matilde is hoping to find: the perfect joke. But good jokes can also mimic sacrifice. They contain a scapegoat in as much as someone or something is generally the object of laughter. That's why they have a cleansing effect.[195] Additionally, a good joke, like sacrifice, is a bridge between the human and the divine. It stands, as Maria puts it, 'somewhere between an angel and a fart.'[196] The phrase perfectly captures the solemnity of the ceremony and the ribald nature of the celebrations that follow it.

But it is the perfect joke which fulfils the highest function of sacrifice, namely the integration of life and death. For one thing it makes you forget yourself and remember yourself – a little psychic expiration and resurrection.[197] Matilde imagines that she was born when her mother told her father a joke[198] and Ana dies when Matilde tells her the 'funniest joke in the world'.[199] Ana's decision to take her death into her own hands is a faint image of how the whole paraphernalia of sacrifice is designed to rob death of its contingency by bringing it under human control. But what is most interesting about both these jokes is that we are not in on them. When Matilde whispers to Ana, we only hear 'sublime music'. This conjures up an air of religious mystery that is lacking in the modern world due to the advances of science and technology. The perfect joke therefore takes on another function of sacrifice, giving existence a numinous quality, intimating that humans may be part of a much greater reality than they can imagine. A more secular version of this is at work in the good joke which depends on acknowledging that our problems are very small and the world is very large.[200]

A further use of jokes in the play is to raise the question of what is funny. Thinking about the arguments between Charles and Ana about whether she should go to hospital, Virginia sighs and says 'Poor Charles.' Lane responds by saying that the adjective is better applied to Ana and even herself before remarking that 'Poor sounds funny if you say it a lot of times.'[201] Does this mean that repetition is a key ingredient of humour? The French philosopher Henri Bergson (1859–1941) claimed that comedy had a mechanical element by which he meant that people did not adapt their behaviour according to their situation, for instance, a person continues to jump up to try and reach an item on a high shelf instead of using a ladder. Lane's question is whether repetition can transform what is horrible into what is humorous. If so then there is no situation that is intrinsically tragic or, for that matter, comic. It is all a question of perspective. A similar point was made in *Humble Boy* when the characters were discussing Jim's death. The issue has been eloquently expressed by the American actress and comedian Carol Burnett (b. 1933) who said that 'comedy is tragedy plus time'.

The perfect joke is free from repetition. 'You only want to heart it once,' says Matilde, 'and then, never again.'[202] That is because death is the punchline. Ana gets her longed-for relationship with the grim reaper when Matilde tells her the perfect joke. The fact that the perfect joke is, so to speak, 'non-repeatable' prevents us from pushing its identification with sacrifice too far. Ritual depends for its efficacy and legitimacy on repetition. It also has an institutional base which is another thing that separates it from the perfect joke. In order to function ritual must be part of a recognized organization that is underpinned by a specific set of beliefs. Moreover, it can only be performed at certain times in certain places and in a certain manner. The perfect joke is under no such constraints. It is a unique phenomenon in a world of reproduction.

The Clean House opens with Matilde telling a joke in Portuguese. The English language audience will be unlikely to understand it. Matilde has a similar experience with her parents' jokes. She is eight years old and in a cafe. Her mother tells her father a dirty joke. They both laugh very hard. Naturally Matilde is too young to understand the joke – something she hates – and naturally her parents will not explain it to her. Her mother, by way of consolation, says 'ask me again when you are thirty'.[203] The incomprehensibility of the perfect joke comes from its profound connection with life and death which are themselves fundamentally mysterious. This gives it a sublime, almost religious quality that is quite different from the bafflement and frustration felt by Matilde and the audience before jokes they do not understand.

What these 'ordinary' jokes dramatize is not awe in the face of cosmic immensity but how some characters, in missing the point of the jokes, also miss the point of their lives. Lane with her professionalism, Virginia with her cleaning and Charles with his adventures are all diverted, or divert themselves, from what can only loosely be called 'reality' in a play that is set, remember, in a 'metaphysical Connecticut'. Fantasy is inherent in *The Clean House*. Matilde spends much of her time *imagining* her parents who seem to relate to each other through jokes. Theirs seems to be the happy marriage comedy always promised. They are played by the actors who play Charles and Ana. This means that when Matilde goes to live with them she is, on a symbolic level at least, going to live with her parents.

Ana says that she can clean their house[204] and, since her parents told dirty jokes, that gives an added significance to the word 'clean'. But Matilde doesn't want to clean; she wants to tell jokes. In particular, she wants to discover the perfect joke. Part of the reason that she wants to find it is because it will remove the anger and impotence she felt at not understanding the joke her mother told her father. As her mother died before she could tell her the joke, always assuming she would have remembered it twenty-two years later, Matilde never did find out what it was. The quest for the perfect joke is therefore, in part, a quest to recreate the original joke which it can never do. And since it was a dirty joke there is also the sense of a search for sexual knowledge which is forever out of reach.

What's more the perfect joke functions as an act of revenge. Matilde kills her mother in the shape of Ana – whose name sounds like 'mama' – in an action that reverses her childhood humiliation. Now she is the one who tells the jokes and her 'mother' finally receives her punishment for having overlooked and then excluded her daughter from an intimate moment between husband and wife. There is much more that can be said on this matter, for example how Ana's desire to die removes any sense of guilt or responsibility that Matilde may feel for her death, but hopefully I have shown that the perfect joke also has a psychological dimension and is very much a feature of the dynamic relation between Matilde and her parents.

The most important thing to remember, though, is that the perfect joke approximates to sacrifice in several respects, particularly in its integration of life and death. The search for a formula that fuses the deepest mysteries of existence testifies at once to the demise of sacrifice and to the need for something to replace it. But perhaps it is an exaggeration to talk of the demise of sacrifice since Matilde is a version of the scapegoat. As a Brazilian, she is an outsider but, instead of being cast out, she finds her way to the centre of a community and acts as its binding force. Moreover, she brings with her the very thing which that community lacks, some model of sacrifice that will, in the form of the joke, rid society of disease as symbolized in Ana and liberate the instinct for life that otherwise struggles for expression. Matilde's role as a scapegoat is inseparable from her status as an immigrant. Immigrants are often made into scapegoats but Matilda shows that the immigrant can actually be a means of renewal. What this demonstrates is that we do not have to choose, when analysing a play between a social or sacrificial approach. The two belong together. Without the social there is no sacrifice, and without sacrifice there is no social.

10

Conclusion: Tragedy, Comedy and Sacrifice in Popular Culture

The idea of sacrifice, its nature and function, remains at the heart of how we think about ourselves and the world. It is the subject of academic study, and of novels and films.[1] The term appears regularly in a variety of contexts from politics[2] to war[3] and its meaning is endlessly pondered in the media.[4] How do we account for this fascination, even reliance on sacrifice? In a recent study, Julia Meszaros and Johannes Zachhuber suggest that it represents the attempt of secular societies to come to terms with their religious heritage.[5] Another possibility is that the interest in sacrifice may be an expression of anxiety about living in a free market economy where profit often comes before people. Or, to put it another way, in consumer society it is goods, not the good which matters. Sacrifice, by contrast, can act as a symbol for social cohesion to the extent that it promotes the ideal of putting ourselves before others.

Whatever the reasons for the hold that sacrifice exercises on the cultural imagination, there can be no doubt that it is an important factor in how we process our experience of the world. The popular press, for example, continue the age-old habit of scapegoating outsiders for social ills,[6] while the meanings and workings of sacrifice pervade the entertainment industry. The question of whether one person should be killed in order to save many recurs throughout the first five seasons of the hit US T.V. show *24* (2001–2014). The series relies on identifying and expelling evil while the hero himself, Jack Bauer, played by Kiefer Sutherland, occasionally resembles the ancient year-god[7] by 'dying' only to be resurrected.[8] Historically, one of the important functions of sacrifice was to discharge aggression and pent-up energies and this notion lies behind films such as *The Purge* (2013), *The Purge: Anarchy* (2014) and *The Purge: Origins* (2016). Written and directed by James Monaco, they depict a future where, on one night of the year, people are free to commit any crime they like without fear of reprisal. They turn the controlled violence of ritual into a chaos of robbery, rape and murder. As such the films differ from sacrifice whose violence was ultimately linked to a sense of renewal.

But this link with sacrifice, and therefore with tragedy and comedy, is evident in other Blockbuster movies. Take the James Bond franchise. The series began in 1962 with *Dr. No*. The generic plot pits Bond against a villain bent on world domination. After a series of setbacks, he succeeds in killing him. The final shot was often of Bond in sexual embrace. It is easy to recognize, even from this brief description, the basic elements of tragedy and comedy. The hero has to remove the evil represented by the villain. This frequently takes the form of an explosion which recalls the spectacular nature of sacrifice. Bond's promiscuity, particularly in the early films, reflects the sexual revolution of the 1960s and 1970s, but it also gestures to the orgiastic celebrations following a sacrifice. The simplistic division between good and evil in the films is pure melodrama, but the introduction of Daniel Craig as Bond introduced an element of psychological complexity into the stories and also resulted in the downplaying of the character's sexual activities. Both may be related to his Oedipal relationship with M, played by Judi Dench, which was at strongest in *Skyfall* (2012), the film in which she met her end. This particular aspect relates the films more to tragedy, where the Oedipal strain has proved remarkably durable, than to comedy.

Comedy has adapted better to historical change than tragedy with the result that, despite its different manifestations, it is still recognizable in a way that tragedy, on the whole, is not. There is a direct line between the leader of the Greek chorus poking fun at members of the audience and the contemporary comedian targeting a person on the front row as the butt of their jokes. Comedy remains a glorious medley of caricature, exaggeration, satire, pratfalls, buffoonery, practical jokes, mistaken identities, misunderstandings, plays on words and so on. Nothing seems to be immune from humour, given the right context and the correct timing. Alan Ayckbourn extracts hilarity from a suicide attempt in Act 2 of *Absurd Person Singular* (1972). Depressed by her marriage and other matters, Eva decides to kill herself on an evening when guests are visiting. As she puts her head into the gas oven, Jane, one of the guests, enters and says brightly: 'Don't you worry about [cleaning] that oven now…shall I have a go at it for you…Would you mind? I mean it's no trouble for me. I quite enjoy it actually-and you'd do the same for me, wouldn't you?'[9]

With its roots in revelry, sex is never far from the surface in comedy. The purpose of marriage in comedy was to tame the sexual instinct. It also reflected the social use of marriage, for example in cementing relations between important families. Beginning at least in the late sixteenth century, marriage, in Western society, has also been regarded as the expression of romantic love. But the sexual revolution, feminism, the rise in the divorce rate and the option of cohabitation have called traditional ideas about the institution into question. One effect has been to weaken the convention that comedies should end in marriage. *Blackadder* (1983–1989) debunked key moments in British history while *One Foot in the Grave* (1990–2000) cast an increasingly brilliant eye on the mayhem masked by respectable suburbia. Both series ended in death. Comedy had become tragedy. As it had to a certain extent in *The Office* UK version (2001–2003) where comedy's powers of renewal seemed to flounder amidst memos, paper clips, and filing cabinets, the empty universe of Beckett made manifest in dreary meetings and pointless training days.

But the age-old connection between comedy and weddings has not completely disappeared as is illustrated by the hit British TV series *Miranda* (2009–2015), which charts the socially awkward heroine's attempts to marry her true love Gary. However, it no longer remains a reliable indicator of the genre. Indeed, what is the genre of comedy? Plays, situation comedies, satirical programmes, spoofs, sketch shows, panel games and stand-up all come under its heading. But it is very hard to see what they have in common beyond the amusement of the audience. And it is almost impossible to detect in them comedy's origins in sacrificial celebrations. Where is the communion with the divine? Where the connection with the cycle of nature? Where the sense of renewal or community? Perhaps such questions only make sense in the context of comedy's relation to tragedy but that is a genre in terminal decline. Nevertheless, comedy has not completely lost its connection to ritual.

The annual event of Red Nose Day in Britain generates a sense of community across the nation as people dance, strip to their underwear, have their heads shaved, carry fridges round Yorkshire, or otherwise do something out of the ordinary to raise money for the poor and disadvantaged. But this institutionalized spontaneity lacks the earthiness and robust defiance of authority that could be found in the popular festivities of earlier times. As for sexual licence, that is now a matter of swinger clubs, dogging enthusiasts and internet search engines. Promiscuity is not unique to the present. What is different is that it has lost its connection to considerations of fertility and divinity. Sexual freedom is now the norm but that may be at the cost of the meaning of sex itself. Of course it is a private affair but the public presence of sex, particularly its easy availability on the net, is one of sensation and commodification. As such, it may be less able to offer that sense of release and renewal on which the health of the social partly depended. But this, like so many issues, needs further investigation.

We are on much stronger ground with the claim that tragedy, at least in its classical or Shakespearean sense, has almost ceased to be.[10] There are many reasons for its decline including urbanization, the rise of science, the development of democracy and the growth of mass culture. But this does not mean that tragedy's characteristic themes have disappeared too. Far from it. They can be found, perhaps surprisingly, in science fiction. The issue of fate and free will, for example, is evident in a number of films such as *Back to the Future* (1985), *Timecop* (1994), *Minority Report* (2002) and, most recently, *Predestination* (2014). Another important theme in tragedy can be summed up in Hamlet's question 'What is man?' It is a question that lies at the heart of The *Alien* films,[11] starring Sigourney Weaver as Warrant Officer Ellen Ripley. The helmet-headed alien is pure instinct. Killing and eating, it is a beast with no civilization, no culture and no technology. But the creature is not simply the other of humans, it also confronts them with their own monstrosity as the later films make clear. In *Alien 3* (1992), Ripley discovers she is carrying an embryo of the creature. She kills herself, but in *Alien Resurrection* (1997) she wakes to find she has been cloned and is now part human, part beast. Her link to the alien is also a reminder of how woman is always the dangerous other even though, in these films, it is a woman who is expelling the evil rather than being the evil which is expelled.

Where the *Alien Quadrilogy* examines human nature in relation to monsters, Ridley Scott's *Blade Runner* (1982) does so in relation to machines, specifically replicants who look and sound so much like humans that it is difficult to tell them apart. The film strikes a religious note when one of the replicants, Roy, confronts his creator and kills him: God destroyed by one of his children. Alex Garland's *Ex-Machina* (2015) also explores the relation between humans and machines. Is it possible to tell the difference between a human and an android? And can humans relate to androids as they would to other humans? This is the challenge Nathan, the CEO of Bluebook, puts to Caleb one of his employees, in regard to Ava, the 'female' robot he has designed and built. The anxieties that surround Ripley are similar to those surrounding Ava. Nathan wants to control her, but she escapes his prison and enters the outside world. The attempt to contain female desire has failed.

As an artificial life form, Ava cannot reproduce. Ripley, on the other hand, is a mother. She has a daughter, Amanda, whom she discovers is dead when she wakes from hypersleep in *Aliens* (1986). She compensates for this by taking a young girl, Newt, under her wing, but she later dies. And it is in the very next film that Ripley discovers she is pregnant. In *Alien Resurrection* she kills the baby alien that regards her as its mother. As a mother, Ripley is more associated with death than new life. This aspect of the *Alien Quadrilogy* touches on the issue of fertility which is central to sacrifice. Sacrifice itself is integral to Michael Bay's *Armageddon* (1998), when the central character, Harry Stamper, gives up his own life to save one of his men, A. J. also the boyfriend of his daughter, Grace. By manually detonating the bomb that will destroy the asteroid hurtling towards earth, Harry saves the human race and gives them the opportunity to appreciate life afresh. The question of sacrifice also lies at the heart of Christopher Nolan's densely embroidered *Interstellar* (2014). Should it be for personal reasons or matters of principle? Moreover, it is closely related to fertility. Earth has become a dustbowl and humanity must emigrate to another planet. The spaceship *Endurance* goes in search of suitable worlds but, in case the human race dies out before one can be found, it carries 50,000 frozen embryos to populate the new Eden.

If science fiction is one home for the various elements of tragedy and sacrifice, the detective story or crime novel is another. This too explores the nature of human identity, often from an ethical point of view. The detective and the criminal are frequently shown to be very similar, almost two sides of the same personality as in Val McDermid's *The Mermaids Singing* (1995). But what links sacrifice and the crime novel – as I shall call it – is death. The crime novel works, in fact, like a secular form of sacrifice. The murderer is the evil who must be expelled. His or her removal is a rough illustration of Girard's thesis that sacrifice, or in this case the law, is designed to maintain social harmony by preventing the spread of violence. More importantly, the crime novel provides us with a way of coming to terms with death in a secular society. That murder becomes the main subject of the crime novel[12] precisely when religion is losing its hold on the popular mind may be nothing more than a coincidence, but it is a revealing one.[13]

One of the functions of religion is to give death a meaning. As the influence of the church declines relative to the power of the global economy and consumer culture, so too does its ability to convince people that it has the right understanding of mortality. Again, cinema provides some evidence of our anxiety about how to conceive of death in a secular age. Uberto Pasolini's *Still Life* (2013), starring Eddie Marsan, tells the story of a council official whose job is to track down the relatives of those who died alone in the borough. It is a film about the problem of how to mark a person's demise in a society of family diasporas and broken neighbourhoods. The American series *The Walking Dead* (2010–2015), about a group of survivors confronting a post-apocalyptic world overrun by zombies, poses a related question. What is to stop the dead returning if we cannot find adequate ways of recognizing and indeed ensuring their passing?

But if popular culture asks such questions, it also attempts to answer them. Sacrifice negotiated the mystery and horror of death by turning it to a spectacle and linking it to fertility. Crime novels, particularly those which feature a serial killer, such as Thomas Harris' *The Silence of the Lambs* (1988), also make death into a spectacle. Indeed, part of the serial killer's appeal is that by his or her quasi-ceremonial slaying of their victims, they restore ritual to the act of death though not in any redemptive way. Nevertheless, the crime novel, by making death into a form of art, gives it the appearance of meaning. In fact, it does more than that for, to turn death into a work of art is, in some sense, to negate it. By becoming an object of aesthetic contemplation death is turned into a form of life. Perhaps that is why crime novels sell so well; they reassure us, at some subconscious level, that death can be transcended.

But there is a tension in crime novels between the drama of death and the humdrum explanation of it. The detective, faced with a murder, tries to solve it. In the process, the sublime, ungraspable fact of mortality is safely brought within the province of the known. It is all a matter of studying the crime scene, following clues, identifying suspects, establishing motives and so on until, at last, the cloud of unknowing has been dispelled and death has lost its existential terror. It is something that can be explained in terms we can all understand, love, greed, ambition; the usual suspects. What's more, it is something that happened to the victim, not to us. As in sacrifice, we are assured of our aliveness by witnessing the death of another. But sometimes we are denied these comforts. The motives of the serial killer are not so easy to discern. There may be reasons for their behaviour but they do not fully explain it. We are unsettled by their opacity, the sense of evil, the feeling that death truly is, in the last analysis, unknowable.

The crime novel then functions like sacrifice in giving death a ritual character and an explanation within the scheme of things. The key difference is that the crime novel is a secular affair and sacrifice a sacred one. But there is one further connection between the two. The convention of multiple suspects for murder may be related to the ancient Athenian sacrifice of Bouphonia, or murder of the ox. The peculiar feature of this ceremony was that, after the creature was killed, all the participants blamed each other before finally making the knife responsible for the deed and throwing it into the sea. This corresponds, in very broad terms, to the detective first suspecting and then eliminating people from his or her enquiry until the murderer has been identified. The murderer can be seen as a modern instance of what Hyam Maccaby calls the 'sacred executioner'.[14] This person is mainly associated with human sacrifice. He was required to perform the act but was then cursed for doing so and banished from society. This, in very schematic terms, is the pattern of the detective story. The victim has been 'sacrificed' by the murderer who is then punished for his crime.

No doubt we could find further examples of how aspects of sacrifice are embedded in contemporary culture but hopefully the point has been made that it continues to exert an influence on how we perceive the world and process our experience. It was very fashionable in the late twentieth century to say that there was no such thing as human nature, that it was different in different cultures and in different periods.[15] The idea of a human nature was fundamentally conservative, critics said. If it didn't change why should society? While I would be wary of claiming that the persistence of a particular mode of thought proves the existence of a fundamental human nature, I would venture that the sacrificial residues we find in literature suggest that it changes only very, very slowly.

What's more I would say that, since the decline of tragedy, we have yet to find a way of confronting the great existential issues of life. We live in a culture that, for the most part, either avoids or trivializes and sensationalizes the key questions of humanity. It also has little concept of death except as a form of entertainment in action movies. Without a sense of death, we have little sense of life, for death is what it makes it precious. This is part of the thinking that underlines sacrifice. It links life and death and, in doing so, relates us to something greater than ourselves. It also confronts us with aspects of our nature – that word again – we may prefer to ignore. When people say that literature is about sex and death, they are closer to the truth than they might imagine.

NOTES

Chapter 1

1   Hegel, G. W. F., *Aesthetics: Lectures on Fine Arts*, trans. T. M. Knox, 2 Volumes, Oxford: Clarendon Press, 1975, Vol. 2, p. 1198.

2   For a brief overview of the development of sacrifice, see Lewis, Brenda Ralph, *Ritual Sacrifice: A Concise History*, Stroud Gloucestershire: Sutton Publishing, 2001.

3   For an overview of current thinking on sacrifice, see Meszaros, Julia and Zachhuber, Johannes (eds.), *Sacrifice and Modern Thought*, Oxford: Oxford University Press, 2013 and for a good discussion of sacrifice, myth and ritual see Ackerman, Robert, *The Myth and Ritual School*, London: Routledge, 2002.

4   Tylor, E. B., 'Primitive Culture' in Carter, Jeffrey, *Understanding Religious Sacrifice: A Reader*, London: Continuum, 2006, pp. 14–38, p. 14.

5   Ibid., p. 15.

6   Ibid., p. 20.

7   Ibid., p. 26.

8   Smith, William Robertson, 'The Religion of the Semites' in Carter, Jeffrey (ed.) *Understanding Religious Sacrifice: A Reader*, op. cit. pp. 53–75, p. 62.

9   Ibid., p. 63.

10 Burkert, Walter, *Homo Necans: The Anthropology of Ancient Greek Sacrificial Ritual and Myth*, Berkley and Los Angeles: University of California Press, 1983, p. 1.

11 Durkheim, Émile, *The Elementary Forms of Religious Life*, translated by Carol, Cosman, Oxford: Oxford University Press, 2008, p. 257.

12 Ibid., p. 258.

13 Girard, René, *The Girard Reader*, edited by James G. Williams, New York: The Crossroad Publishing Company, 1996, p. 77.

14 The novel details the sexual perversions of a pair of teenage lovers. It includes exhibitionism, orgies, mutilation, dismemberment, blasphemy and murder.

15 Bataille, George, 'Sacrifice, the Festival and the Principles of the Sacred Word' in Botting, Fred and Wilson, Scott, *The Bataille Reader*, Oxford: Blackwell, 1997, pp. 210–219, p. 212.

16 Frazer was dubbed an 'armchair anthropologist' because he did little in the way of fieldwork. His way of doing anthropology – which included sending out questionnaires to missionaries – was superseded by the ethnographical

approaches of people like Bronisław Kasper Malinowski (1884–1942), who coined the term 'participatory observation'. For an example of criticism of Frazer's work, see Leach, Edmund, 'Reflections on a visit to Nemi: Did Frazer get it wrong?' *Anthropology Today* 1:2 1985, pp. 2–30. Recently, however, there have been debates about whether some issues, for example blood sacrifice, can be explained solely by empirical knowledge. See, for example, Willerslev, Rane, *Soul Hunters: Hunting, Animism and Personhood among the Siberian Yukaghirs*, Berkeley: University of California Press, 2007.

17   See Freud, Sigmund, 'Civilisation and Its Discontents' in *The Future of an Illusion, Civilisation and Its Discontents and Other Works: The Standard Edition of the Complete Psychological Works of Sigmund Freud Volume XIII* (1927–1931), translated by James Strachey, London: Vintage The Hogarth Press and the Institute of Psychoanalysis, [1961] and 2001, pp. 64–145.

18   For support for this thesis, see Mortimer, Ian, *Centuries of Change: Which Century Saw the Most Change?* London: Bodley Head, 2015.

19   For further details, see Bell, Michael, *Literature, Modernism and Myth: Belief and Responsibility in the Twentieth Century*, Cambridge: Cambridge University Press, 1997.

20   See Vickery, John B., *The Literary Impact of the Golden Bough*, Princeton: Princeton University Press, 1973.

21   Nemi took its name from the Latin *nemus* meaning 'holy wood'.

22   Frazer, James *The Golden Bough: A Study in Magic and Religion*, edited with an introduction and notes by Robert Fraser, Oxford: Oxford University Press, 2009, p. 674.

23   Ibid., p. 556.

24   Ibid., p. 580.

25   Eliot, T. S., 'Burnt Norton' in *The Four Quartets*, London: Faber, 2001, p. 4.

26   Freud, 'Civilisation and Its Discontents', op. cit. pp. 64–65.

27   Smith 'The Religion of the Semites', op. cit. p. 70.

28   Freud, Sigmund, 'Three Essays on the Theory of Sexuality' in *A Case of Hysteria, Three Essays on Sexuality and Other Works: The Standard Edition of the Complete Psychological Works of Sigmund Freud Volume VII* (1901–1905), translated by James Strachey, London: Vintage The Hogarth Press and the Institute of Psychoanalysis, [1953] and 2001, pp. 135–243, esp. pp. 198–199.

29   See 'Beyond the Pleasure Principle' in Freud, Sigmund, *On Metapsychology*, translated by James Strachey, Angela Richards (ed.) (Harmondsworth: Penguin, 1991) pp. 275–338.

30   Freud, Sigmund, *Totem and Taboo and Other Works: The Standard Edition of the Complete Psychological Works of Sigmund Freud Volume XIII* (1913–1914), translated by James Strachey, London: Vintage The Hogarth Press and the Institute of Psychoanalysis, [1955] and 2001, pp. 125–146 and see also Darwin, Charles, *The Descent of Man and Selection in Relation to Sex*, Madison Park: Pacific Publishing Studio, 2011, pp. 63–95.

31   Freud, *Totem and Taboo*, op. cit. 148 p.

32 Ibid., p. 154.

33 Burkert, Walter, *The Creation of the Sacred*, Harvard: Harvard University Press, 1998, pp. 103 and 112.

34 Freud, Sigmund, 'Analysis Terminable and Interminable' in *Moses and Monotheism, An Outline of Psychoanalysis: The Standard Edition of the Complete Psychological Works of Sigmund Freud Volume XXIII* (1937–1939), translated by James Strachey in collaboration with Anna Freud assisted by Alix Strachey and Alan Tyson, London: Vintage The Hogarth Press and the Institute of Psychoanalysis, [1964] and 2001.

35 Two very good books on why we fear death and how cope with that fear are Becker, Earnest, *The Denial of Death*, New York: Simon and Schuster, 1973 and Solomon, Sheldon, Greenberg, Jeff, and Pyszczynski, Tom, *The Worm at the Core: On the Role of Death in Life*, Harmondsworth: Penguin, 2015.

36 Steiner, George, *In Bluebeard's Castle: Some Notes Towards the Re-definition of Culture*, London: Faber, 1971, p. 71.

Chapter 2

1 A lost tragedy by Euripides. It tells the story of Cresphontes and his brothers as they try to follow the pronouncements of the Oracle.

2 Freud, Sigmund, '*The Two Classes of Instinct*' in *The Ego and the Id and Other Works: The Standard Edition of the Complete Psychological Works of Sigmund Freud Volume XIX* 1923–25, translated by James Strachey in collaboration with Anna Freud assisted by Alix Strachey and Alan Tyson, London: Vintage The Hogarth Press and the Institute of Psychoanalysis, [1958] and 2001, p. 41.

3 Pickard-Cambridge, A. W., *Dithyramb, Tragedy and Comedy*, Oxford: Clarendon Press, 1927, p. 130.

4 Segal, Erich, *The Death of Comedy*, Cambridge, MA: Harvard University Press, 2001, p. 4.

5 Ibid., op. cit. p. 7.

6 See Graves, Robert, *The Greek Myths: The Complete and Definitive Edition*, Harmondsworth: Penguin, 2011, p. 107.

7 Frazer, James, *The Golden Bough: A Study in Magic and Religion*, edited with an introduction and notes by Robert Fraser, Oxford: Oxford University Press, 2009, p. 397.

8 For details, see Graves, *The Greek Myths*, op. cit. pp. 104–106.

9 Nietzsche, Friedrich, *The Birth of Tragedy*, translated by Shaun Whiteside and edited by Michael Tanner, Harmondsworth: Penguin, 1993, p. 103.

10 Ibid., p. 50.

11 Ibid., p. 100.

12 Ibid.

13 Ibid., p. 39.

14 Ibid., p. 52

15 Ibid., p. 86.

16 Ibid., pp. 85 and 32.

17 For an assessment of the work of the Cambridge Ritualists, see Calder, William M. ed., *The Cambridge Ritualists Reconsidered*, Atlanta: Scholars Press, 1991. See also Ackerman, Robert, *The Myth and Ritual School: J.G. Frazer and the Cambridge Ritualists*, London: Routledge, 2002.

18 Murray, Gilbert, 'Excursus on the Ritual Forms Preserved in Tragedy' in Harrison, Jane (ed.) *Themis: A Study of the Social Origins of Greek Religion*, London: Merlin Press, [1912] 1989, pp. 341–363, pp. 341–342.

19 Ibid., p. 342.

20 Murray, 'Excursus on the Ritual Forms Preserved in Tragedy' op. cit. p. 34.

21 Aristotle, *The Poetics* in Russell, D. A. and Winterbottom, M. (eds.) *Ancient Literary Criticism: The Principal Texts in New Translations*, Oxford: Oxford University Press, 1972, p. 109.

22 Cornford, Macdonald Francis, *The Origin of Attic Comedy*, Cambridge: Cambridge University Press, [1914 Edward Arnold, 1934 Cambridge] 2010, p. 56.

23 A semicircular space in front of the stage used by the Greek chorus.

24 Cornford, *The Origin of Attic Comedy*, op. cit. pp. 121–122.

25 Ibid., p. 45.

26 Aristophanes, *The Wasps*, in Aristophanes, *The Wasps, The Poet and the Women, The Frogs*, translated with an introduction by David Barrett, Harmondsworth: Penguin, 1964 Act 1, lines 1046–1050.

27 Ibid., lines 1054, 1055–1056.

28 Cleon (died 422 BCE) was an aristocrat and Athenian statesman who was the first prominent representative of the city's commercial class. Aristophanes and the Greek historian Thucydides (c. 460–c. 395 BCE) regarded him as a demagogue and a warmonger, though history has presented a more balanced view.

29 Cornford, *The Origin of Attic Comedy*, op. cit. p. 102.

30 Aristophanes, *The Wasps*, op. cit., Act 1 lines 62–63.

31 Pickard-Cambridge, *Dithyramb, Tragedy and Comedy*, op. cit. p. 188.

32 Pickard-Cambridge, *Dithyramb, Tragedy and Comedy*, op. cit. pp. 8, 104 and 180.

33 Ibid., p. 126.

34 Brecht, Bertolt, 'A Short Organum for the Theatre' in Willets, John (ed. and trans.) *Brecht on Theatre: The Development of an Aesthetic*, London: Methuen, 1964, pp. 179–205, p. 181.

35 See, for example, Rhodes, Colin, *Primitivism and Modern Art*, London: Thames and Hudson, 1994.

36 For these and further 'differences' between ritual and drama, see Csapo, Eric and Miller, Margaret C. 'General Introduction' in Csapo, Eric and Miller, Margaret C. (eds.) *The Origins of Theatre in Ancient Greece and Beyond: From Ritual to Drama*, Cambridge: Cambridge University Press, 2007, pp. 1–38; esp. pp. 4–7.

Chapter 3

1   Aristotle, *Poetics* in Russell, D. A. and Winterbottom, M. (eds.), *Ancient Literary Criticism: The Principal Texts in New Translations*, Oxford: Oxford University Press, 1972, p. 96.

2   For a short account of the development of Athenian democracy, including discussion of the figures mentioned here, see Forrest, George, 'Greece: The History of the Archaic Period' in Boardman, John, Griffin, Jasper and Murray, Oswyn (eds.) *The Oxford History of Greece and the Hellenistic World*, Oxford: Oxford University Press, 1988, pp. 13–46. For a fuller account, see Thorley, John, *Athenian Democracy*, London and New York, 2004.

3   See http://penelope.uchicago.edu/Thayer/E/Roman/Texts/Plutarch/Lives/Solon*.html, Section 29: paragraph 4.

4   See Goldhill, Simon, 'The Audience of Athenian Tragedy' in Easterling, P. E. (ed.) *The Cambridge Companion to Greek Tragedy*, Cambridge: Cambridge University Press, 2004, pp. 54–68, pp. 60–66.

5   Goldhill, Simon, *Love, Sex and Tragedy: Why Classics Matter*, London: John Murray, 2004, p. 227.

6   Hall, Edith, 'The Sociology of Athenian Tragedy' in Easterling, P. E. (ed.), *The Cambridge Companion to Greek Tragedy*, op. cit. pp. 93–126, p. 93.

7   Agamemnon was told by the prophet Calchas that he had to sacrifice Iphigenia; otherwise the Greek fleet would be trapped at Aulis and unable to sail for Troy. It was Artemis who was keeping the fleet at Aulis and she was doing so because she had been offended by the Greeks killing a pregnant hare. In some version of the myth, Artemis substitutes a deer for Iphigenia at the moment the knife descends.

8   The Furies were underworld goddesses of vengeance particularly known for pursuing those who had murdered members of their family.

9   Aeschylus, *Eumenides* in *The Oresteia: A New Version* by Ted Hughes, London: Faber, p. 185.

10   Ibid., p. 187.

11   Ibid., p. 190.

12   See, for example, see Smith, Jonathan Z., 'The Domestication of Sacrifice' in Hamerton-Kelly, Robert G. (ed.), *Violent Origins: Ritual Killing and Cultural Formations*, Stanford: Stanford University Press, 1987, pp. 191–205.

13   Aeschylus, *Eumenides*, op. cit. p. 172.

14   Ibid., p. 183.

15   Ibid., p. 190.

16   See Frazer, James, *The Golden Bough: A Study in Magic and Religion*, edited with an introduction and notes by Robert Fraser, Oxford: Oxford University Press, 2009, p. 162.

17   *Agamemnon* in *The Oresteia*, op. cit. p. 3.

18   For a good introduction to the view of women in the classical world, see Pomeroy, Sarah, *Goddesses, Whores, Wives and Slaves: Women in Classical Antiquity*, London: Pimlico, 2007.

19   The rites of Cybele closely resembled those of Dionysus who himself had
     marked female traits. See Euripides, *The Bacchae* in *The Bacchae and Other
     Plays*, translated by John Davie with an introduction and notes by Richard
     Rutherford, Harmondsworth: Penguin, 2005, lines 79–80.

20   *Eumenides* in *The Oresteia*, op. cit. p. 194.

21   Jay, Nancy, *Throughout Your Generations Forever: Sacrifice, Religion and
     Paternity*, Chicago: Chicago University Press, 1992.

22   Beers, William, *Women and Sacrifice: Male Narcissism and the Psychology of
     Religion*, Detroit: Wayne State University Press, 1992, p. 139.

23   *Agamemnon* in *The Oresteia*, op. cit. p. 73.

24   *Choephori* in *The Oresteia*, op. cit. p. 104.

25   *Agamemnon* in *The Oresteia*, op. cit. p. 51.

26   Ibid., p. 69.

27   See Burkert, Walter, *Homo Necans: The Anthropology of Ancient Greek
     Sacrificial Ritual and Myth*, translated by Peter Bing, Berkley: University of
     California Press, 1983, pp. 12–16 and also Ehrenreich, Barbara, *Dancing in
     the Streets: A History of Collective Joy*, New York: Metropolitan Books, 2006,
     pp. 21–43.

28   Burkert, *Homo Necans*, op. cit. pp. 5–8.

29   See Burkert, *Homo Necans*, op. cit. p. 137 and p. 141.

30   *Agamemnon* in *The Oresteia*, op. cit. p. 68.

31   *Eumenides* in *The Oresteia*, op. cit. p. 134.

32   Ibid., pp. 136–143.

33   See Frazer, *The Golden Bough*, op. cit. pp. 479–480.

34   Cited in Burkert, *Homo Necans*, op. cit. p. 11.

35   *Choephori* in *The Oresteia*, op. cit. p. 113.

36   Ibid., p. 140.

37   *Agamemnon* in *The Oresteia*, op. cit. pp. 6–7.

38   Ibid., p. 10.

39   Sophocles, *Oedipus the King* in *The Three Theban Plays: Antigone,
     Oedipus the King, Oedipus at Colonus*, translated by Robert Fagles with an
     introduction and notes by Bernard Knox, Harmondsworth: Penguin, 1984,
     lines 963–984.

40   Euripides, *Iphigenia at Aulis* in *The Bacchae and Other Plays*, op. cit., lines
     1169–1170.

41   For a good introduction to the varieties of comedy in ancient Greece, see
     Lowe, N.J., *Comedy: New Surveys in the Classics No. 37*, Cambridge:
     Cambridge University Press, 2008 from which most of the information in the
     following paragraphs is drawn.

42   The metre of tragedy developed from the dithyramb (an ecstatic, incantatory
     style) to the iambic trimeter (a line of six syllables, one unstressed followed by
     one stressed, and mostly used in the dialogue sections of tragedy and comedy),
     to the trochaic tetrameter (a line of eight syllables one stressed followed by one

unstressed). The development is broadly from a rapturous to a rational style, from a group to an individual expression. Freud would be the first to note the parallel with the development of the child from an instinctive to a reasonable creature.

43 Aristophanes, *The Acharnians* in *Lysistrata, The Acharnians, The Clouds*, translated with an introduction by Alan H. Sommerstein, Harmondsworth: Penguin, 1973, 1:1, lines 632–633 and 678–681.

44 Demeter and Persephone are actually more complicated figures than can be indicated here. Persephone, for example, is another name for Dionysus and her name means 'she who brings destruction' because she sacrificed the sacred king. See Graves, Robert, *The Greek Myths*, Harmondsworth: Penguin, [1955] and 2011, pp. 56 and 93.

45 Thesmos is also used to 'denote customs or laws'. Demeter introduced laws enabling humans to deal justly with one another. See Warrior, Valerie M., *Greek Religion: A Sourcebook*, Newburyport, MA: Focus Publishing, 2009, pp. 125–129, p. 125.

46 There are more layers to the myth than can be mentioned here. For example, Persephone eats seven seeds of a pomegranate in the underworld which partly explains why she has to return there for six months of the year. See Graves, *The Greek Myths*, op. cit. pp. 91–92.

47 Aristophanes, *Women at the Thesmophoria* in *Frogs and Other Plays*, translated by David Barrett; revised translation with an introduction and notes by Shomit Dutta, Harmondsworth: Penguin, 2007, 1:2, lines 298–299.

48 For contemporary accounts, see Warrior, *Greek Religion: A Sourcebook*, op.cit. pp. 125–129.

49 *Women at the Thesmophoria* in *Frogs and Other Plays*, op. cit., 1:2, lines 389–392.

50 Ibid. 1:2, lines 473–475.

51 Ibid. 1:2, lines 786–787.

52 *The Wasps* in *Frogs and Other Plays*, op. cit. 1:1, lines 144–147.

53 *Women at the Thesmophoria* in *Frogs and Other Plays* op, cit. 1:1 lines 499–502.

54 Freud, Sigmund, *Civilization and Its Discontents*, in *The Future of an Illusion, Civilization and Its Discontents and Other Works, The Standard Edition of the Complete Psychological Works of Sigmund Freud Volume XXI* (1927–1931), translated by James Strachey in collaboration with Anna Freud assisted by Alix Strachey and Alan Tyson, London: Vintage The Hogarth Press and the Institute of Psychoanalysis, [1961] and 2001, p. 64.

55 Ibid., p. 66.

56 Telephus was the son of Heracles. The play has not survived but see Heath, Malcolm, 'Euripides' Telephus' in *Classical Quarterly* 1987, vol. 37, pp. 272–280 for a speculative reconstruction of the work.

57 *Women at the Thesmophoria* in *Frogs and Other Plays* op. cit. 1:1. lines 693–694.

58 Ibid., 1:1, lines 734–735.

59 On this point see Miller, Harold W., 'Euripides' Telephus and the Thesmophoriazusae of Aristophanes', *Classical Philology*, 43:3, July 1948, pp. 174–183.

60 *Women at the Thesmophoria* in *Frogs and Other Plays* op, cit. 2:1, line 1009.

61 Ibid., 2:1, line 1227.

62 Ibid., 2: 1, lines 985–989.

63 Ibid., 1:2, lines 718–719.

64 Euripides' *Helen* is based on that version of the myth that says Helen was never in Troy – Hera sent a phantom in her place. Instead she was transported to Egypt under the protection of King Proteus. When he died his son, Theoclymenus, tried to force Helen to marry him but when Menelaus arrives the couple escape with the help of Theoclymenus' sister, Theonoe.

65 Andromeda was the daughter of King Cepheus of Ethiopia. He had offended Poseidon who sent a flood and a sea monster to destroy his land. The only way Poseidon's wrath could be averted was if Andromeda was sacrificed to the monster. She awaited her fate chained to a rock next to a cave from which her own voice echoed back to her. Andromeda was rescued by Perseus who killed the monster by showing it the head of Medusa.

66 'Let the die be cast,' said Caesar before he crossed the Rubicon. It is apparently a line from a Menander's play, *Arrhephoros* (girl acolyte in the cult of Athena) of which only a few fragments remain. St Paul's expression, 'Be not deceived: evil communications corrupt good manners' (Corinthians 15: 33), has also been attributed to Menander but this is more debatable.

67 Philip of Macedon's conquest of Athens in 355 BCE meant the stage was heavily censored.

68 Lowe, *Comedy: New Surveys in the Classics No. 37*, op. cit. p. 66.

69 Ibid., p. 67.

70 Menander, *The Bad-Tempered Man* in *The Plays and Fragments*, translated with notes by Maurice Balme, with an introduction by Peter Brown, Oxford: Oxford University Press, 2008, Act 2, line 338.

71 Ibid., Act 4, lines 700–701.

72 *Agamemnon* in *The Oresteia*, op. cit. p. 11.

73 *The Bad-Tempered Man*, op. cit., Act 1, lines 230–232.

74 Ibid., Act 2, line 286.

75 Ibid., Act 4, lines 766–767.

76 Ibid., Act 2, line 417.

77 Ibid., Act 3, lines 447–454.

78 Ibid., Act 1, lines 130–131.

79 Ibid., Act 1, lines 154–155.

80 Ibid., Prologue, line 7.

81 Ibid., Act 4, line 715.

82 Ibid., Act 4, lines 680–681.

83 Ibid., Act 4, lines 742–744.

84 Ibid., Act 5, line 957.

85 Ibid., Act 5, line 851.

Chapter 4

1   Horace, 'A Letter to Augustus' in Russell, D. A. and Winterbottom, M. (eds.),
     Ancient Literary Criticism: The Principal Texts in New Translations, Oxford:
     Oxford University Press, 1972, pp. 272–279, p. 276.

2   'The Art of Poetry' in Ibid., pp. 279–291, p. 286.

3   Ibid., p. 287.

4   Cited in Boyle, A. J., *Roman Tragedy*, London and New York: Routledge,
     2006, Ibid., p. 8. I am indebted to Boyle for most of what follows on Roman
     tragedy.

5   See Ibid., p. 14 for details of the different *Ludi*.

6   Ibid., p. 15.

7   For a good introduction to the Games, see Futrell, Alice, *The Roman Games:
     Historical Sources in Translation*, Oxford: Blackwell, 2006.

8   Tertullian, 'Apologetics' 15. 4–6 in Mahoney, Anne, *Roman Sports and Spectacles:
     A Sourcebook*, Newbury Port, MA: Focus Publishing, 2001, p. 53. Attis was a
     god of fertility and vegetation. His castration and death were followed by his
     resurrection. Hercules was renowned for his strength and his twelve labours. He
     died as a result of donning a poisoned shirt that made him catch fire.

9   Boyle, *Roman Tragedy*, op. cit. p. 119.

10   Brockett, Oscar G. and Franklin, J. Hildy, *History of the Theatre*, Boston:
     Allyn and Bacon, 1970, pp. 46–47 and MacCulloch, Diarmaid, *A History of
     Christianity*, Harmondsworth: Penguin, 2010, pp. 189–222.

11   Seneca, 'Moral Letters' and Tertullian, 'On Spectacles' in Mahoney, *Roman
     Sports and Spectacles*, op. cit. pp. 93 and 96.

12   There were two myths of the origin of Rome. The first was that of Romulus
     and Remus, twins who were abandoned at birth and raised by a she-wolf.
     When the brothers grew up they decided to establish a city but Romulus killed
     Remus, an act which was held responsible for Rome's notorious internecine
     strife. The second myth was recounted by Virgil (70–19 BCE) in his *Aeneid*
     (composed 29–19 BCE). The hero, Aeneas, leads a band of survivors from the
     Trojan War who, after many adventures, arrive in Italy where Aeneas becomes
     the ancestor of the Romans.

13   Boyle, *Roman Tragedy*, op. cit. p. 43.

14   Among the many offices that Cato held was that of Censor. The holder was
     responsible for maintaining the census and supervising public morality. Cato
     was noted for trying to combat what he considered to be the degenerate
     influence of Greek culture.

15   Jensen, A. E., *Myth and Cult Among Primitive Peoples*, translated by M. T.
     Choldin, Chicago: Chicago University Press, 1963.

16   Boyle, *Roman Tragedy*, op. cit. p. 171.

17   Ibid., p. 3.

18   A plot led by Gaius Calpurnius Piso to assassinate Nero in 65 CE. The emperor
     ordered many of those implicated in the plot, including Seneca, to commit suicide.

19 Seneca, *Letters from a Stoic*, selected, translated and with an introduction by Robin Campbell, Harmondsworth: Penguin, 2004, p. 199.

20 Seneca, *The Trojan Women in Four Tragedies and Octavia*, translated with an introduction by E. F. Watling, Harmondsworth: Penguin, 1966, p. 173 (no line references in text).

21 Shakespeare, William, *King Lear*, 4: 1 l. 2–4.

22 The two other plays, *Alexandros* and *Palamedes*, were apparently unconnected to *The Trojan Women* but, as they have been lost, we can never know for sure.

23 Seneca, *The Trojan Women*, op. cit. p. 169.

24 Ibid., p. 181.

25 Ibid., p. 188.

26 Ibid., p. 198.

27 Ibid., p. 201.

28 Ibid., p. 202.

29 Ibid., p. 171.

30 Ibid., p. 178.

31 Ibid., p. 157.

32 Ibid., p. 167.

33 Ibid., p. 204.

34 It had another connotations too including 'jealous' or 'coward' and of course it is the root of our modern term 'hypocrite'.

35 See Duckworth, George E., *The Nature of Roman Comedy: A Study in Popular Entertainment*, 1st edn, Princeton: Princeton University Press, 1952, second edition, Norman: University of Oklahoma Press 1994, pp. 8–10. I am greatly indebted to this work from which most of the information in this section is taken.

36 Ibid., pp. 10–11.

37 Cited in Ibid., p. 14.

38 See Duckworth, *The Nature of Roman Comedy*, op. cit. pp. 33–38.

39 See Konstan, David, *Roman Comedy*, Ithaca and London: Cornell University Press, 1983, pp. 23–25.

40 Plautus, *The Rope* in *The Rope and Other Plays*, translated and with an introduction by E. F. Watling, Harmondsworth: Penguin, 1964, l. 71.

41 Ibid., l. 304.

42 Ibid., l. 766–767.

43 Ibid., l. 771–772. The link between women and slaves, hinted at here, is evident throughout *The Rope* and Trachalio's words seem like a plea for an end to the economic exploitation of both. In fact neither slavery nor prostitution is seriously challenged in the play unless the victim is a freeborn Athenian.

44 Ibid., l. 648–650.

45 Ibid., l. 1423.

46 Ibid., l. 407–408.

47 Ibid., l. 1184–1186.

48 Ibid., l. 620–632.

49 Ibid., l. 383.

50 Ibid., l. 864.

51 Ibid., l. 1171–1173.

52 Ibid., l. 1110.

53 Ibid., l. 1117–1118.

54 Ibid., l. 1245–1247.

Chapter 5

1 The dark ages is a conventional description used to cover the period from the fall of Rome to either the tenth, or the mid-fourteenth century, the dawn of the Renaissance. It was the Italian poet Petrarch (1304–1374) who conceived the term, comparing the post-Roman era to the achievements of classical antiquity. His view was reinforced in the eighteenth century by thinkers such as Kant (1724–1804) and Voltaire (1694–1778) who were critical of the major role played by religion in the period. But we should not forget that the so-called dark ages as well as being a time of conflict and urban decay also saw the establishment of universities, innovations in art and architecture and the Byzantine Golden age. The term is rarely used nowadays. See Wells, Peter, *Barbarians to Angels: The Dark Ages Reconsidered*, New York: Norton, 2008.

2 Definitions and descriptions of tragedy and comedy could be found in encyclopaedias and florilegia (a collection of sayings and writings). Two of the most important were Evanthius' *On Drama* and Donatus' *On Comedy*, both written in the fourth century. Evanthius looks at the origins of drama, the etymology of tragedy and its difference from comedy. Donatus takes a similar approach but also describes the formal character of comedy. The rediscovery of classical drama in the fourteenth century sparked an interest in what writers like Donatus and Evanthius and, of course, Aristotle had to say about tragedy and comedy. Although tragedy and comedy did not return to the English stage until approximately the beginning of the sixteenth century, the term 'tragedy' was familiar to Chaucer's readers. It is defined in the 'Prologue' to *The Monk's Tale* as the fall of a rich person into misery whose life ends wretchedly.

3 Tydeman, William, 'An Introduction to Medieval Theatre' in Beadle, Richard (ed.), *The Cambridge Companion to Medieval Theatre*, Cambridge: Cambridge University Press, 1994, pp. 1–36, p. 10.

4 Cited in Hutton, Ronald, *The Rise and Fall of Merry England: The Ritual Year 1400–1700*, Oxford: Oxford University Press, 1996, p. 28.

5 The term 'mumming' has a bewildering number of meanings but is thought to derive from the Danish word *momme* and the Dutch word *mumme*, both signifying disguise. For a good overview of the mumming plays, see Brody, Alan, *The English Mummers and Their Plays: Traces of Ancient Mystery*, Philadelphia: University of Pennsylvania Press, 1970. There were three types

of mumming play: the Hero-Combat, the Sword-Dance and the Wooing Ceremony all of which contain a death and resurrection.

6 *Quête* is an old French word meaning quest or collection of money for a performance.

7 For more detail, see Mills, David, 'Drama and Folk-Ritual', in Cawley, A. C., Jones, Marion, McDonald, Peter F. and Mills, David (eds.), *The Revels History of Drama in English: Volume 1 Medieval Drama*, London: Methuen, 1983, pp. 133–138. For an overview of the story of Robin Hood, see Cawthorne, Nigel, *Robin Hood: The True History behind the Legend*, London: Running Press, 2010.

8 See Hutton, *The Rise and Fall of Merry England*, op. cit. p. 33.

9 For the opposite argument, see Dillon, Janette, *The Cambridge Introduction to Early English Theatre*, Cambridge: Cambridge University Press, 2006, p. 24.

10 See Hutton, *The Rise and Fall of Merry England*, op. cit. p. 72.

11 See Brody, *The English Mummers and Their Plays*, op. cit. pp. 67–71.

12 For more details of the *quête*, see Chambers, E. K., *The English Folk Play*, Oxford: Clarendon Press, 1933, pp. 63–71.

13 Brody, *The English Mummers and Their Plays*, op. cit. p. 59.

14 For a chronology of Shakespeare's plays, see Braunmuller, A. R. and Hattaway, Michael (eds.), *The Cambridge Companion to Renaissance Drama*, Cambridge: Cambridge University Press, 2003, pp. 420–447.

15 Tydeman, 'An Introduction to Medieval Theatre', op. cit. p. 9.

16 Ibid., pp. 19–20.

17 The Mass commemorates the Last Supper, Christ's final meal with his disciples. The term is derived from the Latin *missa*, meaning dismissal. It was used at the end of the service, '*Ite missa est*' (Go: It is the dismissal) but in Christian usage 'dismissal' gradually comes to acquire the sense of 'mission', so that the congregation leave the church with a duty to spread the word of God.

18 For what is still a good overview of the development of the Mass, see Klauser, Theodor, *A Short History of the Western Liturgy*, trans. John Halliburton, Oxford: Oxford University Press, 1979.

19 McDonald, Peter F. 'Drama in the Church' in Cawley, A. C., Jones, Marion, McDonald, Peter F. and Mills, David (eds.), *The Revels History of Drama in English: Volume 1 Medieval Drama*, op. cit. pp. 92–121, p. 117.

20 A more detailed account of the *Regularis Concordia* can be found by following this link to the British Library at http://www.bl.uk/onlinegallery/onlineex/illmanus/cottmanucoll/r/011cottiba00003u00003000.html

21 The Harrowing of Hell refers to Christ's descent into hell between his crucifixion and his resurrection to save the souls of all the righteous who had died since the beginning of the world.

22 Tydeman, 'An Introduction to Medieval Theatre', op. cit. p. 5.

23 See Hardison, O. B. Jr., *Christian Rite and Christian Drama in the Middle Ages: Essays in the Origin and Early History of Modern Drama*, Baltimore: Johns Hopkins University Press, 1965; and Normington, Katie, *Medieval English Drama*, Cambridge: Polity Press, 2009.

24 Jesus' first miracle – in the Gospel of John – is to turn water into wine. See *The Gospel according to St. John*, King James Version, chapter 2 verses 1–11.

25 Ehrenreich, Barbara, *Dancing in the Streets: A History of Collective Joy*, London: Granta, 2007, p. 60. See also pp. 58–64.

26 See *The Gospel According to St. Mark*, King James Version, chapter 14 verses 35–36.

27 Ibid., chapter 6 verses 31–33.

28 Jones, Marion, 'Moral and Secular Drama' in Cawley, A. C., Jones, Marion, McDonald, Peter F. and Mills, David (eds.), *The Revels History of Drama in English: Volume 1 Medieval Drama*, London: Methuen, 1983, pp. 213–291, p. 213.

29 Dillon, *The Cambridge Introduction to Early English Theatre*, op. cit. pp. 144–146.

30 Marion Jones argues that the term 'miracle' is best reserved for 'dramatized account of miraculous happenings not recorded in the Bible, not performed by a saint and not allegorical in treatment'. Jones, 'Moral and Secular Drama', op. cit. p. 214.

31 Bevington, D. M., *From Mankind to Marlowe: Growth of Structure in the Popular Dram of Tudor England*, Cambridge: Massachusetts, 1962, p. 19.

32 'The Fall of the Angels' in Beadle, Richard and King, Pamela M. (eds.) *The York Mystery Plays: A Selection in Modern Spelling*, Oxford: Oxford University Press, 2009, pp. 2–7, l. 91.

33 Joseph's 'Trouble about Mary' in *The York Mystery Plays*, op. cit. pp. 48–58, l. 61.

34 Mills, David, 'Religious Drama and Civic Ceremonial' in Cawley, A. C., Jones, Marion, McDonald, Peter F. and Mills, David (eds.), *The Revels History of Drama in English: Volume 1 Medieval Drama*, op. cit. pp. 152–206, p. 193.

35 'The Flood' in *The York Mystery Plays*, op. cit. pp. 21–32.

36 See Bergson, Henri, *Laughter: An Essay on the Meaning of the Comic*, translated by Cloudesely Brereton and Fred Rothwell, Rockville: Arc Manor, 2008, pp. 28–29.

37 The others are *The Pride of Life* (c. 1350), *The Castle of Perseverance* (c. 1420–1425), *Wisdom* (c. 1460–1470) and *Mankind* (c. 1464).

38 See Tydeman, 'An Introduction to Medieval Theatre', op. cit. pp. 18–24.

39 King, Pamela M., 'Morality Plays' in Beadle, Richard (ed.), *The Cambridge Companion to Medieval Theatre*, op. cit., pp. 240–264, p. 257.

40 *Everyman* in *Three Late Medieval Morality Plays*, Lester, G. A. (ed.), London: A & C Black, 1997, l. 536.

41 Ibid., l. 546.

42 Ibid., l. 851.

43 *The Gospel according to St. Mark*, King James Version, chapter 15 verse 34.

44 *Everyman* in *Three Late Medieval Morality Plays*, op. cit. l. 880.

45 *The Gospel according to St. Luke*, King James Version, chapter 24 verse 46.

46 *Everyman* in *Three Late Medieval Morality Plays*, op. cit. l. 584–585.

47 Ibid., l. 29–35.

48 Ibid., l. 56–57.

49 Ibid., l. 569.

50 Ibid., l. 49.

51 See Bowden, Hugh, *Mystery Cults in the Ancient World*, London: Thames and Hudson, 2010, pp. 14–15.

Chapter 6

1   Shakespeare, William, *As You Like It*, Juliet Dusinberre (ed.), The Arden Shakespeare, London: Thompson, 2006, 2: 7 l. 139–166.

2   This is, of course, an exaggeration. The European Reformation was not something that happened overnight. There had been slow build-up of resentment against the Church's wealth, power and corrupt practices.

3   For a discussion of these different types of tragedy, see Watson, Robert N., 'Tragedy' in Braunmuller, A. R. and Hattaway, Michael (eds.), *The Cambridge Companion to English Renaissance Drama*, 2nd Edition, Cambridge: Cambridge University Press, 2003, pp. 292–343.

4   Belsey, Catherine, *The Subject of Tragedy: Identity and Difference in Renaissance Drama*, London: Routledge, 1985, p. 130.

5   Watson, 'Tragedy', op. cit. p. 295.

6   Ibid., p. 294.

7   Shakespeare, William, *Hamlet*, Ann Thompson and Neil Taylor (eds.), The Arden Shakespeare, London: Thompson, 2007, 3: 2 l. 21–24.

8   Philip, Sidney, 'The Defence of Poetry' in Vickers, Brian, *English Renaissance Literary Criticism*, Oxford: Clarendon Press, 1999, pp. 334–390, p. 347.

9   Cited in Klein, David, *Literary Criticism from the Elizabethan Dramatists*, New York: Sturgis and Walton. 1910, p. 30.

10 Sidney, 'The Defence of Poetry', op. cit. p. 372.

11 Cited in Klein, *Literary Criticism from the Elizabethan Dramatists*, op. cit. p. 24.

12 Hattaway, Michael, 'Drama and Society' in Braunmuller, A. R. and Hattaway, Michael (eds.), *English Renaissance Drama*, op. cit. pp. 93–130, p. 99.

13 Marlowe, Christopher, *Tamburlaine The Great*, J. S. Cunningham, and Eithne Henson (eds.), Revels Student Edition, Manchester: Manchester University Press, Tamburlaine the Great Part 1, 1: 2 l. 41.

14 Shakespeare, *Hamlet*, op. cit. 2: 2 l. 334–336.

15 Shakespeare, William, *King Lear*, R. A. Foakes (ed.), The Arden Shakespeare, London: Bloomsbury, 2014, 5: 3 l. 305–306.

16 Ibid., 1: 4 l. 271.

17 Ibid., 4: 4 l. 3–6.

18 For a full account of the different meanings of nature in *King Lear*, see Danby, John F. *Shakespeare's Doctrine of Nature: A Study of King Lear*, London: Faber, 1965.

19 Shakespeare, *King Lear*, op. cit. 1: 2 l. 2.

20 This distinction is for clarity only. A fuller account would look at the language of the Fool and how this relates to plain speaking, rhetoric and truth. There's also an interesting discussion to be had comparing the 'madness' of Lear, the Fool and Poor Tom.

21 Shakespeare, *King Lear*, op. cit. 1: 1 l. 56.

22 Ibid., 1: 1 l. 93.

23 Ibid., 5: 3 l. 323.

24 Ibid., 1: 1 l. 226–227.

25 Ibid., 1: 1 l. 237–239.

26 Ibid., 2: 2 l. 94–96.

27 Ibid., 1: 4 l. 19.

28 Ibid., 1: 4 l. 16.

29 Ibid., 3: 2 l. 64.

30 Ibid., 2: 2 l. 100–103.

31 Ibid., 4: 4 l. 23–27.

32 See Foakes discussion of the time scheme of the play in 'Appendix 1' in *King Lear*, op. cit. pp. 393–402.

33 Shakespeare, *King Lear*, op. cit. 2: 2 l. 28–29.

34 Ibid., 2: 2 l. 167–168.

35 Ibid., 3: 3 l. 12–13.

36 Ibid., 5: 3 l. 5.

37 Ibid., 3: 4 l. 101–106.

38 Shakespeare, *Hamlet*, op. cit. 3: 4 l. 90–93.

39 Ibid., 3: 2 l. 1–43.

40 Shakespeare, *King Lear*, op. cit. 4: 2 l. 79–81.

41 Ibid., 4: 1 l. 39.

42 Ibid., 5: 2 9–11.

43 Ibid., 1: 2 l. 118.

44 Ibid., 1: 2 l. 126–128.

45 For a full discussion of the gods in the play, see Elton, William R., *King Lear and the Gods*, California: Huntingdon Library, 1968.

46 Middleton, Thomas, *The Revenger's Tragedy*, R. A. Foakes (ed.), Revels Student Editions, Manchester: Manchester University Press, 1996, 1: 1 l. 96.

47 Ibid., 4: 1 l. 54.

48 Ibid., 3: 5 l. 183.

49 Ibid., 3: 1 l. 5–6.

50 Ibid., 1: 4 l. 49–50.

51 Ibid., 4: 1 l. 63–64.

52 See Watson, Robert N., 'Tragedy' in *The Cambridge Companion to English Renaissance Drama*, op. cit. p. 310.

53 Middleton, *The Revenger's Tragedy*, op. cit. 1: 1 l. 1.

54 It means 'lustful' or 'lascivious' in Italian.

55 Ibid., 4: 3 l. 15–16.

56 *Deuteronomy*, King James Version, chapter 32 verse 35.

57 Middleton, *The Revenger's Tragedy*, op. cit. 4: 4 l. 47–48.

58 Frazer, James, *The Golden Bough: A Study in Magic and Religion*, op. cit. p. 101.

59 Middleton, *The Revenger's Tragedy*, op. cit. 4: 1 l. 19.

60 Ibid., 1: 3 l. 61–63.

61 Ibid., 2: 1 l. 128.

62 Ibid., 1: 2 l. 119–121. See Shakespeare, *Hamlet*, op. cit. 1: 2 l. 129–137.

63 The sexual symbolism of Orestes killing his mother with a sword is pertinent here.

64 Freud, Sigmund, *Totem and Taboo and Other Works: The Standard Edition of the Complete Psychological Works of Sigmund Freud Volume XIII* (1913–1914), translated by James Strachey, London: Vintage The Hogarth Press and the Institute of Psychoanalysis, [1955] and 2001, p. 140.

65 For a different view of the comedy of the play, see Foakes' 'Introduction' to *The Revenger's Tragedy*, op. cit. pp. 13–14.

66 Middleton, *The Revenger's Tragedy*, op. cit. 1: 1 l. 23–25.

67 Ibid., 3: 5 l. 96–98.

68 Donne, John, 'An Anatomy of the World' in Smith, A. J. (ed.) *The Complete English Poems*, Harmondsworth: Penguin, pp. 270–283, p. 276, l. 213.

69 Cited in Klein, *Literary Criticism from the Elizabethan Dramatists*, op. cit. p. 21.

70 Ibid.

71 Ibid.

72 Ibid., p. 22.

73 Ibid., p. 100.

74 Levenson, Jill, 'Comedy' in *The Cambridge Companion to English Renaissance Drama*, op. cit. pp. 254–291, p. 256.

75 Barber, C. L., *Shakespeare's Festive Comedy: A Study of Dramatic Form and Its Relation to Social Custom*, op. cit. p. 2.

76 Ibid., p. 7.

77 Cited in Ibid., p. 35.

78 Ibid., p. 134.

79 Ibid., p. 141.

80 *Anatomy of Abuses in England in Shakespeare's Youth*. The full text is available at http://archive.org/stream/phillipstubbessa00stubuoft/phillipstubbessa00stubuoft_djvu.txt.

81 If we were looking at the play in terms of the ongoing tensions between Protestantism and Catholicism then love-in-idleness can be seen as an oblique critique of Catholic idolatry, that is, images of Christ, the Virgin, the saints and various animals. In the opinion of Protestants these diverted attention away from the one true God just as love-in-idleness diverts affection from a true object to a false one, though the case of Demetrius complicates that simple distinction.

82 Shakespeare, William, *A Midsummer Night's Dream*, Harold F. Brooks (ed.), The Arden Shakespeare, London: Methuen Drama, 2007, 4: 1 l. 163–165 and 188–189.

83 Ibid., 4: 1 l. 209–212. Bottom's words are a burlesque of those in 1 Corinthians 2: 9 which describes how the senses cannot convey the mystery of God.

84 Ibid., 1: 1 l. 106–108 and 4: 1 l. 170–171.

85 Ibid., 1: 1 l. 141–149.

86 Ibid., 1: 2 l. 234 and 236.

87 Ibid., 3: 1 l. 138–139.

88 Ibid., 1: 1 l. 232–233.

89 Ibid., 3: 1 l. 124.

90 Ibid., 2: 1 l. 204.

91 Ibid., 3: 2 l. 114–115.

92 Ibid., 5: 1 l. 108.

93 Ibid., 2: 1 l. 70–80.

94 Ibid., 2: 1 l. 123.

95 Ibid., 2: 1 l. 94–95.

96 Ibid., 1: 1 l. 73.

97 Ibid., 5: 1 l. 391–392.

98 Ibid., 2: 1 l. 128–129.

99 Ibid., 2: 1 l. 27 and 4: 1 l. 3.

100 Ibid., 5: 1 l. 37.

101 Barber, *Shakespeare's Festive Comedy: A Study of Dramatic Form and Its Relation to Social Custom*, op. cit. p. 25.

102 See, for example, Aristophanes' *The Clouds* (423 BCE); Plautus' *Pseudolus* (*The Liar* 191 BCE), and the chapter on Greek tragedy and comedy for a quick sketch of Theophrastus.

103 Jonson, Ben, *Every Man Out of His Humour*, London: First Rate Publishers, 2014, 1: 1 l. 118–122.

104 Jonson, Ben, *Every Man in His Humour*, Robert N. Watson (ed.), New Mermaids, A & C Black: London, 1998, 5: 1 l. 202–203.

105 Ibid. 'Prologue' l. 21.

106 Ibid., 1: 2 l. 82–83 and 2: 2 l. 57–66.

107 Ibid., 1: 3 l. 12.

108 Ibid., 3: 2 l. 49–53.

109 Ibid., 1: 1 l. 64–67.

110 Ibid., 2: 3 l. 49–50.

111 Ibid., 2: 2 l. 46–98.

112 Ibid., 3: 3 l. 21–23.

113 Ibid., 2: 1 l. 19–20.

114 Ibid., 3: 3 l. 84–85.

115 Ibid., 3: 2 l. 44.

116 Ibid., 1: 1 l. 179.

117 Ibid., 1: 1 l. 18 and 1: 3 l. 70–71.

118 Ibid., 1: 4 l. 60–65.

119 Ibid., 2: 1 l. 173–201.

110 Ibid., 1: 1 l. 17 and 3: 2 l.21.

121 Ibid., 4: 1 l. 156–158.

122 Ibid., 5: 1 l. 229–231.

123 See Ricks, Christopher, *Essays in Appreciation*, Oxford: Oxford University Press, 1998, p. 4.

124 Jonson, *Every Man in His Humour*, op. cit. 5: 1 l. 250–253.

125 For an expanded view of some of the points raised here, see Tennenhouse, Leonard, *Power on Display: The Politics of Shakespeare's Genres*, London: Routledge, 2005.

126 Clement mocks Bobadill and jokes about cutting off Brainworm's arms, legs and head.

Chapter 7

1 For an overview of the period, see O'Gorman, Frank, *The Long Eighteenth Century: British Political and Social History*, London: Hodder and Arnold, 2007.

2 Shakespeare, William, *King Lear*, R. A. Foakes (ed.), The Arden Shakespeare, London: Bloomsbury, 2014, 4: 1 l. 38–39.

3 See Day, Gary and Keegan, Bridget (eds.), *The Eighteenth Century Literature Handbook*, London: Continuum, 2009.

4 Rymer, Thomas, 'Preface to Rapin' in Spingarn, J. E. (ed.), *Critical Essays of the Seventeenth Century: Volume II 1650–1685*, Oxford: Oxford University Press, 1957, pp. 163–181, p. 167.

5 Rymer, 'A Short View of Tragedy' in Ibid., pp. 208–255, p. 223.

6 Ibid., p. 222.

7 Rymer, 'Tragedies of the Last Age' in *Critical Essays of the Seventeenth Century: Volume II 1650–1685*, op. cit., pp. 181–208, p. 188.

8 Addison, Joseph, 'English Tragedy' in Steele, Richard and Addison, Joseph, *Selections from the Tatler and the Spectator*, edited with introduction and notes by Angus Ross, Harmondsworth: Penguin, 1988, pp. 322–334, p. 322.

9 Dryden, John, 'An Essay on Dramatic Poesy' in Womersley, David (ed.), *Augustan Critical Writing*, Harmondsworth: Penguin, 1997, pp. 15–78, p. 50.

10 Dryden, John, 'Heroic Plays' in Hudson, W. H. (ed.), *Dryden's Essays*, London: J. M. Dent, 1954, pp. 87–94, pp. 90 and 91.

11 Cited in Bevis, Richard W., *English Drama: Restoration and Eighteenth Century*, London: Longman, 1988, p. 130.

12 Ibid.

13 The belief that a merchant's fall could not have consequences for the nation may have been difficult to sustain after the collapse of the South Sea Company in 1720 bringing ruin to many.

14 Otway, Thomas, *The Orphan and Venice Preserved*, Charles F. Mcclumpha (ed.), London: Forgotten Books, 2012, 1: 1 l. 54.

15 Ibid., 2: 1 l. 228–229.

16 See Acasto's speech Ibid. 3: 1 l. 67–96.

17 Ibid, 3: 1 572 and 581.

18 It will be remembered that the 'sacrifice' of Clytemnestra took the form of her murder going unavenged. If the Furies had been allowed to punish her murderer, Orestes, the law would not have come into existence.

19 Otway, *The Orphan*, op. cit., 5: 2 l. 257 and 342–343.

20 Congreve, William, 'Concerning Humour in Comedy' in J. E. Spingarn (ed.), *Critical Essays of the Seventeenth Century: Volume III 1685–1700*, Oxford: Oxford University Press, 1957, pp. 242–252, p. 244.

21 Ibid., p. 252.

22 Addison, 'English Tragedy', op. cit., p. 328.

23 Wycherley, William, *The Country Wife*, edited by James Ogden with a new introduction by Tiffany Stern, London: Bloomsbury Methuen Drama, 2014, 5: 4 l. 92–96.

24 Ibid., 1: 1 l. 24–25.

25 Ibid., 4: 2 l. 54–55.

26 Ibid., 3: 2 l. 324.

27 Ibid., 1: 1 l. 220–221.

28 Ibid., 4: 1 l. 23–25 and 5: 2 l. 75–76.

29 Ibid., 3: 2 l. 79–86.

30 Ibid., 2: 1 l. 21.

31 Ibid., 5: 4 l. 80–82.

32 Ibid., 1: 1 l. 197.

33 Ibid., 4: 2 l. 145–150.

34 Ibid., 3: 2 l. 433–434.

35 Ibid., 5: 4 l. 332–333.

36 Ibid., 4: 2 l. 146–148.

37 Ibid., 1: 1 l. 179–180.

38 Ibid., 1: 1 l. 181–182.

39 Ibid., 1: 1 l. 215.

40 O'Brien, John, 'Pantomime' in Moody, Jane and O'Quinn, Daniel (eds.), *The Cambridge Companion to British Theatre 1730–1830*, Cambridge: Cambridge University Press, 2007, pp. 103–114, p. 103.

41 Bevis, *English Drama: Restoration and Eighteenth Century*, op. cit. p. 254.

Chapter 8

1   See, for example, Bratton, Jacky, *New Readings in Theatre History*, Cambridge: Cambridge University Press, 2003; Newey, Kate, Women's *Theatre Writing in Victorian Britain*, Basingstoke: Palgrave MacMillan, 2005; Foulkes, Richard (ed.), *British Theatre in the 1890s: Essays on Drama and the Stage*, Cambridge: Cambridge University Press, 2009.

2   Mayer, David, 'Encountering Melodrama' in Powell, Kerry (ed.), *Victorian and Edwardian Theatre*, Cambridge: Cambridge University Press, 2004, pp. 145–163, p. 159.

3   Smith, James L., *Melodrama*, London: Routledge, 1973, p. 17.

4   Ibid., p. 54.

5   Mayer, 'Encountering Melodrama', pp. 149–151.

6   Ibid., p. 148.

7   Smith, *Melodrama*, op. cit. p. 39.

8   Smith, *Melodrama*, op. cit. p. 38.

9   Jerrold, Douglas, *Black-Ey'd Susan* in Rowell, George (ed.), *Nineteenth Century Plays*, Oxford: Oxford University Press, 1972, 2:1, p. 19 (no line numbers given).

10 Congreve, William, *The Way of the World*, Brian Gibbons (ed.), London: A & C Black, 2005, 2: 1 l. 287–289.

11 Jerrold, *Black-Ey'd Susan*, op. cit. 3:2, p. 36.

12 Ibid., 1: 3, p. 10.

13 Ibid., 2: 1, p. 17.

14 See Platt, Richard, *Smuggling in the British Isles: A History*, Stroud: The History Press, 2011.

15 See Ibid., pp. 107–114.

16 Jerrold, *Black-Ey'd Susan*, op. cit. 2:3, p. 28.

17 Ibid.

18 The island was colonized by both Spain and France at different times. The British fought a sea battle against the French there during the Napoleonic Wars in 1806.

19 Jerrold, *Black-Ey'd Susan*, op. cit. 1:3, p. 13; 1:2, p. 7; 2:1, p. 21.

20 Booth, Michael, 'Comedy and Farce' in Powell (ed.), *Victorian and Edwardian Theatre*, op. cit. pp. 129–144, p. 129.

21 Thorndike, Ashley H., *English Comedy*, London: Macmillan, 1929, p. 509.

22 See Booth, 'Comedy and Farce', op. cit. p. 130.

23 Rowell, George, *The Victorian Theatre 1792–1914*, Cambridge: Cambridge University Press, 1978, p. 64.

24 See Booth, 'Comedy and Farce', op. cit. p. 130.

25 Booth, Michael, 'Early Victorian Farce: Dionysus Domesticated' in Richards, Kenneth and Thomson, Peter (eds.), *Nineteenth Century British Theatre*, London: Methuen, 1975, pp. 80–93.

26 Cited in Booth, 'Comedy and Farce', op. cit. p. 143.

27 Cited in Ibid., p. 135.

28 Wilde, Oscar, *A Woman of No Importance* in Oscar Wilde, *The Importance of Being Earnest and Other Plays*, edited with an introduction, commentary and notes by Richard Allen Cave, Harmondsworth: Penguin, 2000, Act 3, p. 157 (no division into scenes and no line numbers given).

29 Ibid., Act 2, p. 129.

30 Ibid., Act 4, p. 173.

31 Ibid., Act 2, p. 131 and Act 4, p. 159.

32 Ibid., Act 3, p. 155.

33 Ibid., Act 4, p. 167.

34 Ibid., Act 4, p. 160.

35 Ibid., Act 3, p. 148.

36 Ibid., Act 2, p. 130.

37 Ibid., Act 4, p. 167.

38 Ibid., Act 4, p. 165

39 Ibid., Act 4, p. 166.

40 Ibid., Act 4, p. 173.

41 Ibid., Act 1, p. 112.

42 Ibid., Act 2, p. 140.

43 Ibid., Act 4, p. 167.

44 Ibid., Act 4, p. 161.

45 Ibid., Act 4, pp. 164–165.

46 Ibid., Act 3, p. 143.

47 Ibid., Act 4, p. 166.

48 Ibid., Act 1, p. 120.

49 The sacrificial element in *Ghosts* is related to the inability to resolve issues arising from the past and in *A Doll's House* it is related to the control of female sexuality.

50 Ibsen, *Hedda Gabler* in *Plays: Two*, translated and introduced by Michael Meyer, London: Methuen, 1989 Act 1, p. 266 (no line numbers given). It is also the last line of the play.

51 Ibid., Act 3, p. 317.

52 Ibid., Act 2, pp. 285 and 291.

53 Ibid., Act 2, p. 293.

54 Ibid., Act 2, p. 275.

55 Ibid., Act 2, p. 277.

56 Ibid., Act 4, p. 332.

57 Ibid., Act 3, p. 309.

58 Ibid., Act 4, p. 328.

59   Ibid., Act 3, pp. 316–317.

60   For an overview of the development of music hall, see Bratton, Jacky, 'The Music Hall' in Powell (ed.), *Victorian and Edwardian Theatre*, op. cit. pp. 164–182 and for a fuller version Bailey, Peter (ed.), *Music Hall: The Business of Pleasure*, Milton Keynes: Open University Press, 1986.

61   Major, John, *My Old Man: A Personal History of Music Hall*, London: Harper Press, 2012, p. 81.

62   Ibid., p. 224.

63   Cited in Major, *My Old Man: A Personal History of Music Hall*, op. cit. p. 222.

64   Bratton, 'The Music Hall', op. cit. p. 166.

65   Major, *My Old Man: A Personal History of Music Hall*, op. cit. pp. 223–224.

66   Bratton, 'The Music Hall', op. cit. p. 171

67   See Bailey, 'Introduction' in *Music Hall: The Business of Pleasure*, op. cit., pp. viii–xxiii, p. xiii.

Chapter 9

1   For a view of American tragedy, see Palmer, David, *Visions of Tragedy in Modern American Drama*, London: Bloomsbury (2017).

2   For a general of how the brain evolved, see Plotkin, Henry, *Evolution in Mind: An Introduction to Evolutionary Psychology*, Harmondsworth: Penguin, 1997 and also Buss, David, *Evolutionary Psychology, The New Science of Mind*, London: Routledge, 2016.

3   For a recent account of kitchen-sink drama, see Rebellato, Dan, *1956 And All That: The Making of Modern British Drama*, London: Routledge, 1999.

4   For a discussion of why people may be fascinated with such videos, see http://www.ted.com/talks/frances_larson_why_public_beheadings_get_millions_of _views?utm_campaign=social&utm_medium=referral&utm_source=t.co&utm _content=talk&utm_term=global-social%20issues

5   Esslin, Martin, *The Theatre of the Absurd*, Harmondsworth: Penguin, 1991, p. 22.

6   Mercier, Vivien, *The Irish Times*, 18 February 1956.

7   Cited in Esslin, *The Theatre of the Absurd*, p. 44.

8   For a different views of the theatre of the absurd, see Bennett, Michael Y., *Reassessing the Theatre of the Absurd: Camus, Beckett, Ionesco, Genet and Pinter*, Basingstoke: Palgrave, 2011 and Lavery, Carl and Finburgh, Clare (eds.), *Rethinking the Theatre of the Absurd: Ecology, the Environment and the Greening of the Modern Stage*, London: Bloomsbury, 2015.

9   Esslin, *The Theatre of the Absurd*, p. 24.

10   Beckett, Samuel, *Waiting for Godot*, London: Faber, 2006, Act 1, p. 25 (no line numbers).

11 Ibid., Act 1, p. 1.

12 Ibid., Act 1, p. 11.

13 Ibid., Act 2, p. 82.

14 Ibid., Act 1, p. 34.

15 Ibid., Act 2, p. 83.

16 Ibid., Act 2. p. 86.

17 Shakespeare, William, *King Lear*, R. A. Foakes (ed.), The Arden Shakespeare, London: Bloomsbury, 2014, 3: 4 l. 105–106.

18 Beckett, *Waiting for Godot*, op. cit. Act 2, p. 53.

19 Shakespeare, William, *Hamlet*, Ann Thompson and Neil Taylor (eds.), The Arden Shakespeare, London: Thompson, 2007, 2: 2 l. 274.

20 Beckett, *Waiting for Godot*, op. cit. Act 2, p. 74.

21 Ibid., Act 1, pp. 36–38.

22 Ibid., Act 1, pp. 36–37.

23 Ibid., Act 1, p. 33.

24 Ibid., Act 1, p. 47, Act 2, p. 56.

25 Ibid., Act 1, p. 6, Act 2, p. 54.

26 Ibid., Act 1, p. 12, Act 2, p. 60.

27 Ibid., Act 1, p. 14.

28 Ibid., Act 1, p. 25, Act 2, p. 58.

29 Ibid., Ac 1, p. 3, Act 2, p. 51.

30 Ibid., Act 1, p. 29.

31 Ibid., Act 2, pp. 52 and 53, Act 1, p. 27.

32 Ibid., Act 2, pp. 60 and 68.

33 Santayana, George, *The Life of Reason*, New York: Charles Scribner's Sons, 1905, p. 284.

34 Ibid., Act 2, p. 85.

35 Ibid., Act 1, p. 36.

36 Ibid., Act 1, p. 10.

37 See *The Gospel according to Saint Matthew*, King James Version, chapter 25 verse 32.

38 Beckett, *Waiting for Godot*, op. cit. Act 1, p. 44.

39 Ibid., Act 1, pp. 3–5.

40 Ibid., Act 2, p. 64.

41 Simon Gray (1936–2008) has been credited with the first use of 'in your face' theatre in his 2001 play *Japes*.

42 Sierz, Aleks, *In-Yer-Face Theatre: British Drama Today*, London: Faber, 2001, p. 4.

43 Cited in Ibid., p. 101.

44 Ibid.

45 Kane, Sarah, *Blasted* in *Complete Plays*, Introduced by David Greig, London: Methuen, 2001, scene 3, p. 48 (no line numbers).

46 Ibid., Scene 2, p. 31 and Scene 3, p. 46.

47 Bataille, George, 'The Accursed Share' in Carter, Jeffrey (eds.), *Understanding Religious Sacrifice: A Reader*, London: Continuum, 2006, pp. 162–177, pp. 170–171.

48 Bataille, George, 'Sacrifice, the Festival and the Principles of the Sacred Word' in Botting, Fred and Wilson, Scott (eds.), *The Bataille Reader*, Oxford: Blackwell, 1997, pp. 210–219, p. 213.

49 Ibid., pp. 210, 212, and 214.

50 Bataille, 'The Accursed Share', op. cit. p. 172.

51 Bataille, 'Sacrifice, the Festival and the Principles of the Sacred Word', op. cit. p. 212.

52 Ibid., p. 215.

53 Ibid.

54 Ibid., p. 217.

55 Kane, *Blasted*, op. cit. Scene 3, p. 47. See also Scene 1, pp. 12–13 and Scene 3, pp. 43–47.

56 Ibid., Scene 1, p. 19.

57 Ibid., Scene 1, p. 10. See also Scene 2, p. 23.

58 Ibid., Scene 5, p. 60.

59 Ibid., Scene 3, p. 48.

60 Ibid., Scene 4, p. 54.

61 Ibid., p. 55.

62 Williams, Tennessee, *A Streetcar Named Desire*, London: Methuen Student Edition, 1994, Scene 9, p. 73 (no line numbers).

63 Ibid., Scene 3, p. 30.

64 Ibid., Scene 7, p. 61.

65 Ibid., Scene 2, p. 17.

66 Ibid., Scene 3, p. 29.

67 Ibid., Scene 3, p. 30.

68 Ibid., Scene 8, p. 66.

69 Ibid., Scene 7, pp. 59–61.

70 Ibid., Scene 4, p. 41.

71 Ibid., Scene 4, p. 40.

72 Ibid., Scene 5, p. 45.

73 Ibid., Scene 4, p. 41.

74 Ibid., Scene 4, p. 36.

75 Ibid., Scene 9, p. 68.

76   Ibid., Scene 4, p. 40.

77   Ibid., Scene 5, p. 45.

78   Ibid., Scene 4, p. 40.

79   New Orleans is a port. Its main business in the 1940s was handling port traffic but it also produced and exported iron, steel and petroleum products.

80   Williams, *A Streetcar Named Desire*, Scene 11, p. 88.

81   Ibid. Scene 10, p. 80.

82   Ibid. Scene 11, p. 82.

83   Ibid., 90.

84   Ibid., p. 83.

85   Parks, Suzan-Lori, *Top Dog/Under Dog*, New York: Theatre Communications Group, 2002, Scene 1, p. 24 (no line numbers).

86   Ibid., Scene 2, p. 33.

87   Ibid., p. 29.

88   Ibid., p. 32.

89   Ibid., Scene 1, p. 19.

90   Ibid., Scene 4, p. 54.

91   Ibid., Scene 2, p. 35.

92   Ibid., Scene 6, pp. 83–84.

93   Ibid., Scene 5, p. 74.

94   Ibid., Scene 6, p. 97.

95   Parks, *Top Dog/Under Dog*, op. cit. Scene 1, p. 21.

96   Ibid. Scene 6, p. 93.

97   Williams, *A Streetcar Named Desire*, op. cit. Scene 11, p. 82.

98   Parks, *Top Dog/Under Dog*, op. cit. Scene 2, p. 35.

99   Ibid., Scene 1, p. 9; Scene 2, p. 36; Scene 3, pp. 47–48; pp. 50–52; Scene 5, p. 73.

100 Ibid., Scene 5, p. 68.

101 Ibid., Scene 6, p. 105.

102 Ibid., Scene 2, pp. 40, 43; Scene 4, pp. 64, 66; Scene 5, pp. 81, 86.

103 See Fox, Richard, 'The President Who Died for Us', *New York Times*, 14 April 2006.

104 Holzer, Harold, *President Lincoln Assassinated: The First Hand Story of the Murder, Manhunt Trail and Mourning*, New York Library of America, p. 7.

105 This is a very crude summary of Freud's argument in 'Beyond the Pleasure Principle' in *Sigmund Freud: On Metapsychology*, translated by James Strachey, edited by Angela Richards, Harmondsworth: Penguin, 1991, pp. 275–335.

106 Parks, *Top Dog/Under Dog*, op. cit. Scene 3, p. 45.

107 See, for example, Ibid., Scene 4, p. 41.

108 Ibid., Scene 6, pp. 100–101.

109 Ibid., p. 90.

110 Ibid.

111 Ibid., Scene 3, pp. 39 and 42.

112 Ibid., Scene 3, p. 48 and Scene 6, p. 86.

113 See *Genesis* 4, King James Version.

114 Parks, *Top Dog/Under Dog*, op. cit. Scene 3, pp. 38–40.

115 See, for example, Ibid., p. 40.

116 Jones, Charlotte, *Humble Boy*, London: Faber, 2001, 2: 1, p. 71 (no line numbers).

117 Ibid., p. 77.

118 Ibid., 1: 1, p. 8.

119 *Hamlet*, op. cit. 1: 5 l. 165–166.

120 *Hamlet*, op. cit. 3: 1 l. 55.

121 Jones, *Humble Boy*, op. cit. 1: 3, p. 27.

122 Ibid., 2: 1, p. 81.

123 *Hamlet*, op. cit. 3: 4 l. 89–92.

124 Jones, *Humble Boy*, op. cit. 1: 2, p. 16.

125 Ibid., 2: 1, p. 84 and see *Hamlet*, op. cit. 3: 1 l. 120.

126 Ibid., 1: 1, p. 7.

127 Flora belongs to a tradition in comedy of older women seeking to retain or recapture their youth. One of the most famous examples is Lady Wishfort in William Congreve's *The Way of the World* (1700).

128 Jones, *Humble Boy*, op. cit. 2: 1, p. 73.

129 Wilde, Oscar, 'The Ballad of Reading Gaol' in Gardner, Helen (ed.), *The New Oxford Book of English Verse*, Oxford: Oxford University Press, 1973, p. 797.

130 Jones, *Humble Boy*, op. cit. 2: 1, p. 90.

131 Ibid., 2: 1, p. 76.

132 Ibid., 1: 2, p. 25.

133 Ibid., 1: 4, p. 44.

134 See, for example, *Hamlet*, op. cit. 3: 4 l. 54–61.

135 Jones, *Humble Boy*, op. cit. 1: 3, p. 26.

136 Ibid., 1: 3, pp. 36–39 and 2: 1, pp. 64 and 71.

137 Ibid., 1: 4, p. 44.

138 Ibid., 1: 2, p. 22.

139 Jones, *Humble Boy*, op. cit. 2: 1, p. 95.

140 Shakespeare, William, *The Winter's Tale*, John Pitcher (ed.), The Arden Shakespeare, London: Bloomsbury, 2010, 3: 3, l.

141 Jones, *Humble Boy*, op. cit. 2: 1, p. 100.

142 *Hamlet*, op. cit. 4: 5 l, pp. 175–185.

143   Ibid., 1: 1, p. 6 and 2: 1, p. 59.

144   Ibid., p. 67.

145   Ibid., p. 93.

146   Ibid., 1:3, p. 28; 1:4, p. 51; 2:1, p. 58.

147   It is also a place of corruption (the serpent) and betrayal (Gethsemane) and it is possible to argue that both are present, in a minor way, in Jim's garden.

148   Jones, *Humble Boy*, 1: 4, p. 42.

149   Ibid., 2: 1, p. 79.

150   Ibid., 1: 3, p. 31.

151   Ibid., p. 33.

152   Ibid., p. 32.

153   Ibid., 2: 1, p. 69.

154   Ibid., p. 97.

155   Eliot, T. S., 'Hamlet' in *Selected Essays*, London: Faber, 1976, pp. 141–146, p. 145.

156   Jones, *Humble Boy*, p. 1.

157   Ruhl, Sarah, *The Clean House*, London and New York: Samuel French, 2007, 1: 13, p. 29 (no line numbers).

158   Ibid., p. 5.

159   Ibid., 1: 7, p. 17.

160   Ibid.

161   Ibid., 2: 5, p. 48.

162   Ibid., 1: 12, p. 27.

163   Ibid., 2: 10, p. 73.

164   Ibid., 2: 5, pp. 49–50.

165   Ibid., 1: 14, p. 37.

166   Ibid., 2: 10, p. 72.

167   Ibid., 1: 13, p. 35.

168   Ibid., 1: 10, pp. 22–23.

169   Ibid., 1: 2, p. 7; 1: 7, p. 15 and 1: 13, p. 34.

170   Ibid., 2: 12, p. 76.

171   Ibid., 2: 2, p. 42.

172   Ibid., 2: 5, p. 51.

173   Ibid., p. 52.

174   Ibid., 1: 3, p. 9.

175   Ibid., 1: 10, pp. 22–23.

176   Ibid., 2: 5, p. 51.

177   Ibid., 1: 13, pp. 34–35.

178   Ibid., 1: 10, p. 22.

179   Ibid., 1: 3, p. 8.

180   Ibid., 1: 7, p. 18 and 1: 13, p. 35.

181   Ibid., 1: 7, p. 15.

182   Douglas, Mary, *Purity and Danger: An Analysis of Concepts of Pollution and Taboo*, London: Routledge, 1976, p. 76.

183   Ruhl, *The Clean House*, op. cit. 1: 3, p. 9.

184   Ibid., 1: 13, p. 35.

185   Ibid., 1: 1, p. 11.

186   Ibid.

187   Ibid., 1: 3, p. 8.

188   Ibid., 2: 12, p. 76.

189   Frazer, James, *The Golden Bough: A Study in Magic and Religion*, edited with an introduction and notes by Robert Fraser, Oxford: Oxford University Press, 2009, p. 487.

190   This idea is ubiquitous in Freud's writing. A relatively early expression of it – 'what, in the conscious, is found split into a pair of opposites, often occurs in the unconscious as a unity' – can be found in 'A Special Type of Object Choice Made By Men' in *Five Lectures on Psychoanalysis, Leonardo Da Vinci and Other Works: The Standard Edition of the Complete Psychological Works of Sigmund Freud Volume 11* (1910), translated by James Strachey in collaboration with Anna Freud assisted by Alix Strachey and Alan Tyson, London: Vintage The Hogarth Press and the Institute of Psychoanalysis, [1957] and 2001, pp. 165–175, p. 170.

191   See Freud, Sigmund, 'Obsessive Actions and Religious Practices' in *Jensen's 'Gradvia' and Other Works: The Standard Edition of the Complete Psychological Works of Sigmund Freud Volume IX* (1906–1908), translated by James Strachey in collaboration with Anna Freud assisted by Alix Strachey and Alan Tyson, London: Vintage The Hogarth Press and the Institute of Psychoanalysis, [1959] and 2001, pp. 117–127.

192   Ruhl, *The Clean House*, op. cit. 2: 9, pp. 65.

193   Ibid., p. 67.

194   Ibid., 1: 13, p. 32.

195   Ibid., 1: 10, p. 21.

196   Ibid., 1: 9, p. 20.

197   Ibid., 1: 7, p. 18.

198   Ibid., 2: 14, p. 86.

199   Ibid., 2: 13, p. 83.

200   Ibid., 1: 10, p. 22.

201   Ibid., 2: 7, pp. 61–62.

202   Ibid., 2: 6, p. 58.

203   Ibid., 1: 9, p. 20.

204   Ibid., 2: 5, p. 51.

Chapter 10

1   Examples of academic studies include Hughes, Derek, *Culture and Sacrifice: Ritual Death in Literature and Opera*, Cambridge: Cambridge University Press, 2007; Halbertal, Moshe, *On Sacrifice*, Princeton: Princeton University Press, 2011, O'Leary, Joseph, 'Five Books on Sacrifice; New Approaches to Sacrificial Studies' *Reviews in Religion and Theology*, 21:3, 2014, pp. 289–296. Examples of novels include Boult, Sharon, *Sacrifice*, London: Banta Books, 2008, Oates, Joyce Carol, *The Sacrifice*, New York: Harper Collins, 2015, and, for teenagers, Duble, Kathleen Benner, *The Sacrifice*, New York: Simon Schuster, 2007. Examples of films include *The Sacrifice*, directed by Andrei Tarkovsky, 1986, *Sacrifice*, directed by Chen Kaige, 2010, *Sacrifice*, directed by Damian Lee, 2011.

2   http://www.theguardian.com/politics/2015/jan/26/david-cameron-tax-cuts-reward-for-sacrifice

3   http://www.theguardian.com/lifeandstyle/2015/apr/18/rachel-billington-my-grandfathers-sacrifice-at-gallipoli

4   http://www.theguardian.com/commentisfree/2014/apr/18/sacrifice-easter-human-experience-christians

5   Meszaros, Julia and Zachhuber, Johannes, 'Introduction' in Meszaros, Julia and Zachhuber, Johannes (eds.), *Sacrifice and Modern Thought* (Oxford: Oxford University Press, 2013) pp. 1–11, p. 11.

6   http://www.theguardian.com/commentisfree/2014/jan/01/scapegoating-bulgarian-romanian-migrants-britain-crisis and see Quarmby, Katharine, *Scapegoat: Why We Are Failing Disabled People* (2011), London: Portobello Books, 2011 and Jones, Owen, *Chavs: The Demonization of the Working Class*, London and New York, 2011.

7   See Chapter 2, 'Tragedy, Comedy and Ritual'.

8   This happens in Seasons 2 (2002–2003), 4 (2004) and 5 (2006).

9   Ayckbourn, Alan, *Three Plays: Absurd Person Singular, Absent Friends, Bedroom Farce*, Harmondsworth: Penguin, 1979, p. 54.

10   For a different view at least of American tragedy, see Palmer, David, *Visions of Tragedy in Modern American Drama*, London: Bloomsbury Methuen Drama, 2017.

11   *Alien*, 1979; *Aliens*, 1986; *Alien 3* 1992; *Alien Resurrection*, 1997, Twentieth Century Fox.

12   Knight, Stephen, *Crime Fiction Since 1800: Detection, Death and Diversity*, London: Palgrave, 2010, p. 67.

13   Pugh, Martin, *We Danced All Night: A Social History of Britain Between the Wars*, London: Vintage, 2009, pp. 9–11.

14   Maccoby, Hyam, *The Sacred Executioner: Human Sacrifice and the Legacy of Guilt*, London: Thames and Hudson, 1982.

15   See, for example, Belsey, Catherine, *The Subject of Tragedy: Identity and Difference in Renaissance Drama*, London: Routledge, 1985, Dollimore, Jonathan, *Radical Tragedy: Religion, Ideology and Power in the Drama of Shakespeare and His Contemporaries*, Hertfordshire: Harvester Wheatsheaf, 1989, Hawkes, Terence, *Meaning by Shakespeare*, London: Routledge, 1992.

BIBLIOGRAPHY

Primary sources

Aristophanes, *The Wasps* in Aristophanes, *The Wasps, The Poet and the Women, The Frogs*, translated with an Introduction by David Barrett, Harmondsworth: Penguin, 1964.

Aristophanes, *The Acharnians* in *Lysistrata, The Acharnians, The Clouds*, translated with an Introduction by Alan H. Sommerstein, Harmondsworth: Penguin, 1973.

Aristophanes, *Women at the Thesmophoria* in *Frogs and Other Plays*, translated by David Barrett; revised translation with an Introduction and Notes by Shomit Dutta, Harmondsworth: Penguin, 2007.

Ayckbourn, Alan, *Three Plays: Absurd Person Singular, Absent Friends, Bedroom Farce*, Harmondsworth: Penguin, 1979.

Beadle, Richard and King, Pamela M. (eds.), *The York Mystery Plays: A Selection in Modern Spelling*, Oxford: Oxford University Press, 2009.

Beckett, Samuel, *Waiting for Godot*, London: Faber, 2006.

Congreve, William, *The Way of the World*, edited by Brian Gibbons, London: A & C Black, 2005.

Eliot, T. S., *The Four Quartets*, London: Faber, 2001.

Euripides, *The Bacchae and Other Plays*, translated by John Davie with an Introduction and Notes by Richard Rutherford, Harmondsworth: Penguin, 2005.

Hughes, Ted, *The Oresteia: A New Version*, London: Faber, 1999.

Ibsen, *Hedda Gabler* in *Plays: Two*, translated and introduced by Michael Meyer, London: Methuen, 1989.

Jerrold, Douglas, 'Black-Ey'd Susan' in Rowell, George (ed.), *Nineteenth Century Plays*, Oxford: Oxford University Press, 1972.

Jones, Charlotte, *Humble Boy*, London: Faber, 2001.

Jonson, Ben, *Every Man in His Humour*, edited by Robert N. Watson, London: New Mermaids, A & C Black, 1998.

Jonson, Ben, *Every Man Out of His Humour*, London: First Rate Publishers, 2014.

Kane, Sarah, *Blasted* in *Complete Plays*, Introduced by David Greig, London: Methuen, 2001.

Lester, G. A. (ed.), *Everyman* in *Three Late Medieval Morality Plays*, London: A & C Black, 1997.

Marlowe, Christopher, *Tamburlaine the Great*, edited by J. S. Cunningham & Eithne Henson, Revels Student Edition, Manchester: Manchester University Press, 1998.

Menander, *The Bad-Tempered Man* in *The Plays and Fragments*, translated with notes by Maurice Balme, with an Introduction by Peter Brown, Oxford: Oxford University Press, 2008.

Middleton, Thomas, *The Revenger's Tragedy*, edited by R. A. Foakes, Revels
    Student Editions, Manchester: Manchester University Press, 1996.
Otway, Thomas, *The Orphan and Venice Preserved*, edited by Charles F.
    Mcclumpha, London: Forgotten Books, 2012.
Parks, Suzan-Lori, *Top Dog/Under Dog*, New York: Theatre Communications
    Group, 2002.
Plautus, *The Rope* in *The Rope and Other Plays*, translated and with an
    Introduction by E. F. Watling, Harmondsworth: Penguin, 1964.
Ruhl, Sarah, *The Clean House*, London and New York: Samuel French, 2007.
Seneca, *The Trojan Women in Four Tragedies and Octavia*, translated with an
    Introduction by E. F. Watling, Harmondsworth: Penguin, 1966.
Shakespeare William, *Hamlet*, edited by Ann Thompson and Neil Taylor, The
    Arden Shakespeare, London: Thompson, 2007.
Shakespeare, William, *King Lear*, edited by R. A. Foakes, The Arden Shakespeare,
    London: Bloomsbury, 2014.
Shakespeare, William, *A Midsummer Night's Dream*, edited by Harold F. Brooks,
    The Arden Shakespeare, London: Methuen Drama, 2007.
Shakespeare William, *As You Like It*, edited by Juliet Dusinberre, The Arden
    Shakespeare, London: Thompson, 2006.
Shakespeare, William, *The Winter's Tale*, edited by John Pitcher, The Arden
    Shakespeare, London: Bloomsbury, 2010.
Sophocles, *Oedipus the King* in *The Three Theban Plays: Antigone, Oedipus the
    King, Oedipus at Colonus*, translated by Robert Fagles with an Introduction
    and Notes by Bernard Knox, Harmondsworth: Penguin, 1984.
Wilde, Oscar, *A Woman of No Importance* in Oscar Wilde, *The Importance of
    Being Earnest and Other Plays*, edited with an Introduction, Commentary and
    Notes by Richard Allen Cave, Harmondsworth: Penguin, 2000.
Williams, Tennessee, *A Streetcar Named Desire*, London: Methuen Student Edition,
    1994.
Wycherley, William, *The Country Wife*, edited by James Ogden with a new
    Introduction by Tiffany Stern, London: Bloomsbury Methuen Drama, 2014.

Secondary sources

Ackerman, Robert, *The Myth and Ritual School: J.G. Frazer and the Cambridge
    Ritualists*, London: Routledge, 2002.
Bailey, Peter (ed.), *Music Hall: The Business of Pleasure*, Milton Keynes: Open
    University Press, 1986.
Barber, C. L., *Shakespeare's Festive Comedy: A Study of Dramatic Form and Its
    Relation to Social Custom*, Princeton: Princeton University Press, 1959.
Bataille, George, from 'The Accursed Share' in Carter, Jeffrey (ed.), *Understanding
    Religious Sacrifice: A Reader*, London: Continuum, 2006, pp. 162–177.
Bataille, George, 'Sacrifice, the Festival and the Principles of the Sacred Word' in
    Botting, Fred and Wilson, Scott (eds.), *The Bataille Reader*, Oxford: Blackwell,
    1997, pp. 210–219.
Beadle, Richard (ed.), *The Cambridge Companion to Medieval Theatre*,
    Cambridge: Cambridge University Press, 1994.
Becker, Earnest, *The Denial of Death*, New York: Simon and Schuster, 1973.

Beers, William, *Women and Sacrifice: Male Narcissism and the Psychology of Religion*, Detroit: Wayne State University Press, 1992.

Bell, Michael, *Literature, Modernism and Myth: Belief and Responsibility in the Twentieth Century*, Cambridge: Cambridge University Press, 1997.

Belsey, Catherine, *The Subject of Tragedy: Identity and Difference in Renaissance Drama*, London: Routledge, 1985.

Bennett, Michael Y., *Reassessing The Theatre of the Absurd: Camus, Beckett, Ionesco, Genet and Pinter*, Basingstoke: Palgrave, 2011.

Bergson, Henri, *Laughter: An Essay on the Meaning of the Comic*, translated by Cloudesely Brereton and Fred Rothwell, Rockville: Arc Manor, 2008.

Bevington, D. M., *From Mankind to Marlowe: Growth of Structure in the Popular Drama of Tudor England*, Cambridge, MA: Harvard University Press, 1962.

Bevis, Richard W., *English Drama: Restoration and Eighteenth Century*, London: Longman, 1988.

Boardman, John, Griffin, Jasper and Murray, Oswyn (eds.), *The Oxford History of Greece and the Hellenistic World*, Oxford: Oxford University Press, 1988.

Booth, Michael, 'Early Victorian Farce: Dionysus Domesticated' in Richards, Kenneth and Thomson, Peter (eds.), *Nineteenth Century British Theatre*, London: Methuen, 1975, pp. 80–93.

Booth, Michael, 'Comedy and Farce' in Powell, Kerry (ed.), *The Cambridge Companion to Victorian and Edwardian Theatre*, Cambridge: Cambridge University Press, 2004, pp. 129–144.

Botting, Fred and Wilson, Scott (eds.), *The Bataille Reader*, Oxford: Blackwell, 1997.

Bowden, Hugh, *Mystery Cults in the Ancient World*, London: Thames and Hudson, 2010.

Boyle, A. J., *Roman Tragedy*, London and New York: Routledge, 2006.

Bratton, Jacky, *New Readings in Theatre History*, Cambridge: Cambridge University Press, 2003.

Bratton, Jacky, 'The Music Hall' in Powell, Kerry (ed.), *The Cambridge Companion to Victorian and Edwardian Theatre*, Cambridge: Cambridge University Press, 2004, pp. 164–182.

Braunmuller, A. R. and Hattaway, Michael (eds.), *The Cambridge Companion to English Renaissance Drama*, Cambridge: Cambridge University Press, 2nd edn, 2003.

Brecht, Bertolt, 'A Short Organum for the Theatre' in *Brecht on Theatre: The Development of an Aesthetic*, edited and translated by John Willets, London: Methuen, 1964.

Brockett, Oscar G. and Franklin, J. Hildy, *History of the Theatre*, Boston: Allyn and Bacon, 1970.

Brody, Alan, *The English Mummers and Their Plays: Traces of Ancient Mystery*, Philadelphia: University of Pennsylvania Press, 1970.

Burkert, Walter, *Homo Necans: The Anthropology of Ancient Greek Sacrificial Ritual and Myth*, translated by Peter Bing, Berkley: University of California Press, 1983.

Burkert, Walter, *The Creation of the Sacred*, Harvard: Harvard University Press, 1998.

Buss, David, *Evolutionary Psychology, The New Science of Mind*, London: Routledge, 2016.

Calder, William M. (ed.), *The Cambridge Ritualists Reconsidered*, Atlanta: Scholars Press, 1991.

Carter, Jeffrey, *Understanding Religious Sacrifice: A Reader*, London: Continuum, 2006.

Cawley, A. C., Jones, Marion, McDonald, Peter F. and Mills, David (eds.), *The Revels History of Drama in English: Volume 1 Medieval Drama*, London: Methuen, 1983.

Cawthorne, Nigel, *Robin Hood: The True History behind the Legend*, London: Running Press, 2010.

Chambers, E. K., *The English Folk Play*, Oxford: Clarendon Press, 1933.

Congreve, William, 'Concerning Humour in Comedy' in Spingarn, J. E. (ed.), *Critical Essays of the Seventeenth Century: Volume III 1685–1700*, Oxford: Oxford University Press, 1957, pp. 242–252.

Cornford, Macdonald Francis, *The Origin of Attic Comedy*, Cambridge: Cambridge University Press, [1914 Edward Arnold, 1934 Cambridge] 2010.

Csapo, Eric and Miller, Margaret C. (eds.), *The Origins of Theatre in Ancient Greece and Beyond: From Ritual to Drama*, Cambridge: Cambridge University Press, 2007.

Danby, John F., *Shakespeare's Doctrine of Nature: A Study of King Lear*, London: Faber, 1965.

Day, Gary and Keegan, Bridget (eds.), *The Eighteenth Century Literature Handbook*, London: Continuum, 2009.

Dillon, Janette, *The Cambridge Introduction to Early English Theatre*, Cambridge: Cambridge University Press, 2006.

Dollimore, Jonathan, *Radical Tragedy: Religion, Ideology and Power in the Drama of Shakespeare and His Contemporaries*, Hertfordshire: Harvester Wheatsheaf, 1989.

Douglas, Mary, *Purity and Danger: An Analysis of Concepts of Pollution and Taboo*, London: Routledge, 1976.

Dryden, John, *Dryden's Essays*, edited by W. H. Hudson, London: J. M. Dent, 1954.

Duckworth, George E., *The Nature of Roman Comedy: A Study in Popular Entertainment*, Norman: University of Oklahoma Press, 1994.

Durkheim, Émile, *The Elementary Forms of Religious Life*, translated by Carol Cosman, Oxford: Oxford University Press, 2008.

Easterling, P. E. (ed.), *The Cambridge Companion to Greek Tragedy*, Cambridge: Cambridge University Press, 2004.

Ehrenreich, Barbara, *Dancing in the Streets: A History of Collective Joy*, London: Granta, 2007.

Eliot, T. S., *Selected Essays*, London: Faber, 1976.

Elton, William R., *King Lear and the Gods*, California: Huntingdon Library, 1968.

Esslin, Martin, *The Theatre of the Absurd*, Harmondsworth: Penguin, 1991.

Foulkes, Richard (ed.), *British Theatre in the 1890s: Essays on Drama and the Stage*, Cambridge: Cambridge University Press, 2009.

Fox, Richard, 'The President Who Died for Us', *New York Times*, 14 April 2006

Frazer, James, *The Golden Bough: A Study in Magic and Religion*, edited with an Introduction and Notes by Robert Fraser, Oxford: Oxford University Press, 2009.

Freud, Sigmund, *On Metapsychology*, translated by James Strachey, edited by Angela Richards, Harmondsworth: Penguin, 1991.

Freud, Sigmund, *The Ego and the Id and Other Works: The Standard Edition of the Complete Psychological Works of Sigmund Freud Volume XIX 1923–25*, London: Vintage The Hogarth Press and the Institute of Psychoanalysis, [1958] and 2001.

Freud, Sigmund, *Five Lectures on Psychoanalysis, Leonardo Da Vinci and Other Works: The Standard Edition of the Complete Psychological Works of Sigmund Freud Volume 11* (1910), London: The Hogarth Press and the Institute of Psychoanalysis, [1957] and 2001.

Freud, Sigmund, *The Future of an Illusion, Civilization and its Discontents and Other Works, The Standard Edition of the Complete Psychological Works of Sigmund Freud Volume XXI* (1927–1931), London: Vintage The Hogarth Press and the Institute of Psychoanalysis, [1961] and 2001.

Freud, Sigmund, *Jensen's 'Gradvia' and other works: The Standard Edition of the Complete Psychological Works of Sigmund Freud Volume IX* (1906–1908), London: Vintage the Hogarth Press and the Institute of Psychoanalysis, [1959] and 2001.

Freud, Sigmund, *Moses and Monotheism, An Outline of Psychoanalysis: The Standard Edition of the Complete Psychological Works of Sigmund Freud Volume XXIII* (1937–39), London: Vintage The Hogarth Press and the Institute of Psychoanalysis, [1964] and 2001.

Freud, Sigmund, 'Three Essays on the Theory of Sexuality' in *A Case of Hysteria, Three Essays on Sexuality and Other Works: The Standard Edition of the Complete Psychological Works of Sigmund Freud Volume VII* (1901–1905), translated by James Strachey, London: Vintage The Hogarth Press and the Institute of Psychoanalysis, [1953] and 2001.

Freud, Sigmund, *Totem and Taboo and Other Works: The Standard Edition of the Complete Psychological Works of Sigmund Freud Volume XIII* (1913–1914), London: Vintage The Hogarth Press and the Institute of Psychoanalysis, [1955] and 2001.

Futrell, Alice, *The Roman Games: Historical Sources in Translation*, Oxford: Blackwell, 2006.

Girard, René, *The Girard Reader*, edited by James G. Williams, New York: The Crossroad Publishing Company, 1996.

Goldhill, Simon, *Love, Sex and Tragedy: Why Classics Matter*, London: John Murray, 2004.

Goldhill, Simon, 'The Audience of Athenian Tragedy' in Easterling, P. E. (ed.), *The Cambridge Companion to Greek Tragedy*, Cambridge: Cambridge University Press, 2004 pp. 54–68.

Graves, Robert, *The Greek Myths: The Complete and Definitive Edition*, Harmondsworth: Penguin, 2011.

Halbertal, Moshe, *On Sacrifice*, Princeton: Princeton University Press, 2011.

Hall, Edith, 'The Sociology of Athenian Tragedy' in Easterling, P. E. (ed.), *The Cambridge Companion to Greek Tragedy*, Cambridge: Cambridge University Press, 2004, pp. 93–126.

Hamerton-Kelly, Robert G., *Violent Origins: Ritual Killing and Cultural Formations*, Stanford: Stanford University Press, 1987.

Hardison, O. B. Jr., *Christian Rite and Christian Drama in the Middle Ages: Essays in the Origin and Early History of Modern Drama*, Baltimore: Johns Hopkins University Press, 1965.

Harrison, Jane, *Themis: A Study of the Social Origins of Greek Religion*, London: Merlin Press, [1912] and 1989.

Hattaway, Michael, 'Drama and Society' in Braunmuller, A. R. and Hattaway, Michael (eds.), *The Cambridge Companion to English Renaissance Drama*, Cambridge: Cambridge University Press, 2nd edn, 2003, pp. 93–130.

Hawkes, Terence, *Meaning by Shakespeare*, London: Routledge, 1992.

Heath, Malcolm, 'Euripides' Telephus', *Classical Quarterly* 1987, 37, pp. 272–280.

Hegel, G. W. F., *Aesthetics: Lectures on Fine Arts*, translated by T. M. Knox, 2 Volumes, Oxford: Clarendon Press, 1975.

Hemmer, Bjørn, 'Ibsen and the Realistic Problem Drama' in McFarlane, James (ed.), *The Cambridge Companion to Ibsen*, Cambridge: Cambridge University Press, 1994, pp. 68–87.

Holzer, Harold, *President Lincoln Assassinated: The Firsthand Story of the Murder, Manhunt Trial and Mourning*, New York Library of America, 2015.

Horace, 'A Letter to Augustus' in Russell, D. A. and Winterbottom, M. (eds.), *Ancient Literary Criticism: The Principal Texts in New Translations*, Oxford: Oxford University Press, 1972, pp. 272–279.

Hubert, Henri and Mauss, Marcel, *Sacrifice Its Nature and Functions*, translated by W. D. Halls, Chicago: Chicago University Press, 1981.

Hughes, Derek, *Culture and Sacrifice: Ritual Death in Literature and Opera*, Cambridge: Cambridge University Press, 2007.

Hutton, Ronald, *The Rise and Fall of Merry England: The Ritual Year 1400–1700*, Oxford: Oxford University Press, 1996.

Jay, Nancy, *Throughout Your Generations Forever: Sacrifice, Religion and Paternity*, Chicago: Chicago University Press, 1992.

Jensen, A. E., *Myth and Cult among Primitive Peoples*, translated by M. T. Choldin, Chicago: Chicago University Press, 1963.

Jones, Marion, 'Moral and Secular Drama' in Cawley, A. C., Jones, Marion, McDonald, Peter F. and Mills, David (eds.), *The Revels History of Drama in English: Volume 1 Medieval Drama*, London: Methuen, 1983, pp. 213–291.

Jones, Owen, *Chavs: The Demonization of the Working Class*, London and New York: Verso, 2011.

King, Pamela M., 'Morality Plays' in Beadle, Richard (ed.), *The Cambridge Companion to Medieval Theatre*, Cambridge: Cambridge University Press, 1994, pp. 240–264.

Klauser, Theodor, *A Short History of the Western Liturgy*, translated by John Halliburton, Oxford: Oxford University Press, 1979.

Klein, David, *Literary Criticism from the Elizabethan Dramatists*, New York: Sturgis and Walton, 1910.

Knight, Stephen, *Crime Fiction since 1800: Detection, Death and Diversity*, London: Palgrave, 2010.

Konstan, David, *Roman Comedy*, Ithaca and London Cornell University Press, 1983.

Krasner, David, *American Drama, 1945–2000: An Introduction*, Oxford: Blackwell, 2006.

Lavery, Carl and Finburgh, Clare (eds.), *Rethinking the Theatre of the Absurd: Ecology, the Environment and the Greening of the Modern Stage*, London: Bloomsbury, 2015.

Leach, Edmund, 'Reflections on a Visit to Nemi: Did Frazer Get It Wrong?' *Anthropology Today* 1985, 1:2, pp. 14–21.

Levenson, Jill, 'Comedy' in *The Cambridge Companion to English Renaissance Drama*, Cambridge: Cambridge University Press, 2nd edn, 2003, pp. 254–291.

Lowe, N. J., *Comedy: New Surveys in the Classics No. 37*, Cambridge: Cambridge University Press, 2008.

Maccoby, Hyam, *The Sacred Executioner: Human Sacrifice and the Legacy of Guilt*, London: Thames and Hudson, 1982.

MacCulloch, Diarmaid, *A History of Christianity*, Harmondsworth: Penguin, 2010.

Mahoney, Anne, *Roman Sports and Spectacles: A Sourcebook*, Newbury Port, MA: Focus Publishing, 2001.

Major, John, *My Old Man: A Personal History of Music Hall*, London: Harper Press, 2012.

Mayer, David, 'Encountering Melodrama' in Powell, Kerry (ed.), *The Cambridge Companion to Victorian and Edwardian Theatre*, Cambridge: Cambridge University Press, 2004, pp. 145–163.

McClymond, Kathryn, *Beyond Sacred Violence: A Comparative Study of Sacrifice* Baltimore: Johns Hopkins, 2008.

McDonald, Peter F. 'Drama in the Church' in Cawley, A. C., Jones, Marion, McDonald, Peter F. and Mills, David (eds.), *The Revels History of Drama in English: Volume 1 Medieval Drama*, London: Methuen, 1983, pp. 92–121.

Mercier, Vivien, *The Irish Times*, 18 February 1956.

Meszaros, Julia and Zachhuber, Johannes (eds.), *Sacrifice and Modern Thought*, Oxford: Oxford University Press, 2013.

Miller, Harold W., 'Euripides' Telephus and the Thesmophoriazusae of Aristophanes', *Classical Philology*, July 1948, 43:3, pp. 174–183.

Mills, David, 'Drama and Folk-Ritual' in Cawley, A. C., Jones, Marion, McDonald, Peter F. and Mills, David (eds.), *The Revels History of Drama in English: Volume 1 Medieval Drama*, London: Methuen, 1983, pp. 133–138.

Mills, David, 'Religious Drama and Civic Ceremonial' in Cawley, A. C., Jones, Marion, McDonald, Peter F. and Mills, David (eds.), *The Revels History of Drama in English: Volume 1 Medieval Drama*, London: Methuen, 1983, pp. 152–206.

Moody, Jane and O'Quinn, Daniel, *The Cambridge Companion to British Theatre 1730–1830*, Cambridge: Cambridge University Press, 2007.

Mortimer, Ian, *Centuries of Change: Which Century Saw the Most Change?* London: Bodley Head, 2015.

Murray, Gilbert, 'Excursus on the Ritual Forms Preserved in Tragedy' in Harrison, Jane (ed.), *Themis: A Study of the Social Origins of Greek Religion*, London: Merlin Press, [1912] and 1989, pp. 341–363.

Newey, Kate, Women's *Theatre Writing in Victorian Britain*, Basingstoke: Palgrave MacMillan, 2005.

Nietzsche, Friedrich, *The Birth of Tragedy*, translated by Shaun Whiteside and edited by Michael Tanner, Harmondsworth: Penguin, 1993.

Normington, Katie, *Medieval English Drama*, Cambridge: Polity Press, 2009.

O'Brien, John, 'Pantomime' in Moody, Jane and O'Quinn, Daniel (eds.), *The Cambridge Companion to British Theatre 1730–1830*, Cambridge: Cambridge University Press, 2007, pp. 103–114.

O'Gorman, Frank, *The Long Eighteenth Century: British Political and Social History*, London: Hodder and Arnold, 2007.

Palmer, David (ed.), *Visions of Tragedy in Modern American Drama*, London: Bloomsbury, 2017.

Philip, Sidney, 'The Defence of Poetry' in Vickers, Brian (ed.), *English Renaissance Literary Criticism*, Oxford: Clarendon Press, 1999, pp. 334–390.

Pickard-Cambridge, A. W., *Dithyramb, Tragedy and Comedy*, Oxford: Clarendon Press, 1927.

Platt, Richard, *Smuggling in the British Isles: A History*, Stroud: The History Press, 2011.

Plotkin, Henry, *Evolution in Mind: An Introduction to Evolutionary Psychology*, Penguin: Harmondsworth, 1997.

Pomeroy, Sarah, *Goddesses, Whores, Wives and Slaves: Women in Classical Antiquity*, London: Pimlico, 2007.

Powell, Kerry, *The Cambridge Companion to Victorian and Edwardian Theatre*, Cambridge: Cambridge University Press, 2004.

Pugh, Martin, *We Danced All Night: A Social History of Britain between the Wars*, London: Vintage, 2009.

Rebellato, Dan, *1956 And All That: The Making of Modern British Drama*, London: Routledge, 1999.

Rhodes, Colin, *Primitivism and Modern Art*, London: Thames and Hudson, 1994.

Ricks, Christopher, *Essays in Appreciation*, Oxford: Oxford University Press, 1998.

Rowell, George, *The Victorian Theatre 1792–1914*, Cambridge: Cambridge University Press, 1978.

Russell, D. A. and Winterbottom, M. (eds.), *Ancient Literary Criticism: The Principal Texts in New Translations*, Oxford: Oxford University Press, 1972.

Rymer, Thomas, 'Preface to Rapin' in Spingarn, J. E. (ed.), *Critical Essays of the Seventeenth Century: Volume II 1650–1685*, Oxford: Oxford University Press, 1957, pp. 163–181.

Rymer, Thomas, 'A Short View of Tragedy' in Spingarn, J. E. (ed.), *Critical Essays of the Seventeenth Century: Volume II 1650–1685*, Oxford: Oxford University Press, 1957, pp. 208–255.

Rymer, Thomas, 'Tragedies of the Last Age' in Spingarn, J. E. (ed.), *Critical Essays of the Seventeenth Century: Volume II 1650–1685*, Oxford: Oxford University Press, 1957, pp. 181–208.

Santayana, George, *The Life of Reason*, New York: Charles Scribner's Sons, 1905.

Segal, Erich, *The Death of Comedy*, Cambridge, MA: Harvard University Press, 2001.

Seneca, *Letters from a Stoic*, selected, translated and with an Introduction by Robin Campbell, Harmondsworth: Penguin, 2004.

Seneca, 'Moral Letters' and Tertullian, 'On Spectacles' in Mahoney, Anne (ed.), *Roman Sports and Spectacles: A Sourcebook*, Newbury Port, MA: Focus Publishing, 2001, pp. 93 and 96.

Sierz, Aleks, *In-Yer-Face Theatre: British Drama Today*, London: Faber, 2001.

Smith, James L., *Melodrama*, London: Routledge, 1973.

Smith, Jonathan Z., 'The Domestication of Sacrifice' in Hamerton-Kelly, Robert G. (ed.), *Violent Origins: Ritual Killing and Cultural Formations*, Stanford: Stanford University Press, 1987, pp. 191–205.

Smith, William Robertson, 'The Religion of the Semites' in Carter, Jeffrey (ed.), *Understanding Religious Sacrifice: A Reader*, London: Continuum, 2006, pp. 53–75.

Solomon, Sheldon, Greenberg, Jeff and Pyszczynski, Tom, *The Worm at the Core: On the Role of Death in Life*, Harmondsworth: Penguin, 2015.

Spingarn, J. E. (ed.), *Critical Essays of the Seventeenth Century: Volume II 1650–1685*, Oxford: Oxford University Press, 1957.

Spingarn, J. E. (ed.), *Critical Essays of the Seventeenth Century: Volume III 1685–1700*, Oxford: Oxford University Press, 1957.

Steele, Richard and Addison, Joseph, *Selections from the Tatler and the Spectator*, edited with Introduction and Notes by Angus Ross, Harmondsworth: Penguin, 1988.

Steiner, George, *In Bluebeard's Castle: Some Notes towards the Re-definition of Culture*, London: Faber, 1971.

Tennenhouse, Leonard, *Power on Display: The Politics of Shakespeare's Genres*, London: Routledge, 2005.

Tertullian, 'Apologetics'15. 4–6 in Mahoney, Anne (ed.), *Roman Sports and Spectacles: A Sourcebook*, Newbury Port, MA: Focus Publishing, 2001, p. 53.

Thorley, John, *Athenian Democracy*, London and New York: Routledge, 2004.

Thorndike, Ashley H., *English Comedy*, London: Macmillan, 1929.

Tydeman, William, 'An Introduction to Medieval Theatre' in Beadle, Richard (ed.), *The Cambridge Companion to Medieval Theatre*, Cambridge: Cambridge University Press, 1994, pp. 18–24.

Tylor, E. B., 'Primitive Culture' in Carter, Jeffrey (ed.), *Understanding Religious Sacrifice: A Reader*, London: Continuum, 2006, pp. 14–38.

Vickers, Brian, *English Renaissance Literary Criticism*, Oxford: Clarendon Press, 1999.

Vickery, John B., *The Literary Impact of The Golden Bough*, Princeton: Princeton University Press, 1973.

Warrior, Valerie M., *Greek Religion: A Sourcebook*, Newburyport, MA: Focus Publishing, 2009.

Watson, Robert N., 'Tragedy' in Braunmuller, A. R. and Hattaway, Michael (eds.), *The Cambridge Companion to English Renaissance Drama*, Cambridge: Cambridge University Press, 2nd edn, 2003, pp. 292–343.

Wells, Peter, *Barbarians to Angels: The Dark Ages Reconsidered*, New York: Norton, 2008.

Willerslev, Rane, *Soul Hunters: Hunting, Animism and Personhood among the Siberian Yukaghirs*, Berkeley: University of California Press, 2007.

Womersley, David (ed.), *Augustan Critical Writing*, Harmondsworth: Penguin, 1997.

Websites

Anatomy of Abuses in England in Shakespeare's Youth. The full text is available at http://archive.org/stream/phillipstubbessa00stubuoft/phillipstubbessa00stubuoft_djvu.txt

Plutarch, Lives. http://penelope.uchicago.edu/Thayer/E/Roman/Texts/Plutarch/Lives/Solon*. html Section 29: paragraph 4

Frances Larson, 'Why Public Beheadings Get Millions of Views', http://www.ted.com/talks/frances_larson_why_public_beheadings_get_millions_of_views?utm_campaign=social&utm_medium=referral&utm_source=t.co&utm_content=talk&utm_term=global-social%20issues

http://www.theguardian.com/politics/2015/jan/26/david-cameron-tax-cuts-reward
  -for-sacrifice
http://www.theguardian.com/lifeandstyle/2015/apr/18/rachel-billington-my
  -grandfathers-sacrifice-at-gallipoli
http://www.theguardian.com/commentisfree/2014/apr/18/sacrifice-easter-human
  -experience-christians
http://www.theguardian.com/commentisfree/2014/jan/01/scapegoating-bulgarian
  -romanian-migrants-britain-crisis

ABOUT THE AUTHOR

Gary Day recently retired as principal lecturer at De Montfort University, UK, where he taught courses on the history of drama, the eighteenth century, modernism, contemporary drama and contemporary fiction. He is the author, most recently, of *Literary Criticism: A New History* (2008) and *Modernist Literature: 1890–1950* (2010). He has edited a dozen books, the latest being *The Wiley Encyclopaedia of British Eighteenth Century Literature* (2015) with Jack Lynch. He has contributed to the *Cambridge History of Literary Criticism* and to the *Oxford Guide to Literary Theory and Criticism*. He has also been a regular columnist and reviewer for the *Times Higher*.

INDEX

Note: Literary works and films are listed under the author where known; page references with letter 'n' refer to notes; page references in **bold type** denote main references to topics.